THE FABULOUS IMAGINATION
On Montaigne's Essays

THE FABULOUS
IMAGINATION

On Montaigne's Essays

LAWRENCE D. KRITZMAN

Columbia University Press   *New York*

Columbia University Press
Publishers Since 1893
New York   Chichester, West Sussex
Copyright © 2009 Columbia University Press
Paperback edition, 2012
All rights reserved
Library of Congress Cataloging-in-Publication
Kritzman, Lawrence D.
  The fabulous imagination : on Montaigne's Essays / Lawrence D. Kritzman.
     p. cm.
  Includes bibliographical references and index.
  ISBN 978-0-231-11992-4 (cloth : alk. paper)—ISBN 978-0-231-11993-1 (pbk. :
alk. paper)—ISBN 978-0-231-51251-0 (e-book)
  1. Montaigne, Michel de, 1533-1592. Essais. 2. Imagination (Philosophy) I. Title.
  PQ1643.K75 2009
  844'.3—dc22

                                                                2008045954

Columbia University Press books are printed on permanent and durable acid-free
paper.
This book is printed on paper with recycled content.
Printed in the United States of America
c 10 9 8 7 6 5 4 3 2
p 10 9 8 7 6 5 4 3 2 1
References to Internet Web sites (URLs) were accurate at the time of writing. Neither
the author nor Columbia University Press is responsible for URLs that may have
expired or changed since the manuscript was prepared.

Columbia University Press gratefully acknowledges permission to reprint from the
following: Excerpts from Frame, Donald *The Complete Essays of Montaigne* Copyright © 1958 by the Board of Trustees of the Leland Stanford Junior University.

Earlier versions of some chapters have appeared in the following publications:

"Montaigne's Death Sentences: Narrative and Subjectivity in "De la diversion' (Essais 3.4)," in *Distant Voices Still Heard: Contemporary Readings of French Renaissance Literature,* ed. John O"Brien and Malcolm Quainton (Liverpool, Engl.: Liverpool University Press, 2000), 202–16.

"Montaigne's Fantastic Monsters and the Construction of Gender," in *Writing the
Renaissance,* ed. Raymond C. La Charité (Lexington, Ky.: French Forum, 1992),
183–96.

"Montaigne's Fraternity," in *Etienne de la Boétie: Sage révolutionnaire et poete
périgourdin,* ed. Marcel Tetel (Paris: Champion, 2004), 281–89.

"Of Ashes Born: Montaigne's Surrogate Daughter," *Journal of Medieval and Renaissance Studies* 25, no. 3 (fall 1995): 419–31.

"Representing the Monster: Cognition, Cripples, and Other Limp Parts in Montaigne's 'Des Boyteux,'" in *Monster Theory,* ed. Jeffrey J. Cohen (Minneapolis:
University of Minnesota Press, 1996), 168–82.

"The Socratic Makeover: Montaigne's 'De la physionomie' and the Ethics of the Impossible," *L'Esprit Créateur* 46, no. 1 (spring 2006): 75–85.

To Jeremy,
whose fabulous imagination as actor and comedy writer
gave us so much joy

CONTENTS

ACKNOWLEDGMENTS

The origin of this book stems from two appointments as visiting professor at Harvard and Stanford Universities, where I taught graduate seminars on "Montaigne and the Imagination." I wish to thank my colleagues and students at those institutions for their kind invitations, which enabled me to explore this subject more fully.

I am also grateful to a number of institutions that invited me to present lectures, which helped me to come to terms with my work-in-progress on Montaigne and to clarify my ideas. These include: Columbia, Cornell, Duke, Grinell College, Harvard, Johns Hopkins, New York University, the Universities of Miami, Michigan, and Paris IV (Sorbonne),Stanford, and Whitman College.

I would like to recognize the encouragement and feedback I received from Tom Conley, Kathleen Perry Long, Richard Regosin, and the late Marcel Tetel. Their thoughtful comments helped me to gain a better understanding of Montaigne.

I wish to thank the following friends and colleagues who offered support along the way: Ehsan Ahmed, Faith Beasley, Michel Beaujour, Tom Bishop, Howard Bloch, Christian Delacampagne, Jacques Derrida, Philippe Desan, Nelly Furman, Floyd Gray, Daniel and Janice Gross, Ralph Hester, Vivian Kogan, David La Guardia, Françoise Lionnet, Gisèle Mathieu-Castellani, Pierre Nora, François Noudelmann, John O'Brien, John Rassias, Domna C. Stanton, and Zahi Zalloua.

Jennifer Crewe, associate director of Columbia University Press, has been an exceptional editor. I owe her a special debt of gratitude for her continued advice and encouragement. I also wish to thank freelance copy editor Henry Krawitz for having perfected my manuscript and Malcolm Debevoise for having translated from the French an earlier version of one of the chapters.

Without the constant encouragement of Dr. Stuart Pizer, who enabled me to explore my own imagination, this project would never have been completed. My friend and colleague Brian J. Reilly offered me attentive criticism and editorial advice. One could not have asked for a better intellectual interlocutor. Lastly, I owe a special debt of gratitude to the Pat and John Rosenwald Research Professorship, which enabled me to research and write this book.

Lawrence D. Kritzman
New York and Paris
Winter 2008

THE FABULOUS IMAGINATION

INTRODUCTION
Montaigne Is Theory

Literature begins at the moment that literature becomes
a question.
MAURICE BLANCHOT

Act so that there is no use in a center.
GERTRUDE STEIN

 It has often been said that the French think too
much and that they have invented a theory for al-
most everything. Montaigne represents the beginning of a philosophical tradition in French letters
in which ontological and epistemological concerns
intersect. In his exploration of the self Montaigne
poses the same questions that Socrates posed in antiquity and that
modern psychoanalysis had adapted: How shall I live? How can I
know myself? By posing these questions Montaigne, like Socrates
before him, sought to explore the unexamined life independently of
what one might refer to today as the normative constraints of what it
means to know.

Montaigne was the first thinker in the Western tradition to explore human subjectivity in a profound way. In exploring the self,
Montaigne's *Essays* (*Essais*) reflect vital concerns that continue to
haunt us today: what it means to exist and to follow nature; monsters, nightmares, and traumatic memories; fear of impotence and the
fragility of gender; coping with the death of loved ones and the anticipation of one's own death; thoughts about the future and of what
one leaves behind; and mimicry as a tactic of diversion in coping with
the human condition. The quest for self-knowledge that this enter-

prise entails represents the desire to see and to imagine the self from a variety of vantage points.

For Montaigne philosophy is an impossible engagement since he views thought as a destabilizing agent that is open to constant revision. The essayist doubts the possibility of attaining closure in the act of interpretation: "Qui ne diroit que les glosses augmentent les doubtes et l'ignorance, puis qu'il ne se voit aucun livre, soit humain, soit divin, auquel le monde s'embesongne, duquel l'interpretation face tarir la difficulté? . . . Quand est-il convenu entre nous: ce livres en a assez, il n'y a meshuy plus à dire" (III, 13, 1067) ("Who would not say that glosses increase doubts and ignorance, since there is no book to be found, whether human or divine, with which the world busies itself, whose difficulties are cleared up by interpretation? . . . When do we agree and say, 'There has been enough about this book; henceforth there is nothing more to say about it'?" [817]).[1] The consequences of this phenomenon, in the quest for self-knowledge, suggest that Montaigne must theorize the human subject at the limits of the theorizable. The essayist's self-portrait results from a demand requiring that the quest for signification be maintained and that through this process the grounding of both the thinking subject and knowledge itself be disabled. However, this does not imply that thought becomes arbitrary. On the contrary, intellectual activity becomes a more rigorous way of overcoming the constraints imposed by the exigency to create a purely substantive knowledge. If thought is unable to take hold of itself, it is because the imagination is subject to difference: "Il n'est aucun sens ny visage, ou droit, ou amer, ou doux, ou courbe, que l'esprit humain ne trouve aux escrits qu'il entrepend de fouiller" (II, 12, 585) ("There is no sense or aspect, either straight or bitter, or sweet, or crooked, that the human mind does not find it in the writings it undertakes to search" [442]).

In his commentary on two books by Gilles Deleuze, Michel Foucault writes that philosophy cannot be reduced to mere thought. Instead, he claims that it should be regarded as a form of theater "with multiple scenes that are fleeting and instantaneous."[2] To be sure, the rhetoric of self-portraiture in Montaigne's essays suggests that it is the work of a fabulous imagination predicated on the aporetic relationship between seeing and Being. This cognitive faculty links theory and sight to suggest that self-representation stages itself at the cusp of theorization. If the mind is the site of the imagination, then the space in which it takes shape, within the context of the essays, allows theory's virtual potential to sight and re-cite what it has already seen.

The double entendre of what I call "the mind's I" represents a conflation of the visual and the self within the rhetoric of self-portraiture: "Moy qui m'espie de plus prez, qui ay les yeux incessamment tendus sur moy" (II, 12, 565) ("I who spy on myself more closely, who have my eyes unceasingly intent on myself . . ." [425]). If the Greek notion of *thea,* signifying spectacle and contemplation, evokes the theory that is played out in the mind's eye, then the Latin imagination, from the same root of *imitari,* suggests the terms "idea" and "portrait" that are integral to the essaying process. For Montaigne the mind functions as the locus of visualization, with the essay becoming the space in which the self seeks to see itself. This "staging of thought" thus evokes the inescapable reality that theory can only represent itself in the spectacle constituting the play of the text. The mind's "I" plays itself out on a syntactic stage where the eye refocuses the meaning of things and produces a proliferation of semantic configurations: "Nostre ame regarde la chose d'un autre oeil et se la represente par un autre visage: car chaque chose a plusieurs biais et plusieurs lustres" (I, 38, 235) ("Our soul looks on the thing with a different eye, and represents it to itself in another aspect, for each thing has many angles and many lights" [174]). As Rudolph Gasché suggests, visualizing therefore becomes a process "without end in sight." If Being is primed by seeing, then the self can only take shape through a rhetoric of the visual. The contemplative "I" that is Montaigne becomes the source of many imagined, literally visualized selves: "I see therefore I am" is a thought process modulated by the visual and in excess of all conceptuality either in epistemological or ontological terms. Here Montaigne anticipates the work of psychoanalysis. In his quest for self-knowledge and his attempt to conceive of it in secular terms, the essayist views the human psyche as an optical phenomenon.

The various identificatory modalities performed through self-portraiture allow Montaigne to identify the self through multiple references that never refer to the same self but nevertheless form a loose association: "Nous sommes tous de lopins, et d'une contexture si informe et diverse, que chaque piece, chaque momant, faict son jeu. Et se trouve autant de difference de nous à nous mesmes, que de nous à autruy" (II, 1, 337) ("We are all patchwork, and so shapeless and diverse in composition that each bit, each moment, plays its own game. And there is as much difference between us and ourselves as between us and others" [244]). Yet the epistemological limits of thought's capacity to take hold of things becomes a warning concerning the self's ability to find plenitude and closure in the performance of the mind's "I": "Joint qu'à l'adventure ay-je quelque obligation particuliere à ne dire qu'à demy, à dire confusément, à dire discordamment" (III, 9, 995–96) ("Besides, perhaps I have some personal obligation to speak only by halves, to speak confusedly, to speak discordantly" [762]). The mind's "I" can only engage in consistent processes of identification without ever establishing a singular identity or authority. The kinetic energy of the human psyche, as it attempts to envisage subjectivity, fractures the so-called identity of the self, thereby disallowing the essayist's ability to gaze back on it as a totalizable entity.

If, as I have suggested, Montaigne is theory, it is because theory is enacted in the practice of the essay as it becomes a spectacle on the printed page. The refusal to submit to concepts and essentialize them is totally foreign to the meaning of the word "essay" or its Latin root, *exagium,* which transcribes the kinetic energy of thought. Even though Edmond Huguet's *Dictionnaire de la langue française* does not contain a definition of the word "imagination" per se, it nevertheless contains an entry for the synonymous term "fantasier," which signifies "imaginer, se livrer à son imagination et être soucieux."[3] To deliver oneself to one's imagination is a psychic process that allows thinking to occur; it enables the essayist to explore the heterogeneous nature of things and, in the process, to explore the ontological implications of the void from which the imagination is born.[4] Montaigne's writing entails a convergence of the "theater" of the *Essays* with the imaginary architecture in which the self is figured on a world stage: "Si cherchons nous avidement de recognoistre en ombre mesme et en la fable des Theatres la montre des jeux tragiques de l'humaine fortune" (III, 12, 1046) ("Thus do we eagerly seek to recognize, even in shadow and in the fiction of the theaters, the representation of the tragic play of human fortune" [800]). What is most striking, however, is the way that the contemporary self imagines its own theatrical character in an inherited form.

The essay, as Montaigne suggests, consequently becomes an exercise in approaching a horizon of possibilities: "Il y a des autheurs, desquels la fin c'est dire les evenements. La mienne, si j'y sçavoye advenir, seroit dire sur ce qui peut advenir" (I, 21, 105) ("There are authors whose end is to tell what has happened. Mine, if I could attain it, would be to talk about what can happen" [75]). The force of the imagination is thus predicated on the transgression of limits and the normative notions traditionally associated with epistemological and ontological concerns. For Montaigne the act of submitting concepts to the corrosive practice of the essay undermines the legislating power of absolute forms of knowledge since the multiplicity of its points of reference confounds us. Everything unfolds as the representation of a psychic practice in which different spectacles of thought cannot be reduced or totalized, although in Montaigne's conception it is essentially a visceral phenomenon that decenters itself in the peripatetic movement of writing: "Mes fantasies se suyvent, mais par fois c'est de loing, et se regardent, mais d'une veue oblique" (III, 9, 994) ("My ideas follow one another, but sometimes it is from a distance, and look at each other, but with a side-long glance" [761]).

What we testify to as the result of experience, as Montaigne discovers in the writings of Cicero and Lucretius, can only be seen as both contingent and relative: "Si nous voyons autant du monde comme nous n'en voyons pas, nous apercevrions, comme il est à croire, une perpetuele multiplication et vicissitude de formes" (III, 6, 908) ("If we saw as much of the world as we do not see, we would perceive, it is likely, a perpetual multiplication and vicissitude of forms" [693]). Yet for Montaigne the vicissitudes of personal experience alone will not suffice since the imagination will also engender unconventional examples that will find a reality somewhere to which they might eventually correspond: "Il ne tombe en l'imagination humaine aucune fantasie si forcenée, qui ne rencontre l'exemple de quelque usage public" (I, 23, 111) ("I think that there falls into man's imagination no fantasy so wild that it does not match the example of some public practice" [79]). Montaigne here implies that the imagination can produce fantasies that eventually can be encountered in the world.

On another level, however, Montaigne suggests that the force of our imagination requires us to circumscribe the present moment, a process that results in rendering all readings anachronistic by their very nature: "A chaque minute il me semble que je m'eschape" (I, 20, 88) ("Every minute I seem to be slipping away from myself" [61]). The *aporia* of time is that it is without Being and that it can never simply be present as such. As demonstrated by the narrative performance of self-portraiture, knowledge challenges any form of it that is either self-grounded or self-contained. Theory, conceived as sighting and re-citing, raises epistemological and ontological questions that in practice opens theory to the virtual reality of alterity. "Je sois autre moy-mesmes" (III, 2, 805) ("I am different myself" [611]). The essaying of a particular subject for Montaigne renders it distinct from the positivism associated with the literal objectifications practiced by some. The work of the inquiring mind makes the imagination's peripatetic movement analogous to that of a journey in which the fruits of a bookish voyage to the past enables the "reader spectator" to revise what he has envisioned as the result of reading: "En cette practique des hommes, j'entends y comprendre, et principalement, ceux qui ne vivent qu'en la memoire des livres. Il practiquera, par le moyen des histoires, ces grandes ames des meilleurs siecles" (I, 26, 156) ("In this association with men I mean to include, and foremost, those who live only in the memory of books. He will associate, by means of histories, with those great souls of the best ages" [115]).

Montaigne's preambulatory "Au lecteur" ("To the Reader") poses a curious epistemological problem with far-reaching ontological consequences. He writes as follows of the union between author and text: "Je suis moy-mesmes la matiere de mon livre: ce n'est pas raison que tu employes ton loisir en un subject si frivole et si vain" ("I am myself the matter of my book; you would be unreasonable to suspend your leisure on so frivolous and vain a subject" [2]). What is striking in this context is that at first the essayist suggests that his self-portrait is transparent and subject to authorial intention. In fact, the essayist suggests that the self-portrait presents a Being "en chair et en os," which appears to eradicate the artifice of writing. However, at the same time he describes the self as "the matter of the book." Interestingly, in his *Dictionarie of the French and English Tongues,* Cotgrave ascribes to the word "matiere" several meanings, among which one finds the terms "substance, a matter, a thing, an argument or discourse of."[5] Is the matter of the book that he describes an empirical Being, subject to verification, or is it simply a self that is represented discursively in a text? The symbiosis between author and text advocated by those who subscribe to the idea of consubtantiality in its most literal sense fail to consider the fate of a self inscribed in the archive that the *Essays* have become. For Montaigne the act of reading becomes an act of translation projected beyond the horizion of an indissoluble origin. The question therefore arises whether discursive meaning has a proper term and whether one can recuperate meaning as originally intended: "Il y a plus affaire à interpreter les interpretations qu'à interpreter les choses, et plus de livres sur les livres que sur autre subject: nous ne faisons que nous entregloser" (III, 13, 1069) ("It is more of a job to interpret the interpretations than to interpret the things, and there are more books about books than about any other subject: we do nothing but write glosses about each other" [818]). As Montaigne writes in "De l'experience": "Il n'y a point de fin en nos inquisitions; nostre fin est en l'autre monde" (III, 13, 1068) ("There is no end to our researches; our end is in the other world" [817]). Despite the essayist's claim for the autonomy of the text and the desire for intention and meaning to coincide—"Je entends que la matiere se dsitingue soy-mesmes" (III, 9, 995) ("I want the matter to make its own divisions" [761])—the book nevertheless cannot keep authorial intention intact since our imaginative inquiries as readers render texts subject to change. This dilemma represents the *aporia* of self-portraiture, in which the book continues to live on and have a life of its own. To be sure, the text and the person are discrete and separate entities. The act of reading is an act of translation since it makes a text other than it might have been. Montaigne's writing suggests that the dead do indeed have a future beyond the ontological parameters of their existences. This annotation of Being as it unfolds in the future anterior, through a series of differential re-markings, demystifies the very notion of identity.

When Montaigne speaks about what can be, he is in a sense already speaking about the alterity endemic to what represents the valences of the future. As suggested in "De l'affection des peres aux enfans" ("Of the Affection of Fathers for Their Children") the essayist describes the book as a child of the mind exhibiting virtual potential: "Il peut sçavoir assez de choses que je ne sçay plus, et tenir de moy ce que je n'ay point retenu et qu'il faudroit que, tout ainsi qu'un estranger, j'empruntasse de luy, si besoin m'en venoit" (II, 8, 402) ("It may know a good many things that I no longer know and hold from me what I have not retained and what, just like a stranger, I should have to borrow from it if I came to need it" [293]). Here Montaigne paradoxically depends on the reader to reveal the traces of what may be described as a "textual unconscious." By engaging in a hermeneutic interaction with the text, which Montaigne characterizes in "De la resemblance des enfans aux peres" (Of the Resemblance of Children to Fathers") as "cette peinture morte et muete" (II, 37, 784) ("this dead and mute portrait" [596]), he allows himself the freedom to reinvent himself through the sighting and re-citing of the text: "Je donne à mon ame tantost un visage, tantost un autre, selon le costé où je la couche. Si je parle diversement de moy, c'est que je me regarde diversement.

Toutes les contrarietez s'y trouvent, selon quelque tour, et en quelque façon (II, 1, 335) ("I give my soul now one face, now another, according to which direction I turn it. If I speak of myself in different ways, that is because I look at myself in different ways. All contradictions may be found in me by some twist and in some fashion" [242]).

The narrative self depicted by the writer can never be construed as a self-identical Being. Instead, the revisionary practice associated with the act of "essaying" engenders a narrative that, like the work of the imagination, is always already incomplete. The signature "Montaigne" is associated with the writer who has generated the text and the constructed figure born from the writing of the essay; the latter becomes the character whose representation disfigures the narrator's so-called intentionality. As Richard Regosin has claimed, "the 'Au Lecteur' inscribes and . . . includes a reader [who] ostensibly seeks to dissuade [others] from reading, a reader who has no memory of Montaigne, no referential ground upon which to fix the signs of writing and confirm their meaning."[6] The theatricality of theory, as it is performed in the essay, precludes the possible conjunction of seeing and Being; it acquires a perverse kind of relation that undermines the possibility of transcendence. Montaigne's theater of the imagination thus depicts a desiring subject who is always already in pursuit of something beyond itself because the quest for self-knowledge reveals insufficiency or lack in that which it supplements. With this in mind, the *Essays* unfolds as a virtual narrative in which different narrative spectacles cannot be reduced to a single vantage point.

The intellectual climate in which Montaigne composed the essays had an affinity for classical thought, particularly that of the Stoics.[7] For Plato vision in the sense of *theoria* evokes an idea of vision that is integrally linked to the contemplation of knowledge and is characterized as the most exemplary mode of cognition. In the "Apologie" Montaigne proclaims: "Les yeux humains ne peuvent apercevoir les choses que par les formes de leur cognoissance" (II, 12, 535) ("Human eyes can perceive things only in the forms that they know" [399]). In the *Republic,* for example, Plato makes reference to sight, which, unlike the other senses, needs light from the outside in order to function.

Epistemologically speaking Platonic thought draws a parallel between the eye (*onima*) and the sun (*helios*). The word "vision" as we know it today does not signify the Greek notion *opsis*, which suggests the idea of spectacle. Contemplation as spectacle in the Platonic sense maintains a relationship to Being that is curiously present unto itself; it shifts the visuality of theory from *theoria* to the *theos* that is divinity itself.

The idea of the imagination in Hellenic thought was renewed by Aristotle, with attention focused on the material world.[8] While remaining faithful to the epistemological function of imaging, Aristotle shifted the emphasis in his analysis from metaphysical to psychological concerns. He adhered to the belief that images in the mind result from sense perception as depicted by the imagination (*phantasma*). For Aristotle the image functioned as the mediator between sensation and reason, thereby allowing one to determine the veracity or falsehood of imaginative activities.

To consider the imagination within an Aristotelian framework requires that attention be paid to the notion of mimesis or representation. If the Platonic approach to the imagination is based on the external imitation of a divine ideality, then the Aristotelian imperative suggests that the image be treated as a mental representation (*phantasma*) that views the world and reflects it within.

Interestingly, Aristotle links the imagination to human desire, whose ultimate goal is knowledge. But what Aristotle considers knowledge he describes as a lack that can only be realized through the kinetic energy of desire. For instance, in *De Anima* Aristotle examines the psychological character of images and how the material nature of desire is transcribed within the specularity of the mind. For Aristotle the eye sees itself as it sees its reflection. Montaigne, however, recognizes the importance of sight and what is seen. However, he does so by shifting the emphasis from that which is seen to the gaze of the viewer: "Je dy librement mon advis de toutes choses . . . ce que j'en opine, c'est aussi pour declarer la mesure de ma veue, non la mesure des choses." (II, 10, 410) ("I speak my mind freely on all things. . . . And so the opinion I give of them is to declare the measure of my sight, not the measure of things" [298]).

Although Montaigne draws on Aristotle's concept of psychic mobility, his writing practice fails to account for the veracity of any one thing: "Tous jugemens en gros sont laches et imparfaicts." (III, 8, 943) ("All judgmens in gross are loose and imperfect" [721]). In the essays the spiritual and corporeal aspects of the human subject are seen in a state of mobility, which contradicts any claim to sameness: "[Je] reçoy plus facilement la difference que la ressemblance." (I, 37, 229) ("I more easily admit difference than ressemblance" [169]) The autokinetic nature of the imagination renders it in conflict with reason, which by its very nature parallels Pierre de La Primaudaye's be-lief that "il s'emeut un combant entre l'esprit et l'imagination."[9] With this in mind, the imagination is conceived as a transgressive force that undermines the consistency of the self. The encounter with the self as other reveals a divided condition, which also relates to the endless curiosity and vanity that characterizes the human subject and that Montaigne often reiterates: "[De telles] inquisitions et contempla-tions philosophiques ne servent que d'aliment à nostre curiosité" (III, 13, 1073) ("[Such] philosophical inquiries and meditations serve only as food for our curiosity" [821]). In his writing Montaigne empha-sizes the fluidity of the human imagination in perceiving the external world through the perception of sight and sound, as well as its abil-ity to constitute fictions in the theater of the mind. To be sure, the essay becomes a locus of confrontation of the self with its condition of alterity. In the process, it posits a specular relation that raises the issue of the totalization of self-portraiture: "Moy à cette heure et moy tantost sommes bien deux" (III, 9, 964) ("Myself now and myself a while ago are indeed two." [736]).

Recently John Lyons has demonstrated the role of the imagina-tion among the Stoics and its influence on the writing of the *Essays*.[10] According to Lyons, for Seneca the work of the imagination is inte-grally related to the question of freedom and the ability to confront death with a sense of inner tranquillity. Sometimes, when anticipating death, the imagination makes it appear greater than it is: "Plusieurs choses nous semblent plus grandes par imagination que par effect" (II, 6, 372) ("Many things seem to us greater in imagination than in real-ity" [268]). However, what is required in order to come to terms with mortality is a sense of discipline and order in one's daily life. Lyons's analysis suggests that Montaigne's thought owes much to the Stoic practice of "embedded imagining." The imagination's ability to en-gage with the mysteries of the unknown and to perceive visual images as if they were real in order to anticipate and neutralize what might result from thinking about death allows the essayist to manage his fear of mortality and to accept what his imagination has envisaged as an integral part of human experience.

What is particular to Montaigne's adaptation of the Stoic imagi-nation, however, is not an unmitigated adherence to its ethics. The stoical technique of self-mastery and reason may protect the essayist from the effects of contingency but it does not necessarily produce self-knowledge.

Ostons luy l'estrangeté, pratiquons le, accoustumons le. N'ayons rien si souvent en la teste que la mort. A tous instants representons la à nostre imagination et en tous visages. Au broncher d'un cheval, à la cheute d'une tuille, à la moindre piqueure d'espleingue, remachons soudain: Eh bien, quand ce seroit la mort mesme? (I, 20, 86)

Let us rid it of its strangeness, come to know it, get used to it. Let us have nothing on our minds as often as death. At every moment let us picture it in our imagination in all its aspects. At the stumbling of a horse, the fall of a tile, the slightest pin prick, let us promptly chew on this: Well, what if it were death itself? (60)

Although he opts for a more temperate mastery of the self before the specter of death, he reduces its threat by imagining it as a phenomenon integral to the very movement of life itself: "Aussi ay-je puis en coustume d'avoir non seulement en l'imagination, mais continuellement la mort en la bouche" (I, 20, 90) ("So I have formed the habit of having death continually present, not merely in my imagination, but in my mouth" [62]). The confrontation with death thus requires imagining it otherwise as an atomistic phenomenon reflecting the human subject's elusive relation to itself. Stoicism imparts to the essayist a modus operandi. Yet it is through the flexibility of the imagination and the consciousness of the movement constituting the rhythm of life that the essayist is able to modulate the constancy of the Stoic position. It is therefore not surprising that in "De la force de l'imagination" (I, 21) ("On the Power of the Imagination")—the essay that immediately follows "Que philosopher c'est apprendre à mourir" (I, 20) ("That to Philosophize Is to Learn to Die")—there is the suggestion that the imaginaton cannot remain steady and is, in fact, vulnerable to the vicissitudes of human experience.

Montaigne's desire to create a psychic space, where he could exercise his imagination freely in the solitude of his "arrière boutique," enabled him to modify the self through a series of images:

Il se faut reserver une arriere-boutique toute nostre, toute franche, en laquelle nous establissons nostre vraye liberté et principale retraicte et solitude. En cette-cy faut-il prendre nostre ordinaire entretien de nous à nous mesmes, et si privé que

nulle acointance ou communication estrangiere y trouve place.
(I, 39, 241)

We must reserve a back shop all our own, entirely free, in which
to establish our real liberty and our principal retreat and solitude. Here our ordinary conversation must be between us and
ourselves, and so private that no outside association or communication can find a place. (177)

The theater of the mind becomes the stage upon which the mind's
"I" performs the representation of its inner being. Yet the persona
constructed in the essaying process presents the image of someone more in tune with "les ames communes" than the "autheurs"
from which he wishes to distinguish himself in "Du repentir" ("Of
Repentance").

The Stoic imagination stressed the superiority of the mind over
the body, and in Montaigne we see how the imagination can remove
one from the corporeal displeasures of the present. To be sure, Montaigne asserts intellectual authority by engaging in the ultimate object
of philosophy, namely, to learn how to die or, better yet, how to live
well by accepting the fact that death is not the goal of life but simply
its end. There is indeed something noble in envisaging death, which
"le vulgaire" or "common herd" is incapable of doing.

In "essaying" the topos of death, Montaigne uses the imagination in order to free himself from a painful reality conceived of as an
external danger to the self. The anticipatory anxiety associated with
death results from the imagination's ability to make death appear to
be more epic that it is: "Nous estimons grande chose nostre mort"
(II, 13, 606) ("We consider our death a great thing" [458]). Montaigne identifies himself in the mind's "I" with the physical instability
of the universe. He enables himself to overcome the fear of death by
demystifying its teleological function and reconceiving it as a series
of discrete ephemeral passages. The visceral images associated with
the "danse macabre" are displaced by the imagination's deliberate attempt to disengage itself from a terrifying cathexis and to reinscribe
death within the more felicitous rhythm of daily life: "Le continuel
ouvrage de vostre vie c'est bastir la mort. Vous estes en la mort pendant que vous estes en vie. Car vous estes apres la mort quand vous
n'estes plus en vie" (I, 20, 93) ("The constant work of your life is to

build death. You are in death while you are in life; for you are after death when you are no longer in life" [65]).

What Montaigne inherits from the Stoic tradition can be described as a practice of self-care that depends on an ideality requiring actions to conform to reason. As in the case of Aristotle, Montaigne delineates a relationship between the imagination and perception while drawing on the Stoic practice that enables the imagination to negotiate between body and mind. Yet the ethical imperative associated with the Stoic tradition to create a stable and detached self undergoes a significant transformation in the *Essays* by allowing the self to engage in commerce with otherness:[11] "Les livres m'ont servi non tant d'instruction que d'exercitation" (III, 12, 1039) ("Books have served me not so much for instruction as for exercise" [795]). Insofar as theory is a discourse that opens subjects to the nonidentical, cognitive mastery becomes an impossibility that nevertheless calls for a new kind of responsibility. The impossible creates and keeps open the possibility of the coming of the other, which is beyond the authority of authorship.

If Montaigne adopts from the Stoics the superiority of the mind over the body, he does so by transcending the constraints of reason. Montaigne's writing, as he describes it in "De la vanité" (III, 9) ("Of Vanity"), takes shape according to the peripatetic rhythm of the wandering mind: "Mon stile et mon esprit vont vagabondant des mesmes." (III, 9) ("My style and my mind alike go roaming" [761]) The implication suggested here is that writing seduces or, etymologically speaking, leads astray (se = *ducere*) through the digressions (de-grad, to walk aside), leading to the perversion (to go off track) of an idea.

The exemplarity of the imagination in relation to the body is perhaps most keenly observed in "Sur des vers de Virgile" (III, 5) ("On Some Verses of Virgil"). Here Montaigne demonstrates a preference for Virgil's elliptical evocation of love over Martial's crude representation of it since, metaphorically speaking, it threatens to emasculate him: "Il me semble qu'il me chapone. . . . Celuy qui dict tout, il nous saoule et nous desgouste" (III, 5, 880) ("He who says everything satiates and disgusts us" [671]). If, as Montaigne claims, Virgil's representation of love is more like love than love, it is because the mimetic qualities of his writing succeeds more by "periphrase et peinture" (III, 5, 848) ("roundaboutly and figuratively" [644]) than by "dévolement."(unveiling). The power of the imagination allows Venus, the goddess of love, to project the face of that which is most invisible. To be sure, if, according to the logocentric myth, language can capture referentiality in its process of unveiling, ironically it can only do so through suggestion and by obscuring its empirical point of reference. In the end, less paradoxically becomes more.

As I have demonstrated elsewhere, Montaigne's "Sur des vers de Virgile" is a response to the onset of old age and sexual decline, revealing the latent desires of a subject in search of regeneration through the pleasures of the text:[12] "Puisque c'est le privilege de l'esprit de se r'avoir de la vieillesse, je luy conseille, autant que je puis, de le faire; qu'il verdisse, qu'il fleurisse ce pendant, s'il peut, comme le guy sur un arbre mort" (III, 5, 844) ("Since it is the privilege of the mind to rescue itself from old age, I advise mine to do so as strongly as I can. Let it grow green, let it flourish meanwhile, if it can, like mistletoe on a dead tree" [641]). If the desire for sexual pleasure declines in old age, it is textual exploration that enables the essayist to sustain the pleasure of youth through the materiality of language.

The greatest incitement to Venus's games is to hide them from view; the greatest way to curtail desire is to expose it in all its nudity. From this perspective, desire operates according to the exigencies of metonomy. Art therefore becomes the mediator of erotic stimulation. If Nature, represented as the "mauvais mere," is responsible for the decline of Montaigne's virility, it is in contrast to art, which enables sexual pleasure. If taken seriously, this understanding demands a poetics not of unveiling but of obscurity and diversion: "Est-ce à dire que moins nous en exhalons en parole, d'autant nous avons loy d'en grossir la pensée?" (III, 5, 847) ("Does this mean that the less we breathe of it in words, the more we have the right to swell our thoughts with it?" [644]). The success of Virgil's and Lucretius's fertile allusiveness stems from the power of the imagination to penetrate the secrets nature holds in abeyance: "Celuy qui craint à s'exprimer nous achemine à en penser plus qu'il n'en y a" (III, 5, 880) ("He who is afraid to express himself leads us on to think more than there is" [671]).

In "De l'institution des enfans" ("Of the Education of Children"), for example, the Montaignian imagination envisages an allegorical figure of Philosophy, mannishly dressed like Ariosto's Bradamente, who wears a helmet and is much like Pallas Athena herself. Represented as a composite ideal, the figure of Philosophy accompanies men throughout their lives, even in the decrepitude of old age: "La philosophie a des discours pour la naissance des hommes comme pour la decrepitude. . . . C'est ce que dict Epicurus au commencement de sa lettre à Meniceus: 'Ny le plus jeune refuie à philosopher, ny le plus vieil s'y lasse'" (I, 26, 164) ("Philosophy has lessons for the birth of men as well as for their decrepitude. . . . It is what Epicurus says at the beginning of his letter to Meniceus: 'Neither let the youngest refuse to study philosophy, nor the oldest weary of it" [121]). This improper figure in drag, so to speak, becomes a valued partner despite her boyish dress. If Philosophy becomes a more proper partner in its impropriety, it is because it offers more than those feminine ladies, who disdain old men ("le desdain de ces beaux yeux" (III, 5, 887) ("the disdain of those four eyes" [677]). Without the presence of this voluptuous albeit manly cross-dresser in the theater of the imagination, life would become monstrous; without the presence of Philosophy we would be no better off than beasts: "Mais son office propre et particulier . . . sans lequel tout cours de vie est desnaturé, turbulent, et difforme, et y peut on justement attacher ces escueils, ces hailers, et ces monsters" (I, 26, 162) ("But her own particular task . . . without which the course of any life is denatured, turbulent, and deformed, and fit to be associated with those dangers, those brambles, and those monsters" [120]). Philosophy therefore takes on erotic connotations since it "chatouille ou poigne vostre conscience" (III, 9, 989) ("tickles or pricks your conscience" [757]).

If the imagination can enact a form of theatricality through the power of the will, it can also be acted upon by physical symptoms. In "De l'exercitation" ("Of Practice") the text represents a fantasy in which the physical senses, through the re-membering of an accident, produce psychological speculations resulting from the power of the involuntary will: "Il y a plusieurs mouvemens en nous qui ne partent pas de nostre ordonnance" (II, 6, 375) ("There are movements of ours that do not come from our will" [271]). For Montaigne, however, the power of the imagination can also produce infelicitous consequences that make the thinking subject go astray. Our ability to take hold of the world can only be mimetic and not "vraisemblable" in the Aristotelian sense of the term.

The narrative self depicted in the *Essays,* endlessly reconfigured by the imagination, produces a monstrous form that is forever in a state of crisis because of its inability to assume the shape of a single image. In writing the *Essays* Montaigne comes to perceive the monster within himself as an amorphous spectacle to be seen. The representation of the mind's eye envisages a self depicted as a monster in the etymological sense of the word (*monstrum*). Montaigne insists upon displaying his inadequacies, demonstrating them to the public, and making a spectacle out of his own deformity. The narrator's mise en scène projects a spectacle to see and an imperative to be seen (*monstrare*, to show): "Je n'ay veu monstre et miracle au monde plus expres que moy-mesme. . . . Mais plus je me hante et me connois, plus ma difformité m'estonne, moins je m'entens en moy." (III, 11, 1029) ("I have seen no more evident monstrosity and miracle in the world than myself. . . . But the more I frequent myself and know myself, the more my deformity astonishes me, and the less I understand myself " [787]). In "De l'institution des enfans" Montaigne depicts the child of his mind, with its distinctive failings and deformities: "Quant aux facultez naturelles qui sont en moy, dequoy c'est icy l'essay, je les sens flechir sous la charge. Mes conceptions et mon jugement ne marche qu'à tastons, chancelant, bronchant et chopant" (I, 26, 146) ("As for the natural faculties that are in me, of which this book is the essay, I feel them bending under the load. My conceptions and my judgment move only by groping, staggering, stumbling, and blundering" [107]). If the cogitations of Montaigne's imagination enact an immaculate conception resulting from the imprint of a self-image represented as other, it is in order to show that the creation of an imperfect father, one who was lazy and unable to stick to a single subject, produces a son whose imperfections are quite analogous.

Throughout the essays Montaigne draws on a series of anecdotes, both textual and empirical, using their imaginative potential—sometimes to the point of deformation—to recast its meaning. A key topos that emerges in relation to the imagination is that of monstrosity. In "De l'oisiveté" ("Of Idleness") the project of writing is conceived of as an act of registering the monstrous productions of the mind: "Pour en contempler à mon aise l'ineptie et l'estrangeté, j'ay commencé de les mettre en rolle, esperant avec le temps luy en faire honte à luy mesmes" (I, 8, 70) ("In order to contemplate their ineptitude and strangeness at my pleasure, I have begun to put them in writing, hoping in time to make my mind ashamed of itself" [21]).

The monster, represented by incomprehensible difference, comes to represent the otherness associated with the self; the fantasies of the human mind reveal imaginative peregrinations suggesting that monsters can also be creations of the mind. However, the essayist's desire to contemplate the otherness within the self (an otherness signified by "l'ineptie et l'estrangete") cannot be fully circumvented by the injunction that the mind should be ashamed of itself when confronted with its monsters. If the imagination presupposes the existence of a "reality" that is different from it, it is because the imaginary, while transgressing the limits of what we call reality, creates a space in which the distinguishing features between the real and the imagined are indiscernible.

The condition of alterity that characterizes the mind in its mobility dislocates the specular relation with the particular instance of the mind as it is represented in the text: "Je prononce ma sentence par articles descousus, ainsi que de choses qui ne se peut dire à la fois et en bloc" (III, 13, 1076) ("I speak my meaning in disjointed parts, as something that cannot be said all at once and in a lump" [824]). The *aporia* created by passing from the cognitive fabrication of the grotesque to its transcription in the text allows for a change confirming its protean form. The textual representation of experience has the potential to offer, if not oracular veracity, then at least a future other to which it is connected through a shared experience of alterity. Moreover, the description of the essays provided at the beginning of "De l'amitié" ("Of Friendship") suggests the characteristics of an "écriture informe," a writing of the marginal and difference: "Que sont-ce icy aussi . . . que crotesques et corps monstrueux, rappiecez de divers membres, sans certaine figure, n'ayants ordre, suite ny proportion que fortuite" (I, 28, 183) ("And what are these things of mine, in truth, but grotesques and monstrous bodies, pieced together of divers members, without definite shape, having no order, sequence, or proportion other than accidental?" [135]).

Among the many metaphors Montaigne uses to describe his *Essays*, he seems particularly fond of thinking of them as "les enfantemens de nostre esprit." ("the children of our mind"). In "Du dementir," ("Of Giving the Lie"), for example, he sustains the idea that writing down his wild fancies gives them direction and purpose: "Aux fins de renger ma fantasie à resver mesme par quelque ordre et projet, et la garder de se perdre et extravaguer au vent, il n'est que de donner corps et mettre en registre tant de menues pensées qui se presentent à elle" (II, 18, 665) ("In order to train my fancy even to dream with some order and purpose, and in order to keep it from losing its way and roving with the wind, there is nothing like embodying and registering all the little thoughts that come to it." [504]).

For Montaigne the work of the imagination is also a work of mourning. The question that therefore arises is how we as readers can act ethically, out of a sense of duty, toward Montaigne yet still enable him to speak in his very absence. To be sure, Jacques Derrida tells us that mourning is a discursive performance of sorts that constitutes the acting out of inheritance and, in the process, allows it to become the locus of desire.[13] The reader of Montaigne becomes the guardian of the text's memory and therefore enables us, as John O'Brien suggests, to see the dead:[14] "Tout ainsi que nature nous faict voir, que plusieurs choses mortes ont encore des relations occultes à la vie" (I, 3, 21) ("Even so nature shows us that many dead things still have occult relations to life" [13]). In a text on Roland Barthes Derrida once suggested that it is only "in us that the dead may speak and ultimately reside, thereby revealing that death is not the end of being."[15] If death delivers us to memory and interiorization, it is in order to engage in the performance of a ghostly inheritance and debt. Yet the complex play of virtualization that characterizes the act of reading engenders complex relations of spatiotemporal dislocation that challenge the stability of self-contained realms.

The representation of the text as monument suggests the commemoration of the past (monument as tomb) and the possibility of predicting the future (monument, like *monstrum,* is derived from *monere,* to predict. Conscious of the text's ability to generate future texts from the inheritance of the past, Montaigne invites readers to engage in the same proliferation of writing he produced in the allongeails through the rereading of his essays. Montaigne thus sees reading as a form of seeing. This model appears to be contiguous with the idea of experience, the subject of the penultimate essay. Even though he expresses reticence concerning the reader's penchant to deform the matter of the text, he nevertheless realizes that in the end the work of the imagination always sabotages the authority of authorship. In the "Apologie" he expressed the fear that his work, like that of Tasso, would become deformed and left in a state that would be beyond his capacity to remedy: "J'eus plus de despit encore que de compassion, de le voir à Ferrare en si piteux estat, survivant à soy-mesmes, mesconnoissant et soy et ses ouvrages, lesquels, sans son sçeu, et toutesfois à sa veue, on a mis en lumiere incorrigez et informes" (II, 12, 492) (I felt even more vexation than compassion to see him in Ferrara in so piteous a state, surviving himself, not recognizing himself or his works, which, without his knowledge and yet before his eyes, have been brought out uncorrected and shapeless" [363]).

Referring to the way in which he narrates stories, the essayist declares that "chacun y peut joindre ses exemples" (105) ("everyone can add his own examples to them" [75]). In order to traverse the *aporia,* the textual locus at the limit of past and future, the finite work must contain in its own negation a rewriting that paradoxically constitutes an undoing.

Just as Montaigne inherited the traces of the dead in the form of La Boétie's library, so we, as readers of the *Essays,* are haunted by texts yet enable them to live on as a ghostly inheritance: "Ce qui me sert, peut aussi par accident servir à un autre" (II, 6, 377) ("What is useful to me may also by accident be useful to another" [272]). The survival of Montaigne therefore becomes a question of transcending the original desire, set down in "Au lecteur," to limit the readership of his essays to a small circle of friends and relatives. His survival is also related to the promise of the archive, which exteriorizes what has been deposited there; it re-members a corpus through disfiguration so that rigor mortis might not finally set in. The so-called death of the author paradoxically gives new life beyond the finitude of the text, for it gives a future to a life that will have been through a narrative whose remains might be read otherwise. Like the Freudian concept of repression, our talking through the *Essays,* produced in the paradoxical act of reading, could, in fact, begin to interpret what the essayist might not have known: "En mes escris mesmes je ne retrouve pas tousjours l'air de ma premiere imagination: je ne sçay ce que j'ay voulu dire" (II, 12, 566) ("Even in my own writings I do not always find again the sense of my first thought ; I do not know what I meant to say" [425–26]). The desire to restore the so-called interlocutory scene, a practice that some critics still hold dear, renders the text "Montaigne" hostage to a recuperative impulse, suggesting that we cannot survive with an unconscious. Montaigne may proclaim in "Au Lecteur" that "c'est moy que je peins" ("it is myself that I portray" [2]), but by the end of the book "ce n'est plus moy" (III, 13,1102) ("it is no longer myself" [846]). If the essays constitute the practice of self-portraiture, they nevertheless represent a failure to enact the ideality of the writerly quest. Victim of a hermeneutic disclosure, Montaigne's text claims that the publication of his book "mortgages" it to the world and thereby fails to maintain the authority of authorship: "Celuy qui a hypothecqué au monde son ouvrage, je trouve apparence qu'il n'y aye plus de droict" (III, 9, 963) ("When a man has mortgaged his work to the world, it seems to me that he has no further right to it" [736]). However, knowing how futile it may be to recover intentionality, the essayist responds by wishing to return as a ghostly presence in order to rectify the misreading to which he writing has fallen victim: "Je reviendrois volontiers de l'autre monde pour démentir celuy qui me formeroit autre que je n'estois, fut ce pour m'honorer" (III, 9, 983) ("I would willingly come back from the other world to give the lie to any man who portrayed me other than I was, even if it were to honor me" [751]).

The disparity between the event of thought and its interpretation precludes our ability to recover things as they once were: "[Il] n'y a rien qui demeure, ne qui soit toujours un . . . l'aage et generation subsequente va tousjours desfaisant et gastant la precedente" (II, 12, 602) ("There is nothing that abides and is always the same . . . the subsequent age and generation is always undoing and destroying the preceding one" [456]). If we read because we wish to hear, isn't the goal of reading ideally meant to function as a recuperative act? Interestingly, despite the essayist's belief that La Boétie is more present to him in his absence than in his presence, he suggests that the imaginary dialogue he maintains with his friend merely functions at a loss, imbricated as it is in the movement of difference. Montaigne posits a possible termination of inquiry when he asks: "Le principal et plus fameux sçavoir de nos siecles, est-ce pas sçavoir entendre les sçavans?" (III, 13, 1069) ("Is it not the chief and most reputed learning of our times to learn to understand the learned?" [818]). If understanding is conceived of as a way of attempting to hear, then the possibility of coming into direct contact with the ancients is indeed slight.

The paradigm of interpretation that Montaigne performs in "De l'experience" suggests that the production of meaning occurs over time, resulting in an endless series of hermeneutic complications. The temporalizing effect of reading means that signification can never be self-identical: "Trouvons nous pourtant quelque fin au besoin d'interpreter? S'y voit-il quelque progres et advancement vers la tranquilité? Nous faut-il moins d'advocats et de juges que lors que cette masse de droict estoit encore en sa premiere enfance?" (III, 13, 1068) ("Do we therefore find any end to the need of interpreting? Do we see any progress and advance toward tranquillity? Do we need fewer lawyers and judges than when this mass of law was still in its infancy?"

[817]). If, as the essayist suggests, interpretation and knowability are ephemeral, it is because meaning cannot reconstitute itself exactly as it was contextually. Perhaps interpretation best succeeds when it fails; the work of such an author "n'est vif qu'à demy" (III, 13, 1068) ("is only half alive" [818]).

For Montaigne theory thus opens itself up to the unconditionality of the writing of the essays and, in the process, engages in different ways of eroding what constitutes "reality." The *Essays* represents the consequences of such a vision by refusing to deny the otherness of Being: "Mais nous sommes, je ne sçay comment, doubles en nous-mesmes, qui faict que ce que nous croyons, nous ne le croyons pas, et ne nous pouvons deffaire de ce que nous condamnons" (II, 16, 619) ("But we are, I know not how, double within ourselves, with the result that we do not believe what we believe, and we cannot rid ourselves of what we condemn" [469]). Theorizing is an act of resistance to the redaction of thought; the performance of self-reflexive play cannot contain itself, for the inquiring mind invents yet other theoretical re-visions that undercut the self-grounding necessary for the construction of "identity:" "Moy à cette heure et moy tantost sommes bien deux" (III, 9, 964) ("Myself now and myself a while ago are indeed two" [736]). The paradoxical task of Montaigne's writing is to dismantle the fiction of what is real and instead engage in a form of speculation that projects what may be considered to be "real" into what is other than itself. Montaigne's text aims to transcend the closed circle of representation by permitting the fabulous imagination the possibility of living on: "Autant en fera le second au tiers" (II, 12, 561) ("The second will do as much for the third" [421]). The projection of Being for Montaigne thus produces an archive that can never be fully possessed. Imaginative play nevertheless allows for spatio-temporal renewal by making Montaigne's thought possible as something still to come: "C'est tesmoignage de crudité et indigestion que de regorger la viande comme on l'a avallée. L'estomac n'a pas faict son operation, s'il n'a faict changer la façon et la forme à ce qu'on luy avoit donné à cuire." (I, 26, 151) ("It is a sign of rawness and indigestion to disgorge food just as we swallowed it. The stomach has not done its work if it has not changed the condition and form of what has been given it to cook" [111])

More than three centuries before the birth of psychoanalysis, Montaigne's *Essays* lay bare the workings of the human imagination while performing a pivotal role in the development of the idea of human subjectivity. Harold Bloom suggests that Freud had more in common with Montaigne than with the biological sciences: "Montaigne's defense of the self is also an analysis of the self, and Montaigne appears now to have been the ancestor not only of Emerson and Nietzsche, both of whom acknowledge him, but also of Freud, who did not."[16]

The present study examines how Montaigne, the inventor of the modern essay, signals the emergence of the Western concept of the self by exploring how human desires and fears are represented in writing. In the *Essays* the imagination acts as the generative core of an internal universe that influences both the body and mind and reveals itself as essential to human experience. At times Montaigne's text actually performs a healing function resulting from the playful work of the imagination. The imagination allows the essayist to approach the unknowable and the unswayable. It can cause pain but it can also have a curative effect. Far from being an object of scorn (many sixteenth-century European thinkers disparaged the imagination because of its relationship to the senses and the realm of the body), the imagination is often portrayed positively in Montaigne's work. Although the essayist recognizes that the power of the imagination can blind and confuse us, revealing our inability to grasp things, he often represents it as curative, enabling the mind's "I" to sustain itself in the face of human difficulty.

Montaigne's writing depicts imaginative experiences that test the limits of identity, knowledge, and ethics, such as the beyond of death, the ineffable nature of human desire, and the monstrousness of the self. The work of the imagination realizes possibilities that are discovered in a nature that is not as socially restrictive as one that is socially constructed. The cultural encounters that constitute what is socially *proper* involve moments of impropriety; it is in these moments that the question of difference is explored and thereby affords the imagination the possibility of exploring a world without limits. Through the rhetorical configurations that constitute the search for self-knowledge, the mind's "I" in Montaigne creates a persona that overcomes the contingencies of existence and allows the imagination to invent other selves. The power of the imagination engenders critical fictions in which language points to an ethereal reality created by the mind's "I": "Combien de fois ce n'est plus moy!" (III, 13,1102) ("How irrevocably it is no longer myself" [846]).

The individual chapters of the present study serve as case studies that demonstrate how the essays are expositions of ambivalence and the unresolved tension of living in the world. My goal, therefore, is not to present a unified, static Hegelian account of the *Essays*. Such a master narrative would go against the spirit of the essays.

> Et ne desseigne jamais de les produire entiers. Car je ne voy le tout de rien. . . . De cent membres et visages qu'a chaque chose, j'en prens un tantost à lecher seulement, tantost à effleurer; et par fois à pincer jusqu'à l'os. . . . Semant icy un mot, icy un autre, eschantillons despris de leur piece, sans dessein escortez et sans promesse, je ne suis pas tenu d'en faire bon . . . me rend[ant] au doubte et incertitude, et à ma maistresse forme, qui est l'ignorance. (I, 50, 302)

> And I never plan to develop them completely. . . . Of a hundred members and faces that each thing has, I take one, sometimes only to lick it, sometimes to brush the surface, sometimes to pinch it to the bone. . . . Scattering a word here, there another, samples separated from their context, dispersed, without a plan and without a promise, I am not bound to make something of them . . . giving myself up to doubt and uncertainty and my ruling quality, which is ignorance. (219)

In accordance with Montaigne's desire for his text to remain forever fertile and in balance, the present study delineates the rhetorical choreographics associated with the kinetic energy of the essay, for to do otherwise would be to disable what Montaigne calls "the power of the imagination." Each chapter demonstrates how the imagination functions as an effect of language. To be sure, the "power of the imagination" generates the construction of meaning and enables it to play itself out rhetorically in the performance of the essay. Since Montaigne wished his essays to have a future, he requested that we read them as engaged readers by permitting ourselves to be modern, as he himself was in his own time.

Part I, "Monster Theory," examines the fragility of gender resulting from the peripatetic movement of a fabulous imagination. Utilizing the trope of the monstrous body, it records an alternative to the rigidity associated with what is conceived of as natural and suggests that gender is not solely bound up with sexuality. For Montaigne the human condition is para-doxical, with the marginal coming to characterize the natural. In demonstrating the permeability of the human imagination, Montaigne's text emphasizes the performative construction of gender, suggesting that the active role of gender can call into question the very idea of the "natural" to which difference is meant to be reduced. Chapter 1, containing an analysis of "De la force de l'imagination"(I, 21) ("Of the Power of the Imagination") focuses on the relationship between psychic activity and sexuality, as well as on how the concept of nature is more a question of mind over matter. Montaigne represents the imagination's speculative power in enacting "sex-change operations"; sexual metamorphoses are realized when conventionally developed gender roles are transgressed. By describing varieties of monstrosity, Montaigne's essay "Des boiteux" (III, 11) (Of Cripples"), the subject of chapter 2, first proposes a hermeneutic riddle, disguised as an epistemological question, and finally takes on ontological proportions by revealing the crippled judgment that is endemic to the human condition. Montaigne's essay challenges the illusory nature of masculinity and the authority upon which its rests. The recognition of lameness and monstrosity ironically possesses a potency of its own.

Part II, "Death Sentences" studies the gnawing presence of death in the areas of friendship, writing, and the public world of counsel. It examines how the imagination relates to the act of mourning and how it overcomes the fear of death through diversionary tactics and simulation. Chapter 3, "Montaigne's Fraternity: La Boétie on Trial," examines the ways in which "De l'amitié" functions as a prosthesis of La Boétie's *De la servitude volontaire*. It discusses how that friendship survives and perhaps even dies a second death in the essayist's speculative peregrinations. Chapter 4, "Montaigne on Horseback, or the Simulation of Death," recounts how the practice of death—an existential impossibility—is mediated through the experience of writing and gives meaning to his fall. (Here "on horse back" functions as a play on words; its French equivalent "à cheval" can also be understood as "in-between," as, for example, the impossible passage between life and death or between being and nothingness.) Chapter 5, "The Anxiety of Death: Narrative and Subjectivity in 'De la diversion'," examines how the preoccupation with death functions as the condition of narrative in its diversionary strategy. An analysis of this essay reveals how the imagination enacts the scene that the essay depicts, the vain movement of diversion, by mirroring the theoretical strategy that is the subject of the writing. Chapter 6, "Excavating Montaigne: The Essayist on Trial," discusses the relationship between the essayist and Marie de Gournay, the essayist's adopted daughter and literary executor. This chapter demonstrates how de Gournay imagines Montaigne's desire beyond death, suggesting that death has a procreative function since the imagination has a future as inheritance. By assuming the role of literary executor, de Gournay tries to do for Montaigne what he had done for La Boétie in preserving—and perhaps disfiguring—his literary fortune.

Part III, "Philosophical Impostures," examines questions of philosophy, experience, and the relation of self-portraiture to oblivion. It deals with questions of ethics and its relationship to self-portraiture. Chapter 7, "The Socratic Makeover," explores how, through the power of the imagination, the essayist disfigures his borrowed texts and produces a proliferation of "phisionomies" that enable the essay to become the site (as well as the sight) of a literary portrait. By challenging the notion of authenticity, "De la phisionomie" (III,12) ("Of Physiognomy") depicts an ethically responsible imagination in its resistance to master narratives.

Chapter 8, "Romancing the Stone," studies the themes of diversity and difference in relation to the rhetoric of self-portraiture in "De l'experience" (III, 13) ("Of Experience") in the process suggesting that the imagination is capable of expanding the boundaries in which the cultural expectations of what constitutes masculinity can be re-vised. By going beyond the propriety of what is considered natural, the essay engages in moments of impropriety in which questions of difference are explored and through which the essayist is offered a choice in the construction of the self. This chapter also explores the literary representation of the famous biographical anecdote concerning Montaigne's kidney stone. The metaphor of the kidney stone and the pain of its passage become the subject of a "family romance" in which the imagination permits the essayist to reflect on his mortality. The drama of this passage in the mind's "I" describes the body as an agent that enables the essayist to distance himself from his lineage and go beyond the parameters of what are socially accepted notions of gender.

Finally, this study draws attention to how the essays constitute a theater in which the pursuit of thought plays itself out in the mind's

"I". More often than not the eye sees by imagining that which is not visible. If Montaigne's writerly project returns to the metaphor of sight, it is in order to demonstrate the visual agency that allows us to bring things to light through the mind's "I". The exemplarity of the Montaignian imagination teaches us that we can transcend the dominant positivism of our current age by seeing things otherwise.

PART I

Monster Theory

1

MONTAIGNE'S FANTASTIC MONSTERS AND THE CONSTRUCTION OF GENDER

Je n'ay veu monstre et miracle au monde plus expres que
moy-mesme.
"DES BOYTEUX" (III, 11, 1029)

I have seen no more evident monstrosity and
miracle in the world than myself.
"OF CRIPPLES" (787)

———————————————

Nostre verité de maintenant, ce n'est pas ce qui est
mais ce qui se persuade à autruy.
"DU DEMENTIR" (II, 18, 666)

Our truth of nowadays is not what is, but what others
can be convinced of.
"OF GIVING THE LIE" (505)

 As early as the essay "De l'oisiveté" (I, 8) ("Of Idleness") Montaigne informs the reader of the necessity of controlling the movement of his mind. Instead of producing a sense of spiritual tranquillity, Montaigne's retirement from public life paradoxically generated intense psychic activity embodied in amorphous images of "chimeres" (chimeras) and "monstres fantasques" (fantastic monsters). The condition of idleness allows the imagination to wander about fortuitously so that the mind's performance, as it is recounted in the text, represents a psychic "reality" whose sheer excessiveness translates the unreal or fantastic qualities of the work. Accordingly, the essayist's apprenticeship to a contemplative existence is characterized by a formlessness of thought; the reflective subject risks becoming like a runaway horse, out of control, and always already beyond itself:

Dernierement que je me retiray chez moy, deliberé autant que
je pourroy, ne me mesler d'autre chose que de passer en repos,

et à part, ce peu qui me reste de vie: il me sembloit ne pouvoir faire plus grande faveur à mon esprit, que de le laisser en pleine oysiveté, s'entretenir soy mesmes, et s'arrester et rasseoir en soy: ce que j'esperois qu'il peut meshuy faire plus aisément, devenu avec le temps plus poisant, et plus meur. Mais je trouve,

> variam semper dant otia mentem,

que au rebours, faisant le cheval eschappé, il se donne cent fois plus d'affaire à soy mesmes, qu'il n'en prenoit pour autruy; et m'enfante tant de chimeres et monstres fantasques les uns sur les autres, sans ordre, et sans propos. (I, 8, 33)

Lately when I retired to my home, determined so far as possible to bother about nothing except spending the little life I have left in rest and seclusion, it seemed to me I could do my mind no greater favor than to let it entertain itself in full idleness and stay and settle in itself, which I hoped it might do more easily now, having become weightier and riper with time. But I find

> Ever idle hours breed wandering thoughts. LUCAN

that, on the contrary, like a runaway horse, it gives itself a hundred times more trouble than it took for others, and gives birth to so many chimeras and fantastic monsters, one after another, without order or purpose. (21)

The essays are clearly about the parenting of the self and the monstrousness of selfhood; they serve as a locus where the act of writing becomes the tool by means of which the narrating subject can represent itself to itself: "Encore se faut-il testoner, encore se faut-il ordonner et renger pour sortir en place. Or je me pare sans cesse, car je me descris sans cesse" (II, 6, 378) ("Even so one must spruce up, even so one must present oneself in an orderly arrangement, if one would go out in public. Now, I am constantly adorning myself, for I am constantly describing myself" [273]). In this process of self-portraiture, the text reveals the consequences of a fevered imagination. Montaigne sees language and himself in its deformed images; the self that he views risks following its own course, uncontrolled as it is by the power of the imagination. The chimeras—defined as "idle conceits, frivolous thoughts and fruitless imaginings"—reproduce the image of an essentially empty and vain progenitor whose writerly deformities characterize the unreal or fantastic monster as a difference that resists normative meaning.[1]

For Montaigne, then, writing depends upon a certain kinetic energy, a mobility that is textually represented by an amorphous self capable of undergoing multiple metamorphoses. What began as inactivity becomes a process of self-analysis; in its search for mastery, the figuration of the ego struggles to make sense of the difference within the self. What is striking here is the way in which the mind usurps the female role of engendering and gives birth to a self representing a monstrous narcissism that is transformed into a spectacle or an object to be seen: "Je ne vis jamais pere, pour teigneux ou bossé que fut son fils, qui laissast de l'avoüer" (I, 26, 145) ("I have never seen a father who failed to claim his son, however mangy or hunchbacked he was" [106]).

At the core of Montaigne's writerly practice is the desire to domesticate the excesses and strangeness of the mind's activities. When the essayist explains the shift from reflection to writing in this section he recognizes the need to neutralize what he terms the "monstrousness" within himself. Drawing upon an extended metaphor that comprises images of unplanted fields and infertile women, Montaigne's text discovers the monstrous side of nature as something emanating from what is reproduced without mediation:

> Comme nous voyons des terres oysives, si elles sont grasses et fertilles, foisonner en cent mille sortes d'herbes sauvages et inutiles, et que, pour les tenir en office, il les faut assubjectir et employer à certaines semences, pour nostre service; et comme nous voyons que les femmes produisent bien toutes seules, des amas et pieces de chair informes, mais que pour faire une generation bonne et naturelle, il les faut embesoigner d'une autre semence: ainsin est-il des espris. Si on ne les occupe à certain sujet, qui les bride et contreigne, ils se jettent desreiglez, par-cy par là, dans le vague champ des imaginations. (I, 8, 32)

> Just as we see that fallow land, if rich and fertile, teems with a hundred thousand kinds of wild and useless weeds, and that to set it to work we must subject it and sow it with certain seeds for our service; and as we see that women, all alone, produce mere

shapeless masses and lumps of flesh, but that to create a good
and natural offspring they must be made fertile with a different
kind of seed; so it is with minds. Unless you keep them busy
with some definite subject that will bridle and control them, they
throw themselves in disorder hither and on in the vague field of
imagination. (20–21)

Montaigne's text thus devalues what has not been properly cul-
tivated by *humankind*. Untamed growth motivates a genetic process
that is unequal, irregular, and yet is perceived as completely natural.
The paradox of nature lies in the existence of its monstrous imperfections: the disquieting reality of what appears to be unnatural must
be submitted to a "different kind of seed" that will *create* and not
engender a more perfect nature. Here the use of the maternal metaphor is quite revealing. The biological creation of the mother in the
genetic process is represented as inadequate without the intervention
of a paternal "artistry" that would enable it to transcend the banality
of unmotivated reproduction. When the irregularities of the maternal
body submit to the paternal rule, the idea of naturalness loses its role
as model and origin of beauty. Consequently the figuration of authorship, as it is troped on the image of the maternal body, attests to
the desire for writing to project a paternal "artistry" that creates art
from life.

Montaigne's attempt to give concrete form and order to the
mind's amorphous cogitations is but one way to control the possibility of shaping a life and to displace the otherness within the self
onto the fantasist narratives constituting text production: "que pour
en contempler à mon aise l'ineptie et l'estrangeté, j'ay commancé de
les mettre en rolle, esperant avec le temps luy en faire honte à luy
mesmes" (I, 8, 33) ("that in order to contemplate their ineptitude and
strangeness at my pleasure, I have begun to put them in writing, hoping in time to make my mind ashamed of itself" [21]). Montaigne's
monster can be seen here as a figure for self-portraiture that renders
the text the site of the *unheimlich,* the strange and yet thoroughly
familiar. More than a mere object of shame, as the essayist suggests,
the mind's fantastic monsters attest to the omnipotence of thought
derived from the fictions that the desiring mind "experiences." By
becoming a stranger to himself, in the language of the essay, Montaigne's text ironically transcribes his most intimate secrets in a process of self-alienation. Nevertheless, if he writes to contemplate the

strangeness and ineptness of the mind's activity, he does so in order to neutralize it and to seek relief in the concrete realization of the book: "L'ame qui n'a point de but estably, elle se perd: car, comme on dict, c'est n'estre en aucun lieu, que d'estre par tout" (I, 8, 32) ("The soul that has no fixed goal loses itself; for, as they say, to be everywhere is to be nowhere" ([21]).

The attempt to curtail the unwieldy nature of the essayist's "fantastic" thought is intertextually rooted in the father's moral imperative to manage the family estate wisely. Throughout the *Essays* we witness numerous references to the law of patrimony as it is exemplified in the father's desire to preserve his household from excessive financial waste and decay by keeping "le registre des negoces du mesnage" ("the record of household affairs"): "Il ordonnoit à celuy de ses gens qui lui servoit à escrire, un papier journal à inserer toutes les survenances de quelque remarque, et jour par jour les memoires de l'histoire de sa maison. . . . Usage ancien, que je trouve bon à refraichir, chacun en sa chacuniere. Et me trouve un sot d'y avoir failly" (I, 35, 224) ("He ordered the servant whom he used as his secretary to keep a journal and insert in it all occurrences of any note, and the memorabilia of his family history day by day. . . . An ancient custom, which I think it would be good to revive, each man in each man's home. And I think I am a fool to have neglected it" ([166]).

Elsewhere I have discussed Montaigne's ambivalent relationship to his father regarding the transmission of property and his feeling of inadequacy concerning the administration of the inheritance.[2] The paternal metaphor in "De l'oisiveté," realized through the writerly act of recording, serves as an antidote to the negative connotations associated with idleness and waste; the act of self-portraiture preserves the proper balance between saving and spending. Etymologically linked to the concept of the rule of law, the essayist's "registre" (register) reformulates this writerly practice in terms of the son's submission to the paternal metaphor as it is transcribed through the desired entry into the symbolic order. The "register" is also the *regula* or model of the subject's ideal image of himself that is embodied in another: the father whom he fears he will be unable to live up to. In order to be represented as a totalized and totalizing "self," the Montaignian subject must be positioned in relation to the paternal phallus as a kind of reparative gesture for what is later revealed as the son's failure to record the history of patrimony. The dutiful son wishes to establish his legitimacy in the writerly act "qui s'engage à un registre de durée, de toute sa foy, de toute sa force" (II, 18, 665) ("who binds himself to keep an enduring account, with all his faith, with all his strength" [504]). One might infer that the desiring subject's sought-after "solidity" is an attempt to conform to a standard of what a man should be; it acts as a way to control excessive desire and to limit the illegitimate fantasy produced by the force of the imagination.

However, the enduring account that Montaigne sets forth as the goal of his quest is undone in the writing of the *Essays;* what he terms the "desreglement de nostre esprit" (I, 4, 24) "the unruliness of our mind" [15]) repudiates the image of the father's desire.[3] The monstrous progeny depicted in the text does not reflect a stable identity but rather a multiplicity of selves that is subject to change: "Je ne puis asseurer mon object. Il va trouble et chancelant, d'une yvresse naturelle" (III, 2, 805) ("I cannot keep my subject still. It goes along befuddled and staggering, with a natural drunkenness" [610]). Despite the idealized patriarchal motivation to impose a unified order on the meanderings of the mind, the "living register" inscribed in the text records the self-division of the writing subject. The question of gender identity is signified through tropic self-consciousness and paradoxes; they assert and disrupt meaning and thereby generate tensions between the irregularities of the natural and the unnaturalness of the culturally coded.

RE-VISING THE MONSTROUS

In the essay "D'un enfant monstrueux" (II, 30) ("Of a Monstrous Child") Montaigne records through the trope of the monstrous body an alternative to the rigidity associated with the biologically conceived phallic position; the text allegorizes the possibility of transcending the marginality of the monstrous and the so-called exigencies of gender essentialism. The essayist examines the nature of the monstrous and its relation to the concept of difference. The text begins with a concise yet detailed account—described in "objective" terms—of a Siamese twin with one head that the essayist recently viewed being displayed for money. At first the exemplarity of the monstrous stems from the perception of deviation from the normative; difference, portrayed as a visual "effect," attests to the rarity attributed to the object of the gaze:

Ce conte s'en ira tout simple, car je laisse aux medecins d'en discourir. Je vis avant hier un enfant que deux hommes et une nourrisse, qui se disoient estre le pere, l'oncle et la tante, conduisoyent pour tirer quelque sou de le montrer à cause de son estrangeté. . . . Au dessoubs de ses tetins, il estoit pris et collé à un autre enfant sans teste . . . si vous retroussiez cet enfant imparfait, vous voyez au dessoubs le nombril de l'autre. . . . Le nombril de l'imparfaict ne se pouvoit voir. (II, 30, 712–13)

This story will go its way simply, for I leave it to the doctors to discuss it. The day before yesterday I saw a child that two men and a nurse, who said they were the father, uncle, and aunt, were leading about to get a penny or so from showing him, because of his strangeness. . . . Below the breast he was fastened and stuck to another child, without a head . . . if you turned the imperfect child over and up, you saw the other's navel below. . . . The navel of the imperfect child could not be seen. (538–39)

The scopic drive portrayed here draws one's attention to the unusual and transforms it into a public spectacle of sorts, something to be seen ("de le montrer"; "from showing him"). The identity of the unusual can only be known from the projection of its external features. Representing a composite figure whose boundaries are inadequately differentiated, the monster inscribed in the text calls into question the opposition between self and other. The monster is thus born from the power of the image to evoke what is initially perceived as an abnormal sense of human reality. Vision is presented as a means to reify the sense of the word "monster" by reducing the body to its optical dimensions and by foregrounding the strangeness of its existence.[4]

The representation of the monster in this essay takes on epistemological consequences based on the perception and experience of the viewer. Recognized as an image that resists classification, the monstrous is depicted as lacking consensual practice as a sign: "Nous apelons contre nature ce qui advient contre la coustume" (II, 30, 713) ("We call contrary to nature what happens contrary to custom" [539]). Even though we attribute value to the monstrous by paying to see it, from the perspective of the divine and natural orders the monstrous can be interpreted as unquestionably normal.[5]

Ce que nous appellons monstres, ne le sont pas à Dieu, qui voit
en l'immensité de son ouvrage l'infinité des formes qu'il y a comprinses; et est à croire que cette figure qui nous estonne, se rapporte et tient à quelque autre figure de mesme genre inconnu à
l'homme . . . mais nous n'en voyons pas l'assortiment et la relation. (II, 30, 713)

What we call monsters are not so to God, who sees in the immensity of his work the infinity of forms that he has comprised
in it ; and it is for us to believe that this figure that astonishes
us is related and linked to some other figure of the same kind
unknown to man . . . but we do not see its arrangement and
relationship. (539)

Unlike other Renaissance texts, such as Pierre Boaistuau's *Histoire des prodiges* (1560), where monsters are portrayed as supernatural beings produced by miracles, Montaigne's essay domesticates
the monstrous and consequently veers toward the erasure of the unnatural. The paradoxical reduction of the other to the same—first
through the emblem of the conjoined body and then through the text's
post-1588 metacommentary—returns the body of the "enfant monstrueux" (monstrous child) to itself, in its own image, ironically presented as visually different but still not a shockingly abnormal thing.
Difference is just meant to *be;* the acceptance of diversity neutralizes
difference, strips it of its negative connotations, and figuratively represents the possibility of shaping a life free of what is narrowly conceived of as being "natural": "C'est une hardiesse dangereuse et de
consequence, outre l'absurde temerité qu'elle traine quant et soy, de
mespriser ce que nous ne concevons pas" (I, 27, 181) ("It is a dangerous and fatal presumption, besides the absurd temerity that it implies,
to disdain what we do not comprehend" [134]).

As opposed to the universalizing ethos of reason, the imagination allows for an openness to the particular and the strange. In order to be hospitable toward alterity, however, requires the ability to
transcend the self-contained world of narcissism: "Je n'ay point cette
erreur commune de juger d'un autre selon que je suis. J'en croy ay-
sément des choses diverses à moy . . . et, au rebours du commun,
recoy plus facilement la difference que la ressemblance en nous"
(I, 37, 229) ("I do not share that common error of judging another
by myself. I easily believe that another man may have qualities dif-

ferent from mine . . .; and in contrast with the common run of men, I more easily admit difference than resemblance between us" [169]). By admitting examples of diverse behavior that go beyond accepted norms, the Montaignian subject exempts himself from becoming a self-grounding entity functioning as the measure of the law. The essayist asks the reader to sustain the imperative to be hospitable and requests that the latter contribute to diversity by creating a cornucopia of examples that transgress our horizon of expectations: "Chacun y peut joindre ses exemples: et qui n'en a point, qu'il ne laisse pas de croire qu'il en est, veu le nombre et varieté des accidens" (I, 21, 105) ("Everyone can add his own examples to them; and he who has none, let him not fail to believe that there are plenty, in view of the number and variety of occurences" [75]).

Following the description of the child, an interesting anecdote appears in the essay concerning the representation of another type of monster, namely, one who is monstrous within. The text presents in dramatically visual terms a shepherd with a manly beard but no genitals: "Je viens de voir un pastre en Medoc, de trente ans ou environ, qui n'a aucune montre des parties genitales: il a trois trous par où il rend son eau incessamment; il est barbu, a desir, et recherche l'attouchement des femmes" (III, 30, 713) ("I have just seen a shepherd in Médoc, thirty years old or thereabouts, who has no sign of genital parts. He has three holes by which he continually makes water. He is bearded, has desire, and likes to touch women" [539]). Montaigne's text reveals the apparent discrepancy between inside and outside, or the gap between the ontological and the biological. In constructing the radical otherness of the shepherd's body, the Montaignian text represents a desiring subject whose biological sign of masculinity (the genitals) is missing. Despite the presence of the beard, the man's body becomes the locus of a lack that leaves no self-determined masculinity in place.

This split in the self demonstrates that the question of gender is not solely bound up with the question of sexuality. If identity does not stem from the biologically given (what is considered "natural"), then one may infer that biology is clearly not destiny. Here the concept of the monster (derived from the word *monere*, to portend) loses its prognosticating capacities since what we see (that which is visually absent) does not necessarily represent what we get (desire). In suggesting that the equation between the penis and masculinity and the representation of desire is misrecognized, this anecdote teaches us that the only way to read the signs of gender is "à reculons" (II, 30, 713) ("backward" [539]). Montaigne's text thus implies that desire is capable of producing an invisible signifier without the biological means to represent it; the example suggests that even without anything visible, this absence literally represents the paradoxical presence of the monstrosity of desire.

The shepherd's castration therefore makes him no less a man. Within the chiasmatic logic of the essay, the so-called concept of "normality" is viewed as a consequence of the potency of desire (we are told that he likes to touch women) and not as a biological fact. According to this perspective, the absent penis does not foreclose the functioning of the phallic (an emblem of libidinal [psychic] potency); rather, it redefines masculinity as a biologically nonreferential version of sexualized thought. Consequently, what makes a man a man is placing him in the position of "being" rather than "having." In other words, the penis does not make the man. If the ontological plenitude of desire displaces the anatomical emptiness of the shepherd, it is because phallic potency is more a psychological than a physical "reality."

MONTAIGNE'S SEX-CHANGE OPERATIONS

In "De la force de l'imagination" (I, 21) ("Of the Power of the Imagination") Montaigne's text focuses on the relationship between psychic activity and sexuality, as well as on how the concept of nature is more a question of mind over matter.[6] The essay is composed of a series of tales, each of which carries within it a figural representation of the imagination's power. Attributing anthropomorphic force to the imagination's activity, the essay also demonstrates how it is capable of inflicting various forms of violence: "Son impression me perse. . . . Je ne trouve pas estrange qu'elle donne et les fievres et la mort à ceux qui la laissent faire et qui luy applaudissent" (I, 21, 97–98) ("Its impression on me is piercing. . . . I do not find it strange that imagination brings fevers and death to those who give it a free hand and encourage it" [68]). The imagination, viewed as potentially hostile to the desiring subject, constitutes a threat to its well-being through the illusory force of its destructive drive. However, the unwilled effect of the imagination can also produce its share of pleasure, as in the case of the nocturnal emissions of "boiling youth." Montaigne notes: "Et la jeunesse bouillante s'eschauffe si avant en son harnois tout endormie, qu'elle assouvit en songe ses amoureux désirs" (I, 21, 98) ("And boiling youth, fast asleep, grows so hot in the harness that in dreams it satisfies its amorous desires" [69]).

Nevertheless, Montaigne essay describes the dangers of the imagination's speculative power as capable of producing fictions comparable to the force of the death instinct. From this perspective, the anxiety of anticipation is indeed the cause of the very antagonism inducing the paralysis of the thinking subject. Montaigne cites the Latin quotation "Fortis imaginatio generat casum" (I, 21, 97) ("A strong imagination creates the event" [68]). Montaigne's text presents several case studies in which an overly active and tense imagination submits the ego to an inhibiting and repressive authority. For example, in working too hard to comprehend the nature of madness, Gallus Vibius subjects his mind to such a state of tension that he quickly becomes the victim of the very object of his reflection: "Gallus Vibius *banda* si bien son ame à comprendre l'essence et les mouvemens de la folie, qu'il emporta son jugement hors de son siege, si qu'onques puis il ne l'y peut remettre" (I, 21, 98) "Gallus Vibius strained his mind so hard to understand the essence and impulses of insanity that he dragged his judgement off its seat and never could get it back again" [68]). In another tale a condemned prisoner receives a last-minute pardon, but when he is finally set free to hear his reprieve read aloud he dies of fear: "Et celuy qu'on debandoit pour luy lire sa grace, se trouva roide mort sur l'eschafaut du seul coup de son imagination" (I, 21, 98) ("And one man who was being unbound to have his pardon read him dropped stone dead on the scaffold, struck down by his mere imagination" [69]). The fear generated by an overactive imagination in each of these cases imprisons the anxious subject in the inner theater of affective quiescence. In both examples Montaigne's text foregrounds the effort required by the imagination to realize the self's extinction. The repeated use of the word "bander"—a term that Cotgrave defines as "to bend, to bind, to tie, and to tighten"—translates the paradoxical result of the imagination's drive toward self-expression, namely, the person's subjugation to the omnipotence of thought. However, far from simply limiting the power of the imagination to the paralysis of the subject, Montaigne's text borrows a remarkable example from Ambroise Paré's *Des monstres et des prodiges* to illustrate how the transformative powers of the imagination can enact "sex changes": "Ce n'est pas tant de merveille, que cette sorte d'accident se rencontre frequent: car si l'imagination peut en telles choses, elle est si continuellement et si vigoureusement attachée à ce subject" (I, 21, 99) ("It is not so great a marvel that this sort of accident is frequently met with. For if the imagination has power in such things, it is so continually and vigorously fixed on this subject" [69]). Sexual metamorphoses are realized when conventionally developed gender roles are transgressed. The body, recognized as being anatomically distinct, is nevertheless capable of undergoing transformation through a fashioning of the self that enables one to be perceived as a sexual subject.[7]

In Montaigne's rewriting of Paré's story of Marie-turned-Germain, we learn about a twenty-two-year-old woman who strained herself while jumping, underwent biological metamorphosis by sprouting a penis, and was finally declared a man. The performative construction of gender undercuts the notion of what is considered natural and consequently erases its distinctive marks.

> Passant à Victry le Françoys, je peuz voir un homme que l'Evesque de Soissons avoit nommé Germain en confirmation, lequel tous les habitans de là ont cogneu et veu fille, jusques à l'aage de vingt deux ans, nommée Marie. Il estoit à cett'heure-là fort barbu, et vieil, et point marié. Faisant, dict-il, quelque effort en sautant, ses membres virils se produisirent: et est encore en usage, entre les filles de là, une chanson, par laquelle elles s'entradvertissent de ne faire point de grandes enjambées, de peur de devenir garçons, comme Marie Germain. (I, 21, 99)

> Passing through Vitry-le-François, I might have seen a man whom the bishop of Soissons had named Germain at confirmation, but whom all the inhabitants of that place had seen and known as a girl named Marie until the age of twenty-two. He was now heavily bearded, and old, and not married. Straining himself in some way in jumping, he says, his masculine organs came forth; and among the girls there a song is still current by which they warn each other not to take big strides for fear of becoming boys, like Marie Germain. (69)

In this tale of a girl chasing her pig in Vitry, we learn that not only gender but also sex is variable. If gender is a state of mind, then gender construction can miraculously operate sex changes. Although born Marie, when she acts like a man the robust activity of her inappropriate behavior magically inscribes the marks of sexuality on her body. In becoming a man, Marie/Germain takes on a particular body language that ultimately produces the biological sign of maleness. If gender is actively chosen, then sexuality is passively received as the fatal consequence of thinking difference.

In another example that precedes the Marie/Germain story, Montaigne quotes a line from Ovid's *Metamorphoses* (IX, 793) that refers to the topos of sexual transformation, suggesting the imagination's preoccupation with sex. This line is the conclusion to the tale about a young girl who was born a female and raised as a boy in order to prevent her father from killing her. Engaged to marry a girl, Iphis, the beneficiary of her mother's prayers underwent a metamorphosis and eventually received a penis to reflect the man within her: "Vota puer solvit, que foemina voverat Iphis" ("These offerings, vowed by Iphis as a maid, / By Iphis, now a man, are gladly paid").[8] To become a male thus requires acting like a man. Accordingly, a penis may be the biological mark of masculinity, but it is not the ultimate cause of becoming a man. Viewed from this perspective, the male member is regarded as a mere appendage, an outward sign, a consequence of habit and the potency generated by the force of the imagination.

Montaigne's "sex-change operations" are therefore contingent upon the ways in which we construct ourselves through culturally coded gender roles. As it is represented in the text, gender functions as the variable cultural determinant of sex; it is involved in an ongoing revisionism of corporeal or biological identity. This is perhaps why Montaigne's rewriting of Paré's naturalistic explanation for Marie/Germain's "sex-change operation" is so revealing. According to Paré, "the reason why women can degenerate into men is because women have as much hidden within the body as men have exposed outside; leaving aside, only, that women don't have so much heat, nor the ability to push out what by the coldness of their temperament is held bound to the interior."[9] Paré's so-called clinical observations are physiologically rooted and independent of the performance of gender; sex changes, contingent on the outward movement of the concealed member, depend on bodily heat for their appearance. Of prime importance here is the way in which Paré views sex. Firmly rooted in an androcentric tradition dating back to Greek antiquity, his case study confirms the belief in an archetypal body, with men being more capable of realizing perfection.

Montaigne proceeds otherwise by adding a moral injunction to the denouement of Paré's story. By treating the man trapped in a woman's body as a psychic "reality," the essayist suggests that the only way to control the other within the self is to give women penises as a way to regulate their desire and thereby obliterate the discrepancy between gender and sex:[10] "Pour n'avoir si souvent à rechoir en mesme pensée et aspreté de desir, elle a meilleur compte d'incorporer, une fois pour toutes, cette virile partie aux filles" (I, 21, 99) ("In order not to have to relapse so often into the same thought and sharpness of desire, it is better off if once and for all it incorporates this masculine member in girls" [69]). The consubstantiality that Montaigne seems to be opting for here is merely an allegory of the need to create a more balanced, *natural* self that he conceives of as being thoroughly phallocentric in character. Ironically, the gift of the penis undermines women's capacity to think "difference" by biologically reducing the other to the same and discretely establishing the primacy of the male member. Montaigne's representation of the man within the woman ultimately gives birth to a male identity inscribed on a female body, only to claim for it the universalizing function of sexual *indifference*.

Montaigne's text, however, cannot proceed without introducing ambiguities by suggesting that female desire functions as the generative force of the imagination. In Paré's text the female imagination is described as being capable of giving birth to monstrous offspring. Paré suggests that such children result from the "ardent and obstinate imagination [impuissance] that the mother might receive at the moment she conceived—through some object or fantastic dream."[11] To be sure, Paré's text foregrounds the passive character of the mother, who is forced to focus her gaze on the image of Saint John the Baptist during conception and thereby project the bestiality perceived in that image onto the figure of the child. Playing the role of moralist, Paré ends his observation with a didactic commentary destined to mitigate the power of the female imagination: "It is necessary that women—at the hour of conception when the child is not yet formed . . . not be forced to look at or imagine monstrous things."[12]

In rewriting Paré's text, Montaigne implicitly challenges him for ascribing to the maternal imagination a psychic power that puts into question the supremacy of the biological power of sexual reproduction.

Tant y a que nous voyons par experience les femmes envoyer aux corps des enfans qu'elles portent au ventre des marques de leurs

fantasies, tesmoing celle qui engendra le more. Et il fut presenté
à Charles Roy de Boheme et Empereur [. . .] esté ainsi conceue, à
cause d'un'image de Sainct Jean Baptiste pendue en son lit. Des
animaux il en est de mesmes, tesmoing les brebis de Jacob, et
les perdris et les lièvres, que la neige blanchit aux montaignes.
(I, 21, 105)

Nevertheless, we know by experience that women transmit
marks of their fancies to the bodies of the children they carry in
their womb; witness the one who gave birth to the Moor. And
there was presented to Charles, king of Bohemia and Emperor,
a girl from near Pisa, all hairy and bristly, who her mother said
had been thus conceived because of a picture of Saint John the
Baptist hanging by her bed. With animals it is the same: witness
Jacob's sheep, and the partridges and hares that the snow turns
white in the mountains. (75)

Whereas in Paré's version the female figure is forced to look, Montaigne's account presents the story of a mother who focuses her gaze
on John the Baptist'ss bestial form and thereby enables the power of
her imagination to engender a monster. The result of this re-visionary
practice suggests that the performance of gender, as it is enacted in
this narrative, is one that allows for difference through the staging of
desire. What we accept as natural in this context results from gender
performativity.

The heart of Montaigne's essay involves a discussion of impotence in men and the anxiety associated with sexual performance. In
this context the penis becomes the focal point of the male body, the
corporeal locus from which manliness might conceivably be "measured" and judged. The fear of inadequacy produces tension in the
desiring subject stemming from the inability to conform to a phallic
ideal characterized by strength and potency:

Je suis encore de cette opinion, que ces plaisantes liaisons, dequoy nostre monde se voit si entravé, qu'il ne se parle d'autre
chose, ce sont volontiers des impressions de l'apprehension et
de la crainte. Car je sçay par experience, que tel, de qui je puis
respondre, comme de moy mesme, en qui il ne pouvoit choir
soupçon aucune de foiblesse, et aussi peu d'enchantement, ayant ouy faire le conte à un sien compagnon, d'une defaillance

extraordinaire, en quoy il estoit tombé sur le point, qu'il en avoit le moins de besoin, se trouvant en pareille occasion, l'horreur de ce conte lui vint à coup si rudement frapper l'imagination, qu'il en encourut une fortune pareille. (I, 21, 99–100)

I am still of this opinion, that those comical inhibitions by which our society is so fettered that people talk of nothing else are for the most part the effects of apprehension and fear. For I know by experience that one man, whom I can answer for as for myself, on whom there could fall no suspicion whatever of impotence and just as little of being enchanted, having heard a friend of his tell the story of an extraordinary impotence into which he had fallen at the moment when he needed it least, and finding himself in a similar situation, was all at once so struck in his imagination by the horror of this story that he incurred the same fate. (70)

The paradox of impotence is dramatized in the figurative language of the text, according to which the "tying" of the imagination corresponds to the idea of a decline or symbolic fall; stability is depicted as a form of imaginative impotence. The imagination, considered intermittently as the true seat of power, the place where manliness resides, reveals that the phallus (the symbolic) and the penis (the biological) are not always one and the same.[13] Having a penis and being a male is no guarantee of being able to activate the manliness associated with the functioning of the imagination and the generation of libidinal energy.

Within the context of sixteenth-century thought, Montaigne's essay seeks to distance itself from the more popularly conceived etiology of impotence.[14] Based on the misogynist traditions associated with superstition, impotence was regarded as having roots in demonology. The ligatures, transcribed by the metaphor of "nouer l'aiguillette," are defined as that which "empêche[r] le mari ou la femme . . . de se mettre en état d'accomplir, normalement et utilement, les rapprochements sexuels nécessaires à la propagation de l'espèce."[15] However, in Montaigne's essay this symptomology—the impairment of biological functioning—appears to be a consequence of that which is phantasmatically constructed. Through a curious identification with a hypothetical friend, the subject of the narration (the voice representing Montaigne) describes how the fear evoked by the story of

another's impotence generates the malady itself: "La veue des ango-
isses d'autruy m'angoisse materiellement, et a mon sentiment souvent
usurpé le sentiment d'un tiers" (I, 21, 97) ("The sight of other people's anguish causes very real anguish to me, and my feelings have
often usurped the feelings of others" [68]). In constructing the other
as a masked version of the same, Montaigne's text reveals how narrative (and language) can move the unsuspecting subject away from the
body and paradoxically subjugate it to the effects of a horrific trope
of potency that "lui vint à coup si rudement frapper l'imagination,
qu'il en encourut une fortune pareille" (I, 21, 100) "was all at
once so struck in his imagination . . . that he incurred the same
fate" [70]).

On another level, however, impotence is produced by the conflict between desire and the dangers of intimacy: "Ce malheur n'est à
craindre qu'aux entreprinses, où nostre ame se trouve outre mesure
tandue de desir et respect" (I, 21, 100) ("This mishap is to be feared
only in enterprises where our soul is immoderately tense with desire
and respect" [70]). If respect is evoked as a hindrance to the realization of desire, it is because respect implies the need to control the excesses of sensuality—the monstrous within the self—and to remain
within the boundaries of acceptable behavior. By keeping desire separate from sensuality, Montaigne's text represents the fear of enjoying
a woman's body and experiencing the pleasures derived from making
love. Potency, however, can only be achieved through the relaxation
of the imagination—"sa pensée desbrouillée et desbandée, son corps
se trouvant en son deu" (I, 21, 100) ("with his mind unembroiled and
relaxed and his body in good shape" [70])—a phenomenon producing a fluidity of thought that literally "reembodies" the male subject
with the "tool" of erectile force. In this context, then, the inflation
of the male member operates independently of the biological position of power. Montaigne rewrites male subjectivity here: he brack-
ets tension out of desire and lets the body transcend the masculine
paradigm of erotic pursuit for an erotic responsiveness tempered by
the moderation of female desire: "Or elles ont tort de nous recueillir
de ces contenances mineuses, querelleuses et fuyardes, qui nous este-
ignent en nous allumant" (I, 21, 101) ("Now women are wrong to
greet us with those threatening, quarrelsome, and coy countenances,
which put out our fires even as they light them" [71]).

The "c" version of this essay contains the story of Louis de Foix,
comte de Guerson, who fears impotence but is able to overcome it

through a fantasy of empowerment realized through a surrogate object. Montaigne relates the story of a young friend who marries a woman previously courted by someone else. Frightened by the possibility of having his rival cast a spell on him resulting in impotence, the groom expresses great anxiety to Montaigne before the impending wedding. In a gesture of friendship Montaigne offers the friend a gold medal, a valued object, on which "estoient gravées quelques figures celestes, contre le coup de soleil et oster la douleur de teste" (I, 21, 100) ("were engraved some celestial figures, to protect against sunstroke and take away a headache" [71]). Beyond having the power to relieve bodily pain, the talisman can also induce pleasure by miraculously reversing impotence if the proper ceremonial procedures are adhered to. The gold piece is therefore invested with a surplus value; the inanity of the trick paradoxically grants it the "poids et reverence" (I, 21, 101) ("weight and reverence" [71]) necessary for generating an inflationary economy of desire. The will may well be incapable of curing impotence—"On a raison de remarquer l'indocile liberté de ce membre" (I, 12, 102) ("People are right to notice the unruly liberty of this member" [72])—but the power invested in the talisman by the imagination liberates the paralyzed libido through a cathectic transaction that temporarily shifts the focus of desire from the body to this mediator of magical thinking.

Believing himself the victim of a rival's evildoing, on his wedding night the count is unable to consummate his marriage: "Il avoit eu l'ame et les oreilles si battues, qu'il se trouva lié du trouble de son imagination" (I, 21, 101) ("He had had his soul and his ears so battered that he did find himself fettered by the trouble of his imagination" [71]). Following Montaigne's instructions to tie the gold piece around his waist so that it rests directly above the kidney, the groom "en toute asseurance . . . s'en retournast à son prix faict" (I, 21, 101) ("should return to his business with complete assurance" [71]). The medal thus achieves a desired effect. Virility, as represented here, is the consequence of magical thinking motivated by the psychic investment in a phantasmatic force:

Ces singeries sont le principal de l'effect: nostre pensée ne se pouvant desmesler que moyens si estranges ne viennent de quelqu'abstruse science. . . . Somme, il fut certain que mes characteres se trouverent plus Veneriens que Solaires, plus en action qu'en prohibition. (I, 21, 101)

> These monkey tricks are the main part of the business, our mind being unable to get free of the idea that such strange means must come from some abstruse science. . . . All in all, it is certain that the characters on my medal proved themselves more venereal than solar, more useful for action than for prevention. (71)

However comic this may appear, the realization of potency is nevertheless the work of the wish itself. The medal takes on a counterfeit value, enabling the amorous subject to transcend the paralysis of his own nonbeing. This identificatory bond takes hold of the subject and engages him in a mimetic relation whereby the ego temporarily becomes the object of desire. By displacing the excessive desire for success from the impotent subject to the gold coin, the text "allows the marital act to regain a beneficial and 'natural' indifference"[16] Ironically, the process of naturalization is realized through a fiction-making process, represented as a simulacrum of the "real," a phenomenon that once again blurs the distinction between the biological and the symbolic.

Montaigne's story thus enacts a dramatic scenario in which the desired wish is presented as having been fulfilled by a surrogate object. The subject of the wish—the bridegroom—has no sense of manliness prior to the enactment of a *mediated* fantasy since it is only in fantasy that the desire for potency can be granted. To be sure, the fantasy attached to the gold medal induces desire and directs it. Beyond the confines of the patriarchal power structure, which depends on the other for value to be confirmed, the fantasy of potency put forth here constitutes a simulation of manliness on the part of the desiring subject. Indeed, manliness may be more an illusion and a subterfuge than a "psychic" reality:[17]

> Nostre discours est capable d'estoffer cent autres mondes et d'en trouver les principes et la contexture. Il ne luy faut ny matiere ny baze; laissez le courre: il bastit aussi bien sur le vuide que sur le plain, et de l'inanité que de matiere, *dare pondus idonea fumo.* (III, 11, 1027)

> Our reason is capable of filling out a hundred other worlds and finding their principles and contexture. It needs neither matter nor basis; let it run on; it builds as well on emptiness and on fullness, and with inanity as with matter: Suited to give solidity to smoke. PERSIUS (785)

Montaigne's remedy thus naturalizes the artificiality of the cure by giving it potency in the count's imagination: "Il y a des autheurs, desquels la fin c'est dire les evenemens. La mienne, si j'y sçavoye advenir, seroit dire sur ce qui peut advenir" (I, 21, 105–6) ("There are authors whose end is to tell what has happened. Mine, if I could attain it, would be to talk about what can happen" [75]). In recounting this story, the essayist seeks to satisfy a potentially "threatened" gender role. If the inadequacies of nature are compensated for by the artistry of creative fantasies, it is because manliness is not just a biological issue but one involving storytelling and narrative verisimilitude. Like the essayist's quest to extract artistry from the disorder of the "monstres fantasques," the artificially induced cure for impotence represents the attempt to neutralize difference. It acts as a means of controlling nature and paradoxically demonstrates that the "natural" depends as much on the plausibility of fantasy as it does on anything else. We thus construct nature by means of our imagination, a medium through which reality can assure "being." Or can it? That seems to be the question Montaigne addresses when he suddenly suggests that these narratives of fantastic sex changes might simply be a product of someone else's fantastic imagination, whose "mollesse" leaves the mind vulnerable to errancy: "Il est vray semblable que le principal credit des miracles, des visions, des enchantemens et de tels effects extraordinaire, vienne de la puissance de l'imagination agissant principalement contre les ames du vulgaire, plus molles" (I, 21, 99) ("It is probable that the principal credit of miracles, visions, enchantements, and such extraordinary occurrences comes from the power of imagination, acting principally upon the minds of the common people, which are softer" [70]).

The rhetorical acrobatics in Montaigne's text suggest that the self is figured through an other whose gender differences have their own logic: "Mes fantasies se suyvent, mais par fois c'est de loing, et se regardent, mais d'une veuë oblique" (III, 9, 994) ("My ideas follow one another, but sometimes it is from a distance, and look at each other, but with a sidelong glance" [761]). If the penis does not necessarily make the man in the fictions of the *Essays,* it most certainly can reify the image of the man trapped within a woman's body. To be sure, the workings of nature reveal themselves as much in the unpredictability of the biological as in the consequences generated by the monstrous (from *monere,* the power to portend) predictability of the phantasmatically invested: "Aussi en l'estude que je traitte de noz mœurs et mouvemens, les tesmoignages fabuleux, pourveu qu'ils soient possibles, y servent comme les vrais" (I, 21, 105) ("So in the study that I am making of our behavior and motives, fabulous testimonies, provided they are possible, serve like true ones" [75]).

However, in order to overcome impotence and the resistances within the self, in a post-1588 annotation to the essay Montaigne ultimately proposes the "talking cure" as a way to moderate tension and give form to the monstrous perception of difference in the spectacle of language: "Il trouva quelque remede à cette resverie par une autre resverie. C'est que, advouant luy mesmes et preschant avant la main cette sienne subjection, la contention de son ame se soulageoit sur ce, qu'apportant ce mal comme attendu, son obligation en amoindrissoit et luy en poisoit moins" (I, 21, 100) ("He found some remedy for this fancy by another fancy: which was that by admitting this weakness and speaking about it in advance, he relieved the tension of his soul, for when the trouble had been presented as one to be expected, his sense of responsibility diminished and weighed upon him less" [70]). By speaking about impotence and incorporating it in the natural order of things as something to be expected ("ce mal comme attendu"), the desiring subject makes the speaker known for what he is and makes this self-knowledge somehow less monstrous. This "record" of thought embodied in language not only neutralizes difference but engenders its own set of rules functioning on its own terms: "Les miracles sont selon l'ignorance en quoy nous sommes de la nature, non selon l'etre de la nature. L'asseufaction endort la veuë de nostre jugement" (I, 23, 112) ("Miracles arise from our ignorance of nature, not from the essence of nature. Habituation puts to sleep the eye of our judgment" [80]). In writing, as in speaking, the register of thought represents the unevenness of the human condition and suggests that the paralyzing fancies of the imagination can be recuperated and transformed through discursive formations. Only gradually does one come to realize through a series of exemplary narratives that the idealized orderliness that Montaigne sought to impose on his "fantastic monsters" was but a way of transforming what could be perceived as strangeness into a new measure of gender: "Je n'ay pas plus faict mon livre que mon livre m'a faict" (II, 18, 665) ("I have no more made my book than my book has made me" [504]). If the goal of the book was originally to articulate the "natural," the act of essaying has created yet another, more perfect nature figured in this work of art and destined to tame the monster within: "Me peignant pour autruy, je me suis peint en moy de couleurs plus nettes que n'estoyent les miennes premieres" (II, 18, 665) ("Painting myself for others, I have painted my inward self with colors clearer than my original ones" [504]).

2
REPRESENTING THE MONSTER
Cognition, Cripples, and Other Limp Parts
in "Des boyteux" (III, 11)

Les boiteux sont mal propres aux exercices du corps; et aux
exercices de l'esprit les ames boiteuses; les bastardes et vulgaires
sont indignes de la philosophie. (I, 25, 141)

*Cripples are ill-suited to bodily exercises, and crippled souls to
mental exercises. (104)*

C'est par mon experience que j'accuse l'humaine ignorance, qui
est, à mon advis, le plus seur party de l'escole du monde.
(III, 13, 1075–76)

*It is from experience that I affirm human ignorance, which is, in
my opinion, the most certain fact in the school of the world.
(p. 824)*

Et au plus eslevé throne du monde si ne sommes assis que
sus nostre cul. (III, 13, 1115)

*On the loftiest throne in the world we are still sitting only
on our rump. (857)*

COGNITION, MIRACLES, AND MONSTERS

 The relationship between the exemplum of crip-
ples and the theme of causality is central to Mon-
taigne's representation of the monster in the essay
"Des boyteux" (III, 11) ("On Cripples"). The question of causality is discussed early in the essay in
order to set in motion an epistemological critique
whose target is the weakness of human reason. Montaigne specifically focuses on the defects of human understanding and our need
to shift attention away from things (*choses*) in order to reflect more
closely on their causes (*causes*). Nevertheless, by engaging in this
wordplay the essayist ironically links things to causes and thereby

transforms reason into a form of amusement incorporating fiction and desire:

> Je ravassois presentement, comme je faicts souvant, sur ce, com-
> bien l'humaine raison est un instrument libre et vague. Je vois
> ordinairement que les hommes, aux faicts qu'on leur propose,
> s'amusent plus volontiers à en cercher la raison qu'à en cercher
> la verité: ils laissent là les choses, et s'amusent à traiter les causes!
> plaisants causeurs. (III, 11, 1026)

> I was just now musing, as I often do, on how free and vague
> an instrument human reason is. I see ordinarily that men, when
> facts are put before them, are more ready to amuse themselves
> by inquiring into their reasons than by inquiring into their truth.
> They leave aside the cases and amuse themselves treating the
> causes. Comical Prattlers. (785)

In differentiating between facts and causes, Montaigne wishes to suggest a concept of being that is conditioned by the artificial contriv-
ances of causality. The essay demonstrates how the quest for causes
engages us in a retrospective attempt to inscribe the teleological as
the basis for a purposeful and predetermined development. Engaged
in a logic based on the affinity of a given sign or act with its specific
object, those "comical prattlers" to whom Montaigne refers (as those
"plaisants causeurs") invoke fictions aimed at establishing the sovereignty of reference.

For Montaigne the constitution of meaning for these vanity-
stricken subjects is based on the productive power of the imagination,
which makes judgments circulate and consequently blurs the boundary between representation and reality. Generated by the force of the
imagination, what we call "reason" trades upon naive referential
assumptions whose fabrications are nothing less than the presump-
tive passage from cause to effect: "Ces exemples servent-ils pas à ce
que je disois au commencement: que nos raisons anticipent souvent
l'effect, et ont l'estendue de leur jurisdiction si infinie, qu'elles jugent
et s'exercent en l'inanité mesme et au non estre?" (III, 11, 1034; "Do
not these examples confirm what I was saying at the beginning that
our reasons often anticipate the fact, and extend their jurisdiction so
infinitely that they exercise their judgment even in inanity and non-

being?" [791). The faculty of expression is capable of inventing verbal constructs whose foundation is built upon a simulacrum of richness and plenitude derived from the interaction of signs with other signs. With this in mind, Montaigne situates reason in the hyperreality of simulations where images and spectacles nurture a form of thought frozen in a sterile process of invented logic that introduces an unnatural force into the economy of living nature: "Nostre discours est capable d'estoffer cent autres mondes et d'en trouver les principes et la contexture. Il ne luy faut ny matiere ny baze; laissez le courre!: il bastit aussi bien sur le vuide que sur le plain, et de l'inanité que de matiere" (III, 11, 1027) ("Our reason is capable of filling out a hundred other worlds and finding their principles and contexture. It needs neither matter nor basis; let it run on; it builds as well on emptiness as on fullness, and with inanity as with matter" [785]).

By associating reason with discourse, Montaigne represents defective thinking, the deformities of the mind, through a trope whose conceptual or explanatory force is derived from the idea of running or the random motion produced by the peripatetic energy derived from error (from the Latin *errare*): "Il n'est rien si souple et erratique que nostre entendement" (III, 11, 1034) ("There is nothing so supple and erratic as our understanding" [792]). At the very least, a strong affinity is established here between cognition and the kinetic force of language, where meaning opens itself up to the vertiginous possibilities of referential aberration through the presumptuous activity of human understanding: "Nous sommes tous contraints et amoncellez en nous, et avons la veue racourcie à la longueur de nostre nez. . . . Nous sommes insensiblement tous en cette erreur: erreur de grande suite et prejudice" (I, 26, 157) ("We are all huddled and concentrated in ourselves, and our vision is reduced to the length of our nose. . . . We are all unconsciously in this error, an error of great consequence and harm" [116]). If discourse stands in the service of logic, it is in order to project pseudotruths that are the product of the unbridled wandering of the imagination. In the essay "De l'oisiveté" (I, 8) ("On Idleness") Montaigne describes "tant de chimeres et monstres fantasques les uns sur les autres, sans ordre, et sans propos" (I, 8, 33) ("so many chimeras and fantastic monsters, one after another, without order or purpose" [21]).

In "Des boyteux" Montaigne uses the figure of deformity to describe the monstrous representations that the imagination is capable of engendering though the power of unbridled speculation. The desire to create something out of nothing produces an effect that is the result of reason's error: "Nos raisons anticipent souvent l'effect, et ont l'estendue de leur jurisdiction si infinie, qu'elles jugent et s'exercent en l'inanité mesme et au non estre?" (III, 11, 1034) ("Our reasons often anticipate the fact, and extend their jurisdiction so infinitely that they exercise their judgment even in inanity and non-being?" [791]). In describing the exaggerated shape that his own discourse takes, Montaigne relates the epistemological thrust of the rhetorical dimension of language. The inflationary economy of discourse depicted by Montaigne unsettles the solidity of truth and enables it to reverberate in the inflections of a voice that dissociates cognition from performance. Montaigne dramatically proclaims:

> Moy-mesme, qui faicts singuliere conscience de mentir et qui ne me soucie guiere de donner creance et authorité à ce que je dis, m'apperçoy toutesfois, aux propos que j'ay en main, qu'estant eschauffé ou par la resistance d'un autre ou par la propre chaleur de la narration, je grossis et enfle mon subject par vois, mouvemens, vigueur et force de parolles, et encore par extention et amplification, non sans interest de la verité nayfve. . . . La parole vive et bruyante, comme est la mienne ordinaire, s'emporte volontiers à l'hyperbole. (III, 11, 1028)

> I myself, who am singularly scrupulous about lying and who scarcely concern myself with giving credence and authority to what I say, perceive nevertheless that when I am excited over a matter I have in hand, either by another man's resistance or by the intrinsic heat of the narration, I magnify and inflate my subject by voice, movements, vigor and power of words, and further by extension and amplification, not without prejudice to the simple truth. . . . A lively and noisy way of speaking, such as mine ordinarily is apt to be carried away into hyperbole. (786)

The hyperbolic power of language generates a logic of deformation and a deformation of logic; humankind nurtures this monstrous presence through the construction of differences that are merely the effects of rhetorical transformations. "Les autheurs," claims Montaigne, "mesmes plus serrez et plus sages, voiez autour d'un bon argument combien ils en sement d'autres legers et, qui y regarde de pres, incorporels" (III, 12, 1039–40) ("Authors, even the most compact and the wisest—around one good argument see how many others they strew, trivial ones, and if you look at them closely, bodiless" [795]).

To be sure, the tropological complexities of Montaigne's text puts forth a series of figural exchanges in which architectural metaphors are used to represent the instability of knowledge that is accepted as firmly established. Montaigne draws on an example of so-called fact as it passes from one person to another, in the act undergoing a decentering process whose sheer excessiveness might be qualified as a form of monstrousness: "Ainsi va tout ce bastiment, s'estoffant et formant de main en main: de maniere que le plus esloigné tesmoin en est mieux instruict que le plus voisin, et le dernier informé mieux persuadé que le premier" (III, 11, 1028) ("Thus the whole structure goes on building itself up and shaping itself from hand to hand; so that the remotest witness is better instructed about it than the nearest, and the least informed more convinced of it than the first" [786]). The speed by which knowledge is relayed suggests a process of infinite substitution whereby the repetition of information creates a newly reinvented truth whose differentiality from its site of conception projects a return that is never the same. As stories grow and spread, truth is dissipated, with the "real" deriving from the illusion that the further one strays from the truth the closer one gets to it. As Montaigne suggests, when we are challenged regarding the veracity of what was heard, we get "carried away" by the excitement of speaking to the extent that we defend claims that are unsubstantiated by facts.

Within the context of the essay "Des boyteux," ignorance thus acquires a strikingly positive value at the expense of absolute knowledge, which is represented as a form of mastery that restrains the production of meaning to the finality prefigured in its beginnings. As Montaigne astutely notes:

> Ny le vin n'en est plus plaisant à celuy qui en sçait les facultez premieres. Au contraire!: et le corps et l'ame interrompent et alterent le droit qu'ils ont de l'usage du monde, y meslant l'opinion de science. Le determiner et le sçavoir, comme le donner, appartient à la regence et à la maistrise; à l'inferiorité, subjection et apprentissage appartient le jouyr, l'accepter. (III, 11, 1026)

Nor is wine pleasanter to the man who knows its primary properties. On the contrary, both the body and the soul disturb and alter the right they have to the enjoyment of the world by mixing into it the pretension to learning. Determining and knowing, like giving, appertains to rule and mastery; to inferiority, subjection, and apprenticeship appertains enjoyment and acceptance. (785)

The presumption of knowing inevitably extinguishes pleasure and extricates it from the place where it may achieve a kind of plenitude in the bliss of ignorance. The rejection of mastery situates the subject in a position of apprenticeship (implicitly associated with the act of "essaying") that enables it to transform its inadequacy into a form of enjoyment derived from the absence of "objective" content. Yet humankind's attempt to be causative and to determine meaning provides the basic matrix for the compulsive attitude that imprisons the vain subject in (metaphorically speaking) a "phallic mode" that can never be associated with unmitigated enjoyment. In short, the essay transmits an ethical stance that refuses to ignore the void that is at the core of human subjectivity and that ultimately gives rise to the vicissitudes of desire.

Montaigne begins his essay with a discussion of the reform of the calendar by Gregory XIII in 1582, the inability to establish true chronology, and the difficulty of recording a history of the past. What was conceived of as an apocalyptic transformation in the way time is measured ended up failing to effect any real change at all:

> Il y a deux ou trois ans qu'on acoursit l'an de dix jours en France. Combien de changemens devoient suyvre cette reformation. . . . Mes voisins trouvent l'heure de leurs semences, de leur recolte, l'opportunité de leurs negoces, les jours nuisibles et propices, au mesme point justement où ils les avoyent assignez de tout temps. (III, 11, 1025–26)

> It is two or three years since they shortened the year by ten days in France. How many changes were supposed to follow this reform! . . . My neighbors find the hour for sowing and reaping, the opportune moment for their business, the harmful and propitious days, exactly at the same point to which they had always assigned them. (784)

In essence, the attempt to be causative in reforming the calendar, as Louis Richeome suggests in *Trois discours pour la religion catholique* (1597), is simply an example of a false miracle.[1] Instead of producing a wondrous transformation, what one witnesses in the reform of the calendar is the epistemological importance attributed to the workings of reason and its attempt to regulate the processing of time: "Ny l'erreur ne se sentoit en nostre usage, ny l'amendement ne s'y sent" (II, 11, 1026) ("Neither was the error felt in our habits, nor is the improvement felt" [784]). The artificiality of this so-called scientific invention contrasts strikingly with the natural movement intuited through cyclical time: "Tant il y a d'incertitude par tout, tant nostre apercevance est grossiere, obscure et obtuse" (III, 11, 1026) ("So much uncertainty there is in all things: so gross, obscure, and obtuse is our perception!" [784]). Here Montaigne mocks those who assign cosmic meaning to that which is only a false miracle.

At the center of this essay is a discussion of the nature of miracles. By playing on the etymology of the word *miracle* (derived from the Latin *miraculum,* object of wonder), Montaigne enables it to intersect with the concept of the monster (derived from the Latin *monstrum,* to show) in order to demonstrate how external representations overdetermine the way in which we experience the world: "Si nous appellons monstres ou miracles ce où nostre raison ne peut aller, combien s'en presente il continuellement à nostre veue?" (I, 27, 179) ("If we call prodigies [monsters] or miracles whatever our reason cannot reach, how many of these appear continually to our eyes!" [132]). To be sure, miracles are admirable, a product of the human imagination and a cause for wonderment.[2] As Richard Regosin suggests, "We can say . . . that Montaigne's monster is that which is shown and which shows itself, and which shows what it is, *that* it is."[3] The force of the imagination thus has a mesmerizing effect, leading to the collapse of boundaries between the visual and the cognitive: "Tant il y a d'incertitude par tout, tant nostre apercevance est grossiere, obscure et obtuse" (III, 11, 1026) "So much uncertainty there is in all things: so gross, obscure, and obtuse is our perception!" [784]).

In the writing of the text, the essayist attempts to represent the marvelous as the recognition of an unusual experience, a spectacle that is both different and beyond the scope of our perception. The wonders that give the "strange" sign what value it has are themselves effects of difference that produce a feeling of alienation through a cognitive myopia that draws on our propensity to be fearful: "Nostre veue represente ainsi souvent de loing des images estranges, qui s'esvanouissent en s'approchant." (III, 11, 1029) ("Our sight often represents strange images at a distance which vanish as they approach" [787]). The monstrous stems from the perception of deviation from the normative; difference, portrayed as a visual "effect," attests to the rarity attributed to the object of the gaze.[4] Faced with the monstrosity of difference, one reduces the perceived aberration of otherness through a process of recuperation that has a neutralizing effect: "On s'apprivoise à toute estrangeté par l'usage et le temps" (III, 11, 1029) ("We become habituated to anything strange by use and time" [787]). What is most startling here is the change to which strangeness is subjected rather than that which humanity undergoes. If time and spatial proximity make strangeness familiar, it is because strangeness is but a "symptom" of our own inexperience before the threatening diversity of the world. In "D'un enfant monstrueux" ("Of a Monstrous Child") Montaigne asserts: "Nous apelons contre nature ce qui advient contre la coustume: rien n'est que selon elle, quel qu'il soit" (II, 30, 713) ("We call contrary to nature what happens contrary to custom; nothing is anything but according to nature, whatever it may be" [539]).

Throughout the essay Montaigne's text foregrounds the disintegration of the increasing unreliability of the witness and the ability to represent "experience" in language. Initially deformity is more a function of thinking than it is an anatomical consideration: "C'est merveille, de combien vains commencemens et frivoles causes naissent ordinairement si fameuses impressions" (III, 11, 1029) ("It is a marvel from what empty beginnings and frivolous causes such famous impressions ordinarily spring" [787]). What is characterized as a miracle in Renaissance thought is integrally linked to the notion of *admiratio* (derived from the Latin for "to wonder or marvel at"), a concept combining epistemological and causal concerns and based, more often than not, on the visual processing of knowledge.

Drawing upon models found in Aristotle's *Nicomachean Ethics* and Horace's *Epistles*, Montaigne's essay narrates how testimonial stances, produced by the act of seeing, combine perception with incomprehension and transform them into facts that are the result of ignorance:[5] "Iris est fille de Thaumantis. L'admiration est fondement de toute philosophie, l'inquisition le progrez, l'ignorance le bout" (III, 11, 1030) "Iris is the daughter of Thaumas. Wonder is the foundation of all philosophy, inquiry its progress, ignorance its end" [788]).

By failing to read visual signs with deep understanding, humanity is prone to find greatness in that which is most distant and incomprehensible. To witness a miracle is thus to fall prey to the self-deceiving nature of one's vanity, which ultimately produces a situation in which the viewer looks but does not really quite understand. Montaigne's writerly testimony bears witness to the monstrosity of our judgment and the strangeness of our reason, its "erreur et estonnement." At times he even goes so far as to suggest an epistemological equation between "looking" and "lacking." Yet what is perceived as being truly extraordinary, as in the case of divine miracles, should be distinguished from what is merely admirable: "Ce que nous appellons monstres, ne le sont pas à Dieu, qui voit en l'immensité de son ouvrage l'infinité des formes qu'il y a comprinses; et est à croire que cette figure qui nous estonne, se rapporte et tient à quelque autre figure de mesme genre inconnu à l'homme" (II, 30, 713) ("What we call monsters are not so to God, who sees in the immensity of his work the infinity of forms that he has comprised in it; and it is for us to believe that this figure that astonishes us is related and linked to some other figure of the same kind unknown to man" [539]). Montaigne consequently warns us against trying to understand what is beyond our comprehension without being authorized to do so: "De ce qui est hors de sa conception et d'un effect supernaturel, il en doit estre creu lors seulement qu'une approbation supernaturelle l'a authorisé. Ce privilege qu'il a pleu à Dieu donner à aucuns de nos tesmoignages ne doibt pas estre avily et communiqué legerement" (III, 11, 1031) ("What is beyond his conception and of supernatural effect, he should be believed only when some supernatural approbation has sanctioned him. This privilege that it has pleased God to give to some of our testimonies must not be cheapened and communicated lightly" [789]).

In the context of miracles, Montaigne's essay also explores the phenomenon of witchcraft in early modern France by drawing on arguments found in the preface to Jean Bodin's *De la demonomanie des sorciers* (1580). Bodin here opts for the belief in supernatural effects without grounding them in an accurately defined causality.[6] As Richard Sayce has suggested, Montaigne composed his essay at a time when the belief in witchcraft and the persecution of its followers had reached its peak.[7] In this essay, however, Montaigne indirectly inveighs against Bodin, who attacks those skeptics—the "maistres doubteurs"—concerning the "reality" of witchcraft. Montaigne engages in an epistemic critique of those, such as Bodin, who pursue witches through unusual reasoning and thereby ironically provoke their persecution. The immoderation of the believers in witchcraft permits Montaigne not to condemn them "de fauceté leur opinion" (III, 11, 1031) ("[for] holding a false opinion" [789]). On the contrary, he proclaims with great force: "Je ne l'accuse que de difficulté et de hardiesse, et condamne l'affirmation opposite, egalement avec eux sinon si imperieusement. *Videantur sanè, ne affirmentur modo*" (III, 11, 1031) ("I accuse them only of holding a difficult and rash one [opinion], and condemn the opposite affirmation, just as they do, if not so imperiously. Let them appear as probable, not be affirmed positively [Cicero]" [789]).

To be sure, if Montaigne condemns witch-hunting, his goal is not so much to defend the supernatural acts of the unfortunate witches as it is to question the presumption derived from the belief in certitude: "Les sorcieres de mon voisinage courent hazard de leur vie, sur l'advis de chaque nouvel autheur qui vient donner corps à leurs songes" (III, 11, 1031) ("The witches of my neighborhood are in mortal danger every time some new author comes along and attests to the reality of their visions" [788]). By minimizing the miraculous power of the witches, comparatively speaking, the essayist engages in an unmitigated critique of the irrational discourse of scholars who paradoxically ascribe to witchcraft a potency that does not exist. In an attempt to purge the poison that demonology has become, writers such as Bodin serve to reify the omnipresence of this "folly." Reason itself cannot escape the inanity produced by the errancy of the imagination. As the essay unfolds, it renders the demoniacal somewhat normative so that it may be juxtaposed against the demonization of the monstrous.

In the course of the argument, the supernatural activities of the witches become far less threatening than the monstrous reasoning articulated by their accusers.[8] The abuse of knowledge alluded to here inflicts blindness upon our acts of seeing and functions as an assault on an utterly proofless reality: "Il s'engendre beaucoup d'abus au monde ou, pour le dire plus hardiment, tous les abus du monde s'engendrent de ce qu'on nous apprend à craindre de faire profession de nostre ignorance, et que nous sommes tenus d'accepter tout ce que nous ne pouvons refuter" (III, 11, 1030) ("Many abuses are engendered in the world, or to put it more boldly, all the abuses in the world are engendered by our being taught to be afraid of professing our ignorance and our being bound to accept everything that we cannot refuse" [788]). Abuse derives from our inability to see ourselves for what we are; the power of distortion is demonstrated by the need to know and the desire to tell. General testimony becomes impossible because it proves difficult to distinguish the true from the false. Accordingly, the essayist's desire for moderation and skepticism before the hyperbolic power of the imagination reveals the extent to which he believes that we are caught up in representations and simulations of the monstrous: "On me faict hayr les choses vray-semblables quand on me les plante pour infallibles. J'ayme ces mots, qui amollissent et moderent la temerité de nos propositions!: a l'avanture, aucunement, quelque, on dict, je pense, et semblables" (III, 11, 1030) ("It makes me hate probable things when they are planted on me as infallible. I like these words, which soften and moderate the rashness of our propositions: 'perhaps,' 'to some extent,' 'some,' 'they say,' 'I think,' and the like" [788]).

If the identity of the unusual is known only from the projection of external features, it is because we traditionally witness the monstrous as that which resists understanding and categorization within the taxonomies of what culture defines as natural. Within this framework Montaigne's essay discretely combines epistemological and ontological concerns: "Je n'ay veu monstre et miracle au monde plus expres que moy-mesme. On s'apprivoise à toute estrangeté par l'usage et le temps; mais plus je me hante et me connois, plus ma difformité m'estonne, moins je m'entens en moy" (III, 11, 1029) ("I have no more evident monstrosity and miracle in the world than myself. We become habituated to anything strange by use and time; but the more I frequent myself and know myself, the more my deformity astonishes me, and the less I understand myself" (787). Ironically, the variety of miracles one perceives outside of oneself emanates from the strangeness within the self, the grotesque way in which we process reality and interpret it according to the whims of our imagination. The chimera and monsters that the mind produces make the essayist a narcissistic observer of his mind's monstrous progeny: "Nous aymons à nous embrouiller en la vanité, comme conforme à nostre estre" (III, 11, 1027) "We love to embroil ourselves in vanity, as something in conformity with our being" [786]).

The book that Montaigne writes functions as a receptacle that is, paradoxically, filled with "crotesques" (I, 28, 183), the result of epistemological and ontological emptiness: "Que sont-ce icy aussi, à la verité, que crotesques et corps monstrueux, rappiecez de divers membres, sans certaine figure, n'ayants ordre, suite ny proportion que fortuite?" (I, 28, 138) ("And what are these things of mine, in truth, but grotesques and monstrous bodies, pieced together of divers members, without definite shape, having no order, sequence, or proportion other than accidental?" [135]). Within this context, error is the result of humanity's failure to accept the inadequacies of the self, the errors that make it what it is. Nevertheless, the only way to cope with the crippled judgment endemic to the human condition is to transform oneself into a spectacle, an object to be seen in all its deformity, which ultimately becomes what the word "monster" literally signifies: "Qui veut guerir de l'ignorance, il faut la confesser" (III, 11, 1030) ("Anyone who wants to be cured of ignorance must confess it" [788]). The spectacle that defines the monster and that tries ("essaie") to cure us of the malady of ignorance facilitates an attempt to overcome the problematic relationship of language to truth by conferring form on the text of the essay.[9] Montaigne's acceptance of self-deficiency, represented by the rambling and inconstant motion of his mind, enables him to acquire strength through the power of a writerly gait that proceeds at an uneven pace ("à sauts et à gambades") as it stumbles along the circuitous path to self-knowledge. The assumption of a Socratic *docta ignorantia* enables the essayist to be seen as he is, and in this exhibitionist pose of self-portraiture (from the Latin *protrahere*, to draw out, disclose, or reveal) he is able to come into much closer contact with the monstrous deformities that might otherwise escape him. The desire to write is concomitant with the monstrous externalization of his inner phantasms. Thus, Montaigne's essay confirms that the opposition between the natural and the unnatural is artificially constructed and that the monstrous is but a manifestation of the diversity within nature itself: "Rien n'est que selon elle [nature], quel qu'il soit" (II, 30, 713) ("Nothing is anything but according to nature, wherever it may be" [539]).

MONTAIGNE AND MARTIN GUERRE

In the course of the essay, the acknowledgment of the limitations of human inquiry gains symbolic value; the recognition of impairment carries with it a newly found ability to see. It is therefore not surprising that one finds embedded within the essay "Des boyteux" a selective retelling of the famous sixteenth-century story of Martin Guerre, a tale partly derived from presiding judge Jean de Coras's 1566 legal account, "Arrest memorable du parlement de Tolose." a tale that allegorizes the epistemological and ontological issues in Montaigne's essay. The insertion of the Toulouse case in the essay ostensibly relates to the defense against the persecution of witches. However, as Natalie Zemon Davis points out in her analysis of the story, as a young man Guerre lived in a household where "he had to cope not just with one but with two powerful male personalities who both had fiery tempers."[10] Having married at an early age, Guerre was ashamed of his precarious sexuality, in particular his inability to achieve an erection and consummate his marriage.[11] Bertrande's marriage bed had been the locus of impotence for eight years, during which the couple believed they were the victims of a magic spell. However, even after he had finally consummated his marriage, Guerre abandoned his wife and newborn son, Sanxi, because of his fear of impending paternal punishment for minor theft. He decided to go off and fight a war in Spain, where he was wounded. During his absence, another man named Arnaud Du Tilh appeared, who declared himself to be the "real" Martin Guerre and was accepted by the villagers and by Guerre's wife. When a disagreement over family property ensued and Guerre's impersonator commited a number of blunders, a trial took place, the outcome of which reaffirmed the false identity of the impostor. It was only when the court was on the verge of accepting this travesty of justice that the real Martin Guerre suddenly reappeared, entering the courtroom on crutches, thus belatedly revealing his identity through the visual evidence of lameness. The arrival of the lame man paradoxically dramatizes this exemplary fiction, for it ironically foregrounds Arnaud's "im-posture" by no longer providing him with a "leg" to stand on. The public sentencing of Arnaud du Tilh, who is accused of spreading evil spirits, recalls the earlier referenece in the essay to Bodin's discourse on witchcraft and demonology. Interestingly, the term "imposture" resurfaces to describe Arnaud, as it had once done in characterizing the "sorcerers."

Although Montaigne does not call our attention to the question of Martin Guerre's lameness in his retelling of the narrative, the recognition of lameness and monstrosity for those familiar with the story of the trial become sources of re-vision that ultimately lead to knowledge. Not only does Guerre function as the bearer of truth, but his appearance puts into question the absolutism that characterizes the inflexible nature of our judgment. In a way Martin Guerre's deformity carries with it a kind of strength, for the man who stumbles, limps, and advances slowly, the tardy cripple who appears at the end of the trial, comes to embody truth.

The figure who emerges from the story is both erotically and anatomically different. In this text the delusory nature of conventional masculinity is put into question on a symbolic level, for the monstrosity constituting Guerre's difference derives from the representation of a de-phallicized and imperfect male body. Ironically, the man who was incapable of achieving an erection is responsible for the "arrest" (sentence) that stops, stabilizes, and reifies the so-called truth. Moreover, the man who limps and is phallicly limp (and perhaps impotent) symbolically challenges the hypothesis of what modern terminology refers to as the psychoanalytically anchored phallus/penis equation. Like Montaigne, who draws attention to his own sluggishness, and the cripple, whose arrival is quite long in coming, the essayist proclaims that the education of the ideal student must become an exercise in learning, one whose path toward knowledge must be slow, halting, and nondeliberate: "Et si j'eusse eu à dresser des enfans, je leur eusse tant mis en la bouche cette façon de respondre, enquesteuse, non resolutive!: qu'est-ce à dire? Je ne l'entends pas, il pourroit estre, est-il vray?" (III, 11, 1030) ("If I had to train children, I would have filled their mouths so much with this way of answering, inquiring, not decisive—'What does that mean? I do not understand it. That might be. Is it true?'" [788]). Quite clearly, the de-phallicized approach to knowledge practiced by the essayist is revealed in his relation to the symbolic as it is experienced at the level of the imaginary: "Qui establit son discours par braverie et commandement montre que la raison y est foible" (III, 11, 1031) "He who imposes his argument by bravado and command shows that it is weak in reason" [789]).

Interestingly, although Montaigne appears to valorize lameness indirectly, he is also quick to condemn the excesses of justice, as exemplified by the judge of Toulouse, who condemns a man to be hanged without the benefit of fully substantiated evidence against him. On the contrary, Montaigne would have opted for suspending his judgment before the lameness of his reason:

> Il me souvient (et ne me souvient aussi d'autre chose) qu'il me sembla avoir rendu l'imposture de celuy qu'il jugea coulpable si merveilleuse et excedant de si loing nostre connoissance, et la

sienne qui estoit juge, que je trouvay beaucoup de hardiesse en l'arrest qui l'avoit condamné à estre pendu. Recevons quelque forme d'arrest qui die: la court n'y entend rien, plus librement et ingenuement que ne firent les Areopagites, lesquels, se trouvans pressez d'une cause qu'ils ne pouvoient desveloper, ordonnerent que les parties en viendroient à cent ans. (III, 11, 1030)

He seemed to me, in describing the imposture of the man he judged guilty, to make it so marvelous and so far surpassing our knowledge and his own, who was judge, that I found much rashness in the sentence that has condemned the man to be hanged. Let us accept some form of sentence which says "The court understands nothing of the matter," more freely and ingenuously than did the Areopagites, who, finding themselves hard pressed by a case that they could not unravel, ordered the parties to come back in a hundred years. (788)

If in this essay the cripple is figured as the carrier of truth, the judge is presented as the arrogant enforcer of the law: "Combien ay-je veu de condemnations, plus crimineuses que le crime?" (III, 13, 1071) ("How many condemnations I have seen more criminal than the crime!" [819–20]). In this context, the overriding judicial metaphor contributes significantly to a sense of changelessness and the stability associated with phallic identification. The posture (from the Latin *positura*, position) that Montaigne wishes to put forward derives from the need to eradicate the difference between dominance and opposition: "Je suis d'avis que nous soustenons nostre jugement aussi bien à rejetter qu'à recevoir. . . . Ma creance ne se manie pas à coups de poing." (III, 11, 1030–31) ("It is my opinion that we should suspend our judgment just as much in the direction of rejecting as of accepting . . . My belief is not controlled by anyone's fists" [788, 789]). By adopting a more mediocre posture, the essayist permits himself the flexibility that ironically empowers him.

CRIPPLES AND FEMALE DESIRE

If difference is an issue in this essay, the exemplary rarity constituting the monstrous is used as a tool to valorize the representation of female desire. Near the end of the essay, a direct reference is finally made to cripples and the novelty of corporeal imperfections. Here the essayist transforms the female body into the locus of libidinal investment as well as the object of specular surveillance. He suggests in a somewhat matter-of-fact way the deep pleasure derived from making love with a lame person, whose sexual energy becomes more potent due to the lack of movement of the limbs:

A propos ou hors de propos, il n'importe, on dict en Italie, en commun proverbe, que celuy-là ne cognoit pas venus en sa parfaicte douceur qui n'a couché avec la boiteuse. La fortune, ou quelque particulier accident, ont mis il y a long temps ce mot en la bouche du peuple; et se dict des masles comme des femelles. Car la Royne des amazonnes respondit au scyte qui la convioit à l'amour: arista cholos oiphei, le boiteux le faict le mieux. En cette republique feminine, pour fuir la domination des masles, elles les stropioient des l'enfance, bras, jambes et autres membres qui leur donnoient avantage sur elles, et se servoient d'eux à ce seulement à quoy nous nous servons d'elles par deçà. J'eusse dict que le mouvement detraqué de la boiteuse apportast quelque nouveau plaisir à la besongne et quelque pointe de douceur à ceux qui l'essayent, mais je viens d'apprendre que mesme la philosophie ancienne en a decidé: elle dict que, les jambes et cuisses des boiteuses ne recevant, à cause de leur imperfection, l'aliment qui leur est deu, il en advient que les parties genitales, qui sont au dessus, sont plus plaines, plus nourries et vigoureuses. Ou bien que, ce defaut empeschant l'exercice, ceux qui en sont entachez dissipent moins leurs forces et en viennent plus entiers aux jeux de venus. (III, 11, 1033–34)

Apropos or malapropos, no matter, they say in Italy as a common proverb that he does not know Venus in her perfect sweetness who has not lain with a cripple. In that feminine commonwealth, to escape the domination of the males, they crippled them from childhood—arms, legs, and other parts that gave men an advantage over them—and made use of them only for the purpose for which we made use of women over here. I would have said that the irregular movement of the lame woman brought some new pleasure to the business and a spice of sweetness to those who try it. But I have just learned that ancient philosophy, no less, has decided the question. It says that since the legs and thighs of lame women, because of their imperfection, do not receive the food that is their due, the result is that the genital parts, which are above, are fuller, better nourished, and more vigorous. Or else that, since this defect prevents exercise, those who are tainted by it dissipate their strength less and come more entire to the sports of Venus. (791)

In a way, the defect associated with "le mouvement detraqué de la boiteuse" ("the irregular movement of the lame woman") remarkably acquires an exemplarity by challenging the commensurability of the penis and the phallus in depicting passion. To be sure, the crippling of men by women (Amazons), as the essay suggests, is an attempt to resist the domination associated with the patriarchal order, as played out by Martin Guerre's deficiency. This disfigurement of the male anatomy demystifies the relationship between the phallus and the penis, for the resistance to the phallocentric order can be achieved only through a newfound potency associated with the impaired body. If, as Montaigne claims, in the case of women the genital parts are fuller and better nourished in this state of imperfection, it is because lameness, no longer considered a deficiency, must be regarded as something to be desired. Montaigne's text rhetorically enacts a displacement through which sexual difference is constituted and maintained by the projection of a deficiency onto a male subject. By indirectly aligning himself with the feminine (what Montaigne terms "the pleasure brought to those who try it [l'essayent]"), the essayist can pose a libidinal and identificatory challenge to what is traditionally conceived of as potency through references to epistemological issues. In this context, the category of "man" becomes a movable one, for maleness is subject to mutation and exception.[12]

Todd Reeser has suggested that Montaigne's "essaying" of manliness questions the masculinity derived from excess.[13] The Stoic position, as in the thought of Seneca, organized the question of gender around the binary coupling of masculinity and effeminacy, with the former foregrounding an ethic associated with virile military practices. By adopting a skeptical perspective with respect to the essentialism proposed by the Stoics, the essayist reflected the more temperate thought he had discovered in reading Sextus Empiricus's *Outlines of Scepticism* on gender identification: "The mother of the Gods accepts effeminate men; and the goddess would not have made this judgment if being manly were by nature bad. There is much anomaly about how fine it is to be manly."[14]

I now wish to examine the question of gender in Montaigne's essay from a methodological perspective and engage in a metacommentary of the preceding analysis. As a new historicist, Stephen Greenblatt has engaged in a critical debate concerning the Martin Guerre case and the use of psychoanalysis. He views this critical approach—in the context of an early modern work such as that of Montaigne—to be overdetermined in its need to discover a "principle of unalienable self-possession" and a "unitary position," thereby producing an anachronistic reading of the text.[15] On the contrary, the exploration of gender in this essay yields a hybrid human subject whose agency is shaped by the tensions it encounted in a patriarchial culture and the subject's resistance to what was accepted as a socially consecrated norm within sixteenth-century culture. Montaigne's engagement with the intertexts that his archive has become produces an essay that severs the constraints imposed by the normative process of subjugation in the name of a world of difference. What matters above all else is the way in which Montaigne responds to the Martin Guerre narrative and the manner in which he addresses the question of alterity from an ethical perspective. By his refusal to reduce the other to the same Montaigne is able to transcend what John O'Brien has characterized as "the compulsive urge to narrate."[16]

A narrative interlude near the end of "Des boyteux" presents an interesting anecdote that combines the topoi of cripples, lovemaking, and writing: "Qui est aussi la raison pourquoy les Grecs descrioient les tisserandes d'estre plus chaudes que les autres femmes: à cause du mestier sedentaire qu'elles font, sans grand exercice du corps. . . . Ce tremoussement que leur ouvrage leur donne ainsin assises les esveille et sollicite, comme faict les dames le crolement et tremblement de leurs coches" (III, 11, 1034) ("The Greeks decried women weavers as being hotter than other woman: because of the sedentary trade they perform, without much bodily exercise. . . . The joggling that their work gives them as they are thus seated arouses and solicits them, as the shaking and trembling of their coaches does the ladies" (791). The women weavers'(tisserandes, derived from the curious conversion of the Latin texere, to weave, and the Latin textus, tissue of a literary work) activity, like that of Montaigne composing his essays, thematizes the symbolic positioning of desire and the denial of castration. The act of braiding, as it is described here, is tantamount to motivating the drive and the energy that are the source of desire. Far from being negatively conceived, this representation of the sedentary female dramatically portrays the passion and strength that is the result of the art of weaving.

Through the figuration of the monster Montaigne's essay thus demonstrates a tacit challenge not only to the will to totality but to conventional male subjectivity and the very "nature" of gender identity. Post-Freudian psychoanalysis teaches that identity is based on the internalization of a series of images that are first perceived as external to the desiring subject. In the essay "Des boyteux" the psychic mapping of the male subject is based upon the identification with unconventionally deformed bodily images and, later, with the introjection of a female presence attuned to unrestrained libidinal pleasure. The narrative constructed in this essay finds its power of persuasion in its capacity to illuminate the buried history of the essayist. The politics of desire and identification as foregrounded here therefore presents a revisionist theory of male gender in which the exemplary figures of rarity represented in the text aim at deforming the dominant fictions put forth in the name of the father, while constituting a counterdiscourse that indirectly expresses defiance of existing conventions. The resistance to the artificially created authority of man is but an attempt by desire to portray itself in the naturalness of its writerly deformations, and in so doing to combine the desiring subject with the idealized yet imperfect image of the cripple in a kind of specular bliss. The representation of the monster is therefore not based on its isolation from the symbolic order of language but rather on its inability easily to be inscribed within the paradigms of conventional gender identity. By describing the so-called myth of monstrosity, Montaigne's text proposes a hermeneutic riddle, which is first disguised as an epistemological question and finally takes on ontological proportions that suggest that the cultural system in which individual subjects are inscribed is monstrously artificial. In the end, Montaigne's exemplarity derives from the projection of a marvelously imperfect self.

PART II

Death Sentences

3

MONTAIGNE'S FRATERNITY
La Boétie on Trial

"Mon frere, mon frere, me refusez vous doncques une place?"
My brother, my brother, do you refuse me a place? (1055)
ETIENNE DE LA BOÉTIE

FRAGMENT D'UNE LETTRE QUE MONSIEUR LE CONSEILLER DE MONTAIGNE ESCRIT À MONSEIGNEUR DE MONTAIGNE SON PÈRE, CONCERNANT QUELQUES PARTICULARITEZ QU'IL REMARQUA EN LA MALADIE & MORT DE FEU MONSIEUR DE LA BOETIE.

(Lettre datée du mois d'août 1563 et publiée par Montaigne dans La Boétie, La Mesnagerie de Xenophon. Les Regles de mariage, de Plutarque. Lettre de consolation de Plutarque à sa femme. Le tout traduict de Grec en François par feu M. Estienne De la Boetie . . . item, un Discours sur la mort dudit Seigneur De la Boètie par M. de Montaigne, édition établie par M. de Montaigne [Paris: Frederic Morel, 1571])

Although Derrida's *Politiques de l'amitié* (*Politics of Friendship*) makes scant reference to La Boétie's work *La Servitude volontaire* (*On Voluntary Servitude*), the spectrality of that work impinges on his analysis of Montaigne's "De l'amitié" (I, 28) ("Of Friendship"). This intertextual ghost puts the essayist's ethics and politics to the test.[1] To be sure, it has become a critical commonplace to evoke Montaigne's act of mourning in the writing of the *Essays* as a compensation and a *dénégation* (disavowal) of the loss of his beloved friend Etienne de La Boétie. This literary practice, which might be regarded as an attempt to incorporate or encrypt the spectral remains of La Boétie's corpus, also conflates the figure of the friend with that of the brother, who belongs to what Derrida calls a "homosocial political configuration."[2] What is at stake in this literary performance of friendship is its deliteralization, which goes far beyond the simple parameters of fraternity. In the process, it allegorizes the possibility of the political as a democratic phenomenon while suggesting that friendship, like democracy, is neither simple nor pure. According to Derrida, the question of politics is inextricably related to the state of the family. Within this context, friendship can be regarded as a trope for the political or metaphoric matrix of a family romance ("une configuration familiale, fraterniste" (12) "a familial, fraternalist configuration" [viii]). From this perspective the friend would be like the brother, and the possibility of fraternization would associate this relationship with the topoi of equality, freedom, and democracy. As Derrida states: "Pas de démocratie sans respect de la singularité ou l'altérité irréductible, mais pas de démocratie sans 'communauté des amis'. . . sans calcul des majorités, sans sujets identifiables, stabilisables, représentables et égaux entre eux" (40) ("There is no democracy without respect for irreducible singularity or alterity, but there is no democracy without the 'community of friends' . . . without the calculation of majorities, without identifiable, stabilizable, representable subjects, all equal" [22]).

What is foregrounded here is the political translation of friendship not only between friendship and the idea of brotherhood but between La Boétie and Montaigne, who—like Aristotle and Cicero before them—have linked the friend-brother phenomenon to questions of virtue, justice, and political reason. For example, Aristotle's *Politics* stresses that the life of the *polis* is the work of friendship (*philas ergon*) and that sociability is based on the idea of *philia*.

In examining the ways in which Montaigne's "De l'amitié" functions as the "prosthesis" of La Boétie's *Servitude volontaire*, I wish to discuss how that friendship survives or lives on and perhaps even dies once again in the essayist's text by rendering friendship itself problematic.[3] Among the great philosophical meditations on friendship as an experience of mourning, the Montaignian testimony to friendship—recalling Aristotle's haunting exclamation, "O my friends, there is no friend"—functions as a remembrance that simultaneously forgets. Moreover, Montaigne's encryption of La Boétie's discourse into his own demonstrates how a textual metamorphosis can reveal the way in which the psychic and the social intermingle to produce symbolic representations derived from tropes of nourishment and communion.

It might at first appear that the missing corpse, the political treatise against tyranny thematized in *La Servitude volontaire*—initially framed by the discourse on friendship between Montaigne and La Boétie and subsequently abandoned—is tangential. For how can a compelling argument, composed at a time of political turmoil (the religious civil conflicts) and rejecting the willing obedience of subjects to the power of a single ruler, metonymically mesh with relations of friendship? As a dialogic phenomenon the "essaying" of friendship becomes more complex, whereby the figure of the dead friend lives on (the Ciceronian adage "mortiu uiuunt," found in *Laelius de Amicitia*) and survives by becoming subject to a process that transforms *philia* into *necrophilia*, a metamorphosis that ultimately represents a drama of ambivalence.

La Boétie begins *La Servitude voluntaire* by questioning the parameters of political authority and its relationship to nature. It contains an early reference to Ulysses' assertion in the *Iliad* that a soldier must obey his commander out of a sense of duty. This intertextual fragment sets the stage for an evaluation of the pros and cons of monarchy and absolute power. La Boétie declares that freedom is a natural right. However, he also foregrounds the paradox that although men are free by nature, they subject themselves to a singular authority empowered by them through a self-imposed blindness reflected in the oxymoronic trope of voluntary servitude: "Disons donc ainsi, qu'à l'homme toutes choses lui sont comme naturelles . . . à quoy la nature simple et non altérée l'appelle; ainsi la premiere raison de la servitude volontaire c'est la coutume" (150) ("Let us then say that although all things to which man trains and accustoms himself are natural to him, that alone is innate in him to which his simple and unaltered nature calls him. Thus the first reason for voluntary servitude is custom" [205]). La Boétie's text is predicated on a concept of nature and social relations that acquires universal dimensions of companionship and fraternity: "La nature, le ministre de dieu, la gouvernante des hommes, nous a tous faits de même forme, et comme il semble, à même moule, afin de nous entreconnaitre tous pour compagnons ou plutôt pour frères" (140) ("Nature, the minister of God, the governess of human beings, has made us all of the same form, and as it seems, from the same mold, so that all of us should recognize one another as companions or rather as brothers" [197]).

Anthropomorphically conceived as a benevolent maternal force, nature is represented in La Boétie's discourse as a collective entity in which the individual is subsumed by the socializing drive of the human species: "Puis donc que cette bonne mère nous a donné tous logés à tous la terre pour demeure, nous a tous logés aucunement en même maison, nous a tous figurés à même patron afin que chacun se pût mirer et quasi reconnoître l'un dans l'autre" (140–41) ("Because this good mother has given us all the whole earth to live in, has lodged us, in a way, in the same house, has made us all of the same clay, so that each one should be able to look into the other [as into a mirror] and recognize himself" [197–98]). Paradoxically, La Boétie's vision of universal brotherhood, which is partially based on the Aristotelian concept of nature, projects an imaginary community in which the identity of each individual is correlated with self-identity, or a "fraternelle affection" without difference: "Ceste bonne mere . . . nous a tous figure a mesme patron afin que chacun se peust mirer et quasi reconnoiste l'un dans l'autres" (119) ("This good mother . . . has made us all of the same clay, so that each one should be able to look into the other [as into a mirror] and recognize himself" [197–98]). Yet the magnetic attraction of this socializing affinity renders the desire for fraternity subject to nature's inadequacy to make freedom whole. Exemplification of the human subject as theoretical abstraction, while drawing from what we refer to today as "reason," nevertheless emerges as naturally subject to contingency or change: "La nature de l'homme est d'être franc et de le vouloir être, mais aussi sa nature est telle que naturellement il tient le pli que la nourriture lui donne" (150) ("Man's nature is surely to be free, and to want to be free; but his nature is also such that he retains the bias that his upbringing gives him" [205]).

Freedom, as described by La Boétie, has an ironic dimension to it whereby the natural quest for liberty and the unnatural desire to serve coexist: "Or, est-il donc certain qu'avec la liberté, se perd tout en un coup la vaillance: les gens sujets n'ont point d'allégresse au combat ni d'âpreté: ils vont au danger quasi comme attachés et tous engourdis, par manière d'acquit" (153) ("Now it is therefore certain that with the loss of liberty, courage completely disappears. Subjected peoples have no eagerness or spirit for combat. They meet danger as if they were tied up and completely numb as a matter of course" [207]). If servitude risks becoming a universalized phenomena in La Boétie's discourse, it is because our natural inclinations and innate

reason are conceived of as being far less powerful than the imprison-
ing force of custom. The ungrounded nature of custom differentiates
it from justice and allows it to become a second nature capable of
enabling servitude to overcome freedom: "La premiere raison pourquoy les hommes servent volontiers, est parce qu'ils naissent serfs et
sont nourris tel" (153) "The first reason why men willingly serve is
that they are born slaves and are reared as such" [207]). Within this
scheme of things freedom refers not to the rule of law but to a situation sanctioned by the force of habit.

The ideal that La Boétie puts forward rests upon the notion of
a utopian community rooted in freedom and equality. With this in
mind, La Boétie conceives of friendship in relation to tyranny, which,
he suggests, forecloses the possibility of sociability; servility is presented as that which friendship is not:

> L'amitié, c'est un nom sacré, c'est une chose sainte; elle ne se met
> jamais qu'entre gens de bien, et ne se prend que par une mutuelle
> estime; elle s'entretient non tant par bienfaits, que par la bonne
> vie. Ce qui rend un ami assuré de l'autre c'est la connoissance
> qu'il a de son intégrité: les répondens qu'il en a, c'est en son bon
> naturel, la foi et la constance. Il ne peut avoir d'amitié là où est
> la cruauté, là ou est desloyauté, là où est l'injustice; et entre les
> méchants, quand ils s'assemblent c'est un complot, non pas une
> compaignie; ils ne s'entr'aiment pas, mais ils s'entrecraignent; ils
> ne sont pas amis, mais ils sont complices. (168–69)

> Friendship is a sacred word; it is a holy thing. It never occurs ex-
> cept between honorable people, and it arises only from mutual
> esteem. It maintains itself not so much by means of good turns
> as by a good life. What renders a friend assured of the other is
> the knowledge he has of his integrity. The guarantee he has from
> him are his good nature, faith [in each other], and constancy.
> There cannot be friendship where there is cruelty, where there is
> disloyalty, where there is injustice. Among the wicked when they
> assemble, there is a plot, not companionship. They do not pro-
> vide for one another, but fear one another. They are not friends
> but accomplices. (220)

In opting for friendship through the negativity of these restrictive
clauses, La Boétie's text idealizes harmony through a model of a col-

lective subject in control of its fate. Such a model, however, precludes tyrants, who inspire fear and are never worthy of "estime." As for the latter, the tyranny of monarchical rule might possibly embrace injustice rather than the autonomy of its subjects and in so doing subvert the possibility of equal exchange and reciprocity: "Estant au dessus de tous [the tyranical leader] et n'ayant point de compaignon, il est déjà au delà de l'amitié, qui a son vrai gibier en l'équalité et ne veut jamais clocher ainsi est toujours égale" (169) ("Because being above all [other people], and not having any peer, he is already beyond the bounds of friendship, which has its true foundation in equality, which does not ever want to be unbalanced, but is always even" [220]). If for La Boétie community, as a plenitudinous entity, is contingent upon communication, the inoperative or "unworked community" is one in which there are neither equals nor friends.

From La Boétie's perspective friendship is ostensibly a political phenomenon. In its own way La Boétie's lament affects clear symptoms of a cultural melancholia. This leads him to transform his work of mourning into one of survival, portraying a cannibalistic practice that betrays the presuppositions of innate reason. At the end of his text La Boétie invokes the latent fear of the servants of tyranny, for whom friendship and community are foreign entities. In the passage that follows La Boétie ascribes responsibility for revenge to "le peuple" and memoralistic testimony to subsequent generations as a form of ethico-political volition. As La Boétie's narrative reveals, the possibility of evil (unmitigated violence) ironically becomes the condition—the limit and the de-limitation—of good:

> Mais c'est plaisir de considérer qu'est ce qui leur revient de ce grand tourment, et le bien qu'ils peuvent attendre de leur peine et de leur misérable vie. . . . Volontiers le peuple, du mal qu'il souffre, n'en accuse point le tiran, amis ceux qui le gouvernent . . . quand chacun aurait une pièce de leur corps, ils ne seraient pas encore, ce leur semble assez satisfait, ni à demi saoulés de leur peine, mais certes encore apres qu'ils sont morts, ceux qui viennent après ne sont jamais si paresseux que le nom de ce mange-peuples ne soit noirci de l'encre de mille plumes, et leur reputation déchirée dans mille livres, et les os même par manière de dire, trainés par la postérité, les punissant encore après leur mort de leur méchante vie. (170–71)

But it is pleasant to consider what it is that they get from this great torment, and the benefit that they can expect for their pain and from their wretched life. Usually the people does not blame the tyrant for the wrong that it endures, but accuses those who manage him . . . each of whom would still not be satisfied, it seems, even if he had a piece of their [torn] bodies, nor half satisfied with their punishment. But certainly, even after they are dead, those who come after are never so lazy that the names of these devourers of peoples may not be blackened by the ink of a thousand pens, their reputation torn apart in a thousand books, and even their bones, so to speak, dragged [through the dirt] by posterity, punishing them still after their death for their wicked life. (221)

Clearly this fantasy of destruction reflects a fascination with evil, perhaps even suggesting what Jean-Luc Nancy has characterized in another context as "a proper positivity of evil."[4] In a way, this giving of death and evil temporarily suspends the ethical ideal of friendship for an absolute obligation, namely, the righting of a wrong. The powerful historical memory revises the identity of friendship through violence and paradoxically demonstrates how such dislocation opens up the possibility of doing justice to the past by projecting it into the future. Ironically, La Boétie's text enacts what might be termed an uncanny freedom; it reveals the unsettling figure of alterity in the human subject, whereby an appetite for enslavement undercuts the ideality originally proposed. The value of locating friendship in a specific locality (the ideal community) comes undone and paradoxically reifies itself once again by putting the dead in their place. By doing this, La Boétie's text enacts a rupture with the idea of community as unified entity. He engages in a cathartic process, an ethico-political cleansing of sorts that differentiates and redraws the boundaries of civility ("le nom de ces mange-peuples ne soit noirci de l'encre de mille plumes" ("the names of these devourers of peoples may not be blackened by the ink of a thousand pens"). Interestingly, La Boétie ascribes a certain degree of exemplarity to figures such as Brutus, Cassius, and Hamodius, whose sense of friendship manifested itself in regicide to re-form the values of the polis.

At the core of Montaigne's writing project is a nostalgic ideal based on an intersubjective communion between two men. This relationship identifies its singularity by situating alterity outside of itself. To be sure, the friendship characterized by Montaigne as "un'ame en deux corps" (I, 28, 190) ("one soul in two bodies" [141]) evokes Aristotle's argument as reported by Diogenes Laertius. What Derrida terms the "doubly singular definition of the friend" raises important issues as to the political and ethical ramifications concerning the logic of reciprocity in La Boétie's text; it also foregrounds the exigencies of the homosocial nature of a friendship that desires to make itself safe from an alien other.

Throughout "De l'amitié" one encounters the uncanny spectral impact of La Boétie's discursive force. One should bear in mind, however, that Montaigne first comes into contact with La Boétie by way of the signature inscribed on *La Servitude volontaire*. The friendship, as Montaigne suggests, is motivated by a name that precedes an encounter: "Car elle [La Boétie's text] me fut montrée longue piece avant que je l'eusse veu, et me donna la premiere connoissance de son nom, acheminant ainsi cette amitié" (I, 28, 184) ("For it was shown to me long before I had seen him, and gave me my first knowledge of his name, thus starting on its way this friendship" [136]). The metonymic chain between pre-text and essay demonstrates how the transportive power of language moves from page to name and realizes, through the power of the imagination, a perfect friendship "si entiere et si parfaite que certainement il ne s'en lit guiere de pareilles [. . .] entre nos hommes" (I, 28, 184) ("so entire and so perfect that certainly you will hardly read of the like" [136]). The words that inaugurated the process have not disappeared; the thing has not entirely overcome its mediation. Despite everything, Montaigne declares himself "obligé particulierement à cette piece" (I, 28, 184) ("particularly obligated to this work" [136]) Accordingly, *La Servitude volontaire* still retains its value as a "relique" (relic), serving not only as a reminder of La Boétie's existence but also as an affective support mediating the most perfect of friendships. Around the crypt occupying the space of the essay the traces or letters of the incursion of death in life emerge. This writerly relic of things past produces the pleasures of necrophilia enacted as a form of literary cannibalism.

"De l'amitié" bears witness to the legacy of a double absence realized as a work of mourning: the death of the friend and the excision of *La Servitude volontaire*. The essay performs this loss and attempts to account for the absence at its center. As a sign of friendship for La Boétie (the essayist's desire to protect his friend's text from its counterfeited appropriation by the Protestants' having renamed it *Le Contre Un*), Montaigne's essay not only excises *La Servitude volontaire* but reveals that it is not even the perfectly elaborated work that it was said to be: "Si y a il bien à dire que ce ne soit le mieux qu' il [La Boétie] peut faire; et si, en l'aage que je l'ay conneu, plus avancé, il eut pris un tel desseing que le mien de mettre par escrit ses fantasies, nous verrions plusieurs choses rares" (I, 28, 184) ("Still, it is far from being the best he could do; and if at the more mature age when I knew him, he had adopted a plan such as mine, of putting his ideas in writing, we should see many rare things" [135]). La Boétie's text is thus scarcely "élabouré de toute sa suffisance" (I, 28, 183) ("elaborated with all his skill" [135]). It is no more than an example of juvenilia, perhaps impressive but by no means corresponding to the description with which, just a few lines earlier, Montaigne had revealed his inferiority in relation to his painter's masterpiece.

In this extraordinary friendship born in letters—La Boétie, "la mort entre les dents" (I, 28, 184) ("with death in his throat" [136]) bequeaths his library to Montaigne—the mourner has yet to find the words to adequately describe it: "Si on me presse de dire pourquoy je l'aymois, je sens que cela ne se peut exprimer" (I, 28, 188) ("If you press me to tell why I loved him, I feel that this cannot be expressed" [139]). To be sure, by engaging in the tropological representation of the sovereignty of friendship, Montaigne's text disfigures the political thought of La Boétie by transforming the topos of voluntary servitude ("servitude volontaire") into one of free will ("liberté volontaire"). The dream of perfect presence, of "one soul in two bodies," has now been dissolved, in the wake of La Boétie's demise, into the elusiveness of pure smoke ("la fumée," I, 28, 193): "Tout estant par effect commun entre eux, volontez, pensemens, jugemens, biens, femmes, enfans, honneur et vie . . . et leur convenance n'estant qu'un'ame en deux corps . . . ils ne se peuvent ny prester ny donner rien" (I, 28, 190) ("Everything actually being in common between them—wills, thoughts, judgments, goods, wives, children, honor, and life—and their relationship being that of one soul in two bodies . . . they can neither lend nor give anything to each other" [141]). This elimination of alterity veers toward transparent communication—"la chose la plus une et unie" (I, 28, 191) ("the most singular and unified of all things" [142])—in which perfect friendship is one that can only be one: "Le secret que j'ay juré ne deceller à nul autre, je le puis, sans parjure, communiquer à celuy qui n'est pas autre: c'est moy"

(I, 28, 191) ("The secret I have sworn to reveal to no other man, I can impart without perjury to the one who is not another man: he is myself" [142]). Given its exclusivity, this idealized friendship has nothing left to share.

Montaigne engages in an implicit critique of La Boétie's idea of "voluntary servitude," which he regards as a political concept based on a series of social obligations. The "voluntary freedom" that Montaigne refers to in "De l'amitié" is selected as the result of free will and out of affection for the beloved friend. The book that Montaigne had chosen as being responsible for their friendship is now the one to which he responds. La Boétie comes to realize—as Montaigne certainly has discovered—that nature is not an essential matter, nor is it the basis for all that's good. It has a dark side that succumbs to the poison of enslavement: "Il me semble maintenant que l'amour mesme de la liberté ne soit pas si naturelle" (117) "It now seems that the very love of liberty might not be natural" [197]). If the discourse of friendship is based on reciprocity, the relation that results from political expediency in La Boétie's text emphasizes subordination. Essaying the concept of friendship enables Montaigne to engage in the simulation of a dialogic encounter that renders the friend otherwise. In dialoguing about friendship, Montaigne draws on the same critical topoi deployed by La Boétie in *La Servitude volontaire*, namely, friendship, liberty, and tyranny. Unlike La Boétie, however, Montaigne removes his discourse from the public arena and reinscribes it in the privatized space of self-reflection: "Car cette parfaicte amitié dequoy je parle, est indivisble; chacun se donne si entire à son amy, qu'il ne luy reste rien à departir ailleurs" (191) ("For this perfect friendship of which I speak is indivisible; each one gives himself so wholly to his friend that he has nothing left to distribute elsewhere" [141]).

If for La Boétie friendship is a virtue that facilitates the passage to sociability, for Montaigne it is something that is simply extraordinary—"une fois en trois siecles" (I, 28, 184) ("once in three centuries" [136])—since it can only be realized in a privatized locus situated beyond the confines of the public realm. As the essay proceeds, it reveals friendship to be "homo-fraternal" in the sense that its paradigm is always brotherly love or friendship between males, which, as Trevor Hope suggests, is "the foundation of hermeneutic enterprises in the service of the mandate that is central to the disciplinary regime of modernity."[5] Through the restrictive syntax describing what friendship is not, Montaigne's model of brotherly fraternity, which is also one of passion, designates in its sovereign indivisibility where each man gives wholly of himself—"où l' homme fust engagé tout entier" (I, 28, 186) ("so that the entire man would be engaged" [138])—to the exclusion of an other. With this in mind, "De l'amitié" thematizes the question of aurality as it relates to the correspondence (convenance) constituting this absolute community of souls. If hearing is central to the communicative utopia of friendship, as suggested in the closing reference to Catullus (II, 28 194) [144]), aural gratification can only be realized as a phenomenon that is thoroughly androcentric: "A dire vray la suffisance ordinaire des femmes n'est pas pour respondre à cette conference et communication" (I, 28, 186) ("To tell the truth, the ordinary capacity of women is inadequate for that communion and fellowship" [138]).

When, in *Politiques de l'amitié,* Derrida foregrounds the "double exclusion of the feminine" in Montaigne's text and ascribes to it "the sublime figure of virile homosexuality," he suggests a mode of male "intercourse" in which self-limitation is built right into the idea of friendship. Not surprisingly, in an *allongeail* of the Bordeaux edition the assertion of the ineffable quality of friendship is dramatically revised: "Si on me presse de dire pourquoy je l'aymois, je sens que cela ne se peut exprimer qu'en respondant: 'Par ce que c'estoit luy; par ce que c'estoit moy'" (I, 28, 188) (" If you press me to tell why I loved him, I feel that this cannot be expressed, except by answering: Because it was he, because it was I" [139]). This sentence expresses in its terseness and in the balance of its self-identity the harmonious albeit limited parameters of this friendship; it mimetically reproduces the restrictiveness and the exclusivity of perfect friendship.

On another level, however, the ambivalence of Montaigne's discourse in terms of La Boétie's model of social communion gives rise to a representation whose effect is power; it is simultaneously the imaginary satisfaction of this desire and its deferred satisfaction. Bearing this in mind, it is important to consider that from a psychoanalytic perspective the introjection of one's "word thing" functions as a process emanating from primitive fantasies of cannibalistic incorporation and as a defense against loss. What in another context I have termed "Montaigne's reader's digest"[6] provides the locus for the projection of La Boétie's "word thing," yet it also involves the subject's writerly violence against the lost object that is the result of the essaying process.

Here let us recall the dramatic account of La Boétie's death as narrated by Montaigne in a letter to his father.[7] In "Extraict d'une lettre" the essayist's "extreme friendship" is used as a pretext to recount the death scene in the name of the divine Father ("que si Dieu vouloit qu'il empirast"; "that if God willed that he get worse") while ironically remaining the director and main character of the drama ("le dommage serait à moy" [1350]; "the loss would be mine" [1048]):

Ce mesme jour, par ce qu'il fut trouvé bon, je luy dis, qu'il me sieroit mal pour l'extreme amitié que je luy portais si je ne me souciois que comme en sa santé on avoit veu toutes ses actions pleines de prudence & de bon conseil, autant qu'à l'homme du monde, qu'il les continuast encore en sa maladie: & que si Dieu vouloit qu'il empirast, je serais tresmarry qu'à faute d'advisement il eust laissé nul de ses affaires domestiques décousu. [1349–50])[8]

This same day, because it was judged suitable to do so, I said to him that because of the extreme friendship I bore him, it would be unbecoming to me if I did not take care that, as all his actions in health had been seen to be as full of wisdom and good counsel as those of anyone else in the world, he should continue them still in his sickness; and that if God willed that he get worse, I would be very sorry if for lack of advice he should leave any of his domestic affairs at loose ends. (1048)

Montaigne's story of La Boétie's demise, his "prise de la parole" (capture of speech), translates the symbolic death that his narrative is meant to effect. By displacing his violent desire onto the Heavenly Father, Montaigne's text captures the death scene as the locus of an agonistic encounter and the place from which La Boétie's sacrifice will commence.

In an apparent gesture to defend *La Servitude volontaire* against its opportunistic appropriation by Huguenot propagandists, such as Simon Goulard, near the end of "De l'amitié" the essayist lends voice to his dead friend and in so doing problematizes his text, rendering it "implexe," or folded within itself. The following passage reveals a discrepancy between La Boétie's theoretical reflections and his political practice and signifies a scission in the so-called harmony of thought.

Je ne fay nul doubte qu'il ne creust ce qu'il escrivoit, car il estoit assez conscientieux pour ne mentir pas mesmes en se jouant. Et sçay davantage que, s'il eust eu à choisir, il eut mieux aimé estre nay à Venise qu'à Sarlac: et avec raison. Mais il avoit un'autre maxime souverainement empreinte en son ame, d'obeyr et de se soubmettre tres-religieusement aux loix sous lesquelles il estoit nay. Il ne fut jamais un meilleur citoyen, ny plus affectionné au repos de son païs, ny plus ennemy des remuements et nouvel-letez de son temps. (I, 28, 194)

I have no doubt that he believed what he wrote, for he was so conscientious as not to lie even in jest. And I know further that if he had had the choice, he would rather have been born in Ven-ice than in Sarlat, and with reason. But he had another maxim sovereignly imprinted in his soul, to obey and submit most reli-giously to the laws under which he was born. There never was a better citizen, or one more devoted to the tranquillity of his country, or more hostile to the commotions and innovations of his time. (144)

Here Montaigne's rhetoric engages in the very balancing act that defines the textual practice associated with the genre of the essay. This text simultaneously exculpates the friend from any possible ac-cusation of disloyalty and draws our attention to La Boétie's enthu-siasm for aristocratic republicanism. At the very least this passage foregrounds an ambivalence that simultaneously supports and ques-tions the integrity (in the sense of wholeness) of the friend before the inquiring gaze of the other. In memorializing the lost friend, Mon-taigne becomes the brother who functions like a pater familias. As a result, the brother is transformed into a support of the essayist's self-projection in what is represented as a Montaignian stance of indeci-sion ("Il l'escrivit par maniere d'essay" I, 28, 183–84) ("He wrote it by way of essay" [135]). No longer characterized as what Donald Frame once referred to as Montaigne's "moral mentor,"[9] La Boétie now becomes subordinate to the words of another. The so-called equal engagement of friendship is subject to a revisionary rhetoric that puts the friend on trial ("à l'épreuve") and makes the discourse on friendship question the exigencies of communion in order for it to become the vehicle for amour-propre. Perhaps here Montaigne puts into effect a topos found in Cicero's *De Amicitia* where Laelius suggests that friendship abhors subservience.

By the end of "De l'amitié" Montaigne has been forced to go public with his friendship for La Boétie since it now has to answer to an agency beyond itself (the imperatives of the patriarchal order) while breaking the bond of silence. The death of the friend and the political situation provokes an "outing" of sorts from the indivisibility of friendship, a betrayal of the secrecy that once held this sovereign relationship together but now causes it to unravel. Montaigne's text projects a "prosthesis" that renders the propriety of La Boétie's corpse improper due to its re-membering as it is grafted onto the Montaignian corpus. This grafting constitutes an answering for and to the other and accordingly functions as the undoing of the solidity of the sacred bond.

By shifting the focus from "servitude volontaire" to the "liberté volontaire" of friendship, Montaigne's desire to defend the brother takes on paternalistic proportions; it reveals how this revisionary gesture of friendship, translated through the disfiguration of the missing corpse, requires both the good will and the fratricidal sacrifice represented in *La Servitude volontaire*.[10] In the end we are left with the impression that for friendship to exist it must transcend its self-protected communion in the etymological sense of "common" (com) and "defense" (munis) whereby Montaigne's citation of Aristotle's maxim, "O mes amis il n'y a nul amy" (I, 28, 190) ("Oh my friends, there is no friend." [140]) becomes a declaration of individuation, a mark of distinction that enables the essayist's text to assert its priority.

4

MONTAIGNE ON HORSEBACK, OR THE SIMULATION OF DEATH

Je ne puis tenir registre de ma vie par mes actions: fortune les met
trop bas: je le tiens par mes fantasies. (III, 9, 945–46)

I cannot keep a record of my life by my actions; fortune places
them too low. I keep it by my thoughts. (721)

To die, to sleep; / To sleep; perchance to dream: ay, there's the rub;
/ For in that sleep of death what dreams may come / When we have
shuffled off this mortal coil, Must give us pause.
SHAKESPEARE, *HAMLET*, III, I, 64–68

 In the essay "De l'exercitation" (II, 6) ("Of Prac-
tice") Montaigne tries to find a way around the im-
possibility of describing the experience of death by
foregrounding the relationship between the imagination and the body: "Je n'imagine aucun estat
pour moy si insupportable et horrible, que d'avoir
l'ame vifve et affligée, sans moyen de se declarer" (II, 6, 375) ("I can
imagine no state so horrible and unbearable for me as to have my
soul alive and afflicted, without means to express itself" [270]). At
the beginning of the essay Montaigne intends to reconcile the phenomenon of death with practice, which is to say the habit of experiment or trial. If trial is essentially a matter of *exagium*, of balance and
passage, then death, by contrast, is located in the domain of aporia
and nonpassage:[1]

Mais à mourir, qui est la plus grande besoigne que nous ayons
à faire, l'exercitation ne nous y peut ayder. . . . Mais, quant à la
mort, nous ne la pouvons essayer qu'une fois; nous y sommes
tous apprentifs quand nous y venons. . . . Si nous ne la pouvons
joindre, nous la pouvons approcher, nous la pouvons reconnois-

tre; et, si nous ne donnons jusques à son fort, au moins verrons nous et en prattiquerons les advenuës. (II, 6, 371–72)

But for dying, which is the greatest task we have to perform, practice cannot help us. . . . But as for death, we can try it only once: we are all apprentices when we come to it. . . . If we cannot reach it, we can approach it, we can reconnoiter it; and if we do not penetrate as far as its fort, at least we shall see and become acquainted with the approaches to it. (267)

In adopting the classic topos of death, Montaigne finds a way of entering into a paradoxically dynamic relationship with it. To be sure, the subject in question recognizes the indeterminacy of death; he is conscious of the impossibility of grasping it as such. If he embarks on an inquiry into his own knowledge through a semantic network that refers to the act of trying (exercising, experimenting, testing, tasting), how can he evoke the experience of death when death constitutes absolute difference and inaction? If the moment of death eludes consciousness, and if one then disappears in the nonpassage of death, how can one explain what can be grasped only in this ungraspable impasse? How can one take into account evidence of a nonexperienced phenomenon, an abyss of thought, in a discourse that claims to report the "trials" of a life?

In "De l'exercitation" Montaigne attempts to submit death to an experiment—a notion that in itself is paradoxical since death is a singular, nonrepeatable phenomenon. A test or trial is based on repetition and the examination of difference. This implies a lapse in time, not the absence of time that is inherent in death; in other words, a gap between the temporality associated with one's "experience" of the test and the atemporal finality of death. Montaigne relies on this distinction in order to provide an existential analysis of death that precedes any biological consideration or ontological assumption.

"De l'exercitation" presents the reader with a simulated vision of death based on the rhetorical claim that in this case testing is only a form of practice, an exercise to illuminate the mystery of death. In order to narrate the experience of dying, he must be able to imagine it. To hold forth on death is therefore a kind of protection in which the desire for transgression clashes with the anguish it produces: "Il me semble toutefois qu'il y a quelque façon de nous apprivoiser à elle et de l'essayer aucunement" (II, 6, 371) ("It seems to me, however, that

there is a certain way of familiarizing ourselves with death and trying it out to some extent" [268]). As Freud suggested, the taboo that
prohibits talk of death is born of an affective ambivalence; it is the
product of a conscious sorrow and the satisfaction of being able to
rid oneself of it.[2] This suffering is therefore reexperienced when Montaigne describes it. The text portrays death as a place foreign to consciousness, which the latter attains only by asking rhetoric to provide
a description of it. In this context, the test becomes an inquiry into
the movement of the soul, a substitute for examining death directly
that transforms itself in the process of existing despite death. The
advantage it affords the essayist is that it provides a writerly space
where death can be simulated in a manner similar to the mental activity deployed while dreaming: "Ce n'est pas sans raison," Montaigne
proclaims, "qu'on nous fait regarder à nostre sommeil mesme, pour
la ressemblance qu'il a de la mort" (II, 6, 372) ("It is not without reason that we are taught to study even our sleep for the resemblance it
has with death" [268]).

Montaigne begins his essay by referring to the Roman nobleman
Julius Canius. Like the essayist with his "tests," Canius wished to
study himself in order to know himself better. Sentenced to death,
Canius aimed at discerning the moment of its arrival. In asserting the
existence of a fixed boundary between life and death, Canius challenged the usual assumptions regarding the two:

> Je pensois, luy respondit-il, à me tenir prest et bandé de toute
> ma force, pour voir si, en cet instant de la mort, si court et si
> brief, je pourray appercevoir quelque deslogement de l'ame, et si
> elle aura quelque ressentiment de son yssuë, pour, si j'en aprens
> quelque chose, en revenir donner apres, si je puis, advertissement
> à mes amis. (II, 6, 371)

> "I was thinking," he replied, "about holding myself ready and
> with all my powers intent to see whether in that instant of death,
> so short and brief, I shall be able to perceive any dislodgment of
> the soul, and whether it will have any feeling of its departure; so
> that, if I learn anything about it, I may return later, if I can, to
> give the information to my friends." (267)

The example of Canius sheds light upon the enigmatic relationship
between dying and witnessing. Death cannot be perceived, for the

sudden stop it puts to life eliminates temporality altogether, so that all awareness of oneself disappears in the singular limit constituted by the ending of time. The notion of transposing the atemporal to the sphere of repeatable experience would appear to involve a striking contradiction. Canius nonetheless proposed to do the impossible: to transform the end of life and the stopping of thought by passing beyond the limit; to transcend the difference that constitutes the narrative framework of life.

Canius was thus attempting to be in life and death simultaneously. He therefore imagined a paradoxical death—a death that is not a death. In trying to see "que c'estoit de ce passage" (II, 6, 371) ("what this passage was [267]) and to grasp "l'instant et au point de passage" (II, 6, 372) ("the instant and point of passing away" [268]), Canius sought to exploit a magic form of thought by means of which the difference between life and death could be erased. The hypothetical experience he envisioned requires a transcendence capable of blurring the boundary between passage and nonpassage. If the semantic value of the word "passage" is complicated here, it is because the word is related to the idea of crossing, which signifies both movement (passing from the other side, from life) and stability (finishing life). Conceived of as an active phenomenon, philosophizing implies for Canius the possibility of shifting the demarcation of the end, thereby dispelling some of the finality associated with death; it is a means of transforming death, the voyage without return, into a perpetual voyage: "Cettuy-cy philosophe non seulement jusqu'à la mort, mais en la mort mesme" (II, 6, 371) "This man philosophizes not only unto death, but even in death itself" [267]).

The Montaigne who writes about himself in this essay is intent on imitating Canius's example; the desire to face up to what he finds lacking in himself amounts to a determination to "form[er] nostre ame" (II, 6, 370) ("form our soul" [267]) and thereby to strengthen himself: "Nous en pouvons avoir experience, sinon entiere et parfaicte, au moins telle, qu'elle ne soit pas inutile, et qui nous rende plus fortifiez et asseurez" (II, 6, 371–72) ("We can have an experience of it that is, if not entire and perfect, at least not useless, and that makes us more fortified and assured" [268]). Montaigne cites this historical example and incorporates it in his discourse in order to assure himself of a freedom of examination that he could not discover otherwise.

Montaigne investigates the paradoxical phenomenon of temporary death through an account that recreates what he believes to have taken place after an accident caused him to lose consciousness. To describe this episode as though it were a lucid experience involves situating himself in a space in which temporality cannot exist. Montaigne devises an imaginary account that inquires into the unknown; he seeks to explore the boundary that divides death from life.

In relating the incident of Montaigne's fall from a horse—an accident caused by one of his men, who, eager to make a show of his daring, came up galloping behind him at full speed—the text draws attention to the danger that arises when the essayist is no longer at home, namely, a loss of balance.[3] The progress of his horse was marked by a false *step* ("faux pas"), a fatal accident that triggered an episode of mental aberration. The following passage retrospectively dramatizes the narrative interlocking of what ontologically must escape consciousness:

> Pendant nos troisiesmes troubles ou deuxiesmes (il ne me souvient pas bien de cela), m'estant allé un jour promener à une lieue de chez moy, qui suis assis dans le moiau de tout le trouble des guerres civiles de France, estimant estre en toute seureté et si voisin de ma retraicte que je n'avoy point besoin de meilleur equipage, j'avoy pris un cheval bien aisé, mais non guiere ferme. A mon retour, une occasion soudaine s'estant presentée de m'aider de ce cheval à un service qui n'estoit pas bien de son usage, un de mes gens, grand et fort, monté sur un puissant roussin qui avoit une bouche desesperée, frais au demeurant et vigoureux, pour faire le hardy et devancer ses compaignons vint à le pousser à toute bride droict dans ma route, et fondre comme un colosse sur le petit homme et petit cheval, et le foudroier de sa roideur et de sa pesanteur, nous envoyant l'un et l'autre les pieds contremont: si que voilà le cheval abbatu et couché tout estourdy, moy dix ou douze pas au delà, mort, estendu à la renverse, le visage tout meurtry et tout escorché, mon espée que j'avoy à la main, à plus de dix pas au delà, ma ceinture en pieces, n'ayant ny mouvement ny sentiment, non plus qu'une souche. (II, 6, 373)

During our third civil war, or the second (I do not quite remember which), I went riding one day about a league from my house, which is situated at the very hub of all the turmoil of the civil wars of France. Thinking myself perfectly safe, and so near my home that I needed no better equipage, I took a very easy but not very strong horse. On my return, when a sudden occasion came up for me to use this horse for a service to which it was not accustomed, one of my men, big and strong, riding a powerful work horse who had a desperately hard mouth and was moreover fresh and vigorous—this man, in order to show his daring and get ahead of his companions, spurred his horse at full speed up the path behind me, came down like a colossus on the little man and little horse, and hit us like a thunderbolt with all his strength and weight, sending us both head over heels. So that there lay the horse bowled over and stunned, and I ten or twelve paces beyond, dead, stretched on my back, my face all bruised and skinned, my sword, which I had in my hand, more than ten paces away, my belt in pieces, having no more motion or feeling than a log. (268–69)

In this description of a being "dead and skinned," the text presents the image of a body in a state of temporary rigor mortis. Represented now as a "thing" through the image of a log, this being-for-death is inserted in a space marking a limit. Deprived of movement and consciousness, the mental for-oneself gives the impression of being locked into an in-oneself lying outside reflective vitality. Curiously, the text conveys the distance that separates the represented object from its narrative vantage point. The simulation of death occurs in a place where memory appeals to a figurative language to transcribe an "experience" that otherwise escapes it. The image of Montaigne on horseback is the driving force behind the allegorical transformation that the text carries out in connection with someone who finds himself "sur le trottoir" (II, 6, 378) ("prominently displayed" [273]). This disturbed being who no longer feels at home in his own skin ("bien dans sa peau")—indeed, he describes himself as skinned ("escorché") (II, 6, 373)—is the product of an imaginary act in which the abdicated self searches for its way in a fiction of alterity.

The narrative voice thus functions as both witness and spokesman of the apparently departed subject. The insistence on the inexactitude of Montaigne's memory at the very beginning of the passage just quoted underscores the fictive process that underlies his perception of this equestrian episode. The technique is obvious. Through the voice of a rhetorical intermediary, the essay presents the experience of death as one of a disturbed consciousness that, in spite of the derangement it has suffered, is sure of itself. Even though Montaigne does not recollect speaking, his narrative engages in a form of ventriloquism that functions as a reflex action independent of himself. In seeking to deny the void that arises from the defects of consciousness, Montaigne's account supplies a detailed narrative that bridges the gap associated with death. Suddenly the vacancy of the self is filled with words that lend a certain degree of plausibility to the account. Gradually the "practice" produced by the application of this technique anticipates the return of the departed soul through a transposition of the narcissistic representation of death as a vital force: "Sur le chemin, et après avoir esté plus de deux grosses heures tenu pour trespassé, je commençay à me mouvoir et respirer. . . . Je commençay à reprendre un peu de vie" (II, 6, 373) ("On the way, and after I had been taken for dead for more than two full hours, I began to move and breathe. . . . I began to recover a little life" [269]). Suffering thus disappears behind a suspended consciousness in which the body acts independently of thought and paradoxically has a "life" of its own.

After the description of his fall from the horse and the blackout that followed, Montaigne considers the experience of passing over into death. However, instead of representing death as a limit, it describes it as a place of paradoxical passage, with the "locus" of nonpassage suddenly becoming an unbounded space incapable of respecting distinctions between life and death as we know them. Simulation, one could say, aims at suppressing the meaning of latent symptoms in the face of the threat of death. The ineffable in the temporal world suddenly springs forth and creates a two-sided illusion:

Il me sembloit que ma vie ne me tenoit plus qu'au bout des lèvres: je fermois les yeux pour ayder, ce me sembloit, à la pousser hors, et prenois plaisir à m'alanguir et à me laisser aller. C'estoit une imagination qui ne faisoit que nager superficiellement en mon ame, aussi tendre et aussi foible que tout le reste, mais à la verité non seulement exempte de desplaisir, ains meslée à cette douceur que sentent ceux qui se laissent glisser au sommeil. (II, 6, 374)

It seemed to me that my life was hanging only by the tip of my lips; I closed my eyes in order, it seemed to me, to help push it out, and took pleasure in growing languid and letting myself go.

It was an idea that was only floating on the surface of my soul, as delicate and feeble as all the rest, but in truth not only free from distress but mingled with that sweet feeling that people have who let themselves slide into sleep. (269–70)

The ending contemplated here reveals a refusal to arrive at a resolution. The essayist's swan song describes the sensory aspects of finishing out life, but it does so in an almost erotic manner that introduces an image of death exceeding the limits of the concept itself. Thanks to the evocative power of Montaigne's imagination, this scene paradoxically brings him a measure of added existence. These "approaches to death" set us on the road toward the unattainable aporia of death— toward what Derrida ironically characterizes as "a coming without steps"[4]—in the paradoxical movement of nonmovement: "La constance mesme n'est autre chose qu'un branle plus languissant" (III, 2, 805) ("Stability itself is nothing but a more languid motion" [610]).

This text opens up an imaginary space, namely, that of the unconscious, and thereby discloses another world: "Nostre monde vient d'en trouver un autre" (III, 6, 908) ("Our world has just discovered another world" [693]). As in the case of dreaming, the scene described here unfolds under the force of desire. The repetition of forms considered at the beginning of the passage suggests the coming of death that constitutes the narration itself. The virtually dead subject is transferred to a space that is closed off to consciousness. The being caught between life and death nonetheless acts by means of reflex gestures that give his body a vital movement, albeit one that lies outside his will: "Chacun sçait par experience qu'il y a des parties qui se branslent, dressent et couchent souvent sans son congé. Or ces passions qui ne nous touchent que par l'escorse, ne se peuvent dire nostres. . . . Les douleurs que le pied ou la main sentent pendant que nous dormons, ne sont pas à nous" (II, 6, 376) ("Every man knows by experience that there are parts that often move, stand up, and lie down, without his leave. Now these passions which touch only the rind of us cannot be called ours. . . . The pains which the foot or the hand feel while we are asleep are not ours" [271]).

The relation that Montaigne sustains with death as represented here is the product of desire. Ironically, death literally engenders a renaissance or rebirth of a subject who this time is taken over by an imagined self. Located "sur le beguayement du sommeil" (II, 6, 375) ("in the early stages of sleep" [271]), the figure who sleeps in a blurred state slips "aux bords de l'ame" (II, 6, 375) ("on the edges of the soul" [271]), into the sweetness of unknown pleasures. This hypothetical past is symbolically reconstructed at the price of a certain trickery, through the illusion of a lived experience that ought to be, in his own view, out of reach: "Je ne sçavoy pourtant ny d'où je venoy, ny où j'aloy; ni ne pouvois poiser et considerer ce que on me demandoit" (II, 6, 376) ("I did not know, for all that, where I was coming from or where I was going, nor could I weigh and consider what I was asked" [271]).

In alluding to the sweetness of this experience, the text brings into play chimeras that enhance the subject's pleasure. As Tom Conley suggests, Montaigne "slides into oblivion through discourse and diction."[5] Dreaming gives him the illusion of directing his will in inventing consciousness of the dream. Ironically, the movement toward death proceeds by means of the detour of a paradoxical resurrection whose driving force passes into the illusion of nonpassage. The belief in the experience of death depends on a movement capable of traversing the no-man's-land of the aporia while transforming the moment of death into an illusory regeneration. The simulated experience, like that of a dream, discloses a scene where the "reality" of death is changed by crossing an imaginary boundary. The narrative invention implicitly questions our biological and psychological assumptions about death. If life consists in an increase in tension, death, conversely, is pictured here as the consequence of a calming of this tension. For Montaigne pleasure could be defined as the avoidance of displeasure and the search for a voluptuous relaxation. The figurative ballet of the text, tracing the contours of this state, suggests that the elimination of pain is an illusion that requires an abandonment of the self, and in this way produces a pleasure corresponding to the free flow of energy.

The rebirth of this phantom subject becomes an effect of language. It establishes a rhetorical function capable of arousing a cathartic process in reverse. The text rids itself of the nothingness of death, which for this reason is found to be slightly less annihilated. The access to dying and the sensation of vacillation perceived at its threshold suggests that the possibility of passing away is a strategy for going forward by means of a certain *step*. Speech pierces consciousness without its being perceived.

What occurs in the field of speech in Montaigne's text is therefore sustained by its movement as it is passively received as a series of sensations. The image of pushing life outside oneself gives rise to a psychic phenomenon through which a phantasmic subject results from a figurative configuration capable of accounting for desire as an accomplished fact: "Je me laissoy couler si doucement et d'une façon si douce et si aisée que je ne sens guiere autre action moins poisante que celle-là estoit" (II, 6, 377) ("I was letting myself slip away so gently, so gradually and easily, that I hardly ever did anything with less of a feeling of effort" [272]). This slipping away is governed by a satisfaction that is represented between an imagined perception and what was to have been its beyond. The phantom subject establishes the desire of being not only as it is perceived but also, both on this side and the beyond, as it traverses the mental space dramatized by the portrayal of his demise.

The fear of death is weakened through rhetorical excess. Burying death in a "writerly shroud" plays the illusory experience of death off against death itself. The dream of eliminating all negative feeling associated with death is the symptom of a will to embrace an aberration of desire. Such symptoms are small "tests" of death that are added to each other in order to confront it and, at the same time, to engage in a Pascalian "divertissement" (from the Latin *divertire*), meaning to turn away from. In any case, the illusion weakens fear since it evades the "real" world. Montaigne's narration exceeds reality and thus grasps death in the illusion of sleep. Paradoxically, the subject depicted in this text lives in terms of an absence and savors the pleasure of a virtual history: "Cependant mon assiete estoit à la vérité tres-douce et paisible; je n'avoy affliction ny pour autruy ny pour moy: c'estoit une langueur et une extreme foiblesse, sans aucune douleur" (II, 6, 376) ("Meanwhile my condition was, in truth, very pleasant and peaceful; I felt no affliction either for others or for myself; it was a languor and an extreme weakness, without any pain [272]).

If, in reality, the essayist never experienced the fall he describes, memory will furnish him with the occasion to invent an account of it. In this context, it is a question of impression, for writing contemplates "the impressed effect" of the imagined situation. The use of this rhetorical tool conveys the feeling of crossing over, in which a change of affect takes place that hides itself in the void of temporality. It needs to be witnessed in a state of semiconsciousness. The mirror of limbo is distorted to reveal the sensations that pierce the heart of his soul:

Mais long temps apres, et le lendemain, quand ma memoire vint
à s'entr'ouvrir et me representer l'estat où je m'estoy trouvé en
l'instant que j'avoy aperçeu ce cheval fondant sur moy (car je
l'avoy veu à mes talons et me tins pour mort, mais ce pensement
avoit esté si soudain que la peur n'eut pas loisir de s'y engen-
drer), il me sembla que c'estoit un esclair qui me frapoit l'ame de
secousse et que je revenoy de l'autre monde. (II, 6, 377)

But a long time after, and the next day, when my memory came
to open up and picture to me the state I had been in at the instant I perceived that horse bearing down on me (for I had seen
him at my heels and thought I was a dead man, but that thought
had been so sudden that I had no time to be afraid), it seemed to
me that a flash of lightning was striking my soul with a violent
shock, and that I was coming back from the other world. (272)

The opening up of his memory permitted the essayist to situate himself in a scenario somewhere between the familiar and the unknown.
Although the past was partially imperceptible, what was accessible to
recollection made an impression thanks to a language that cannot be
identical with the instant of the accident. The sudden emergence of
this memory creates a fictive past in the present that fills in the gaps
surrounding the fall. The essayist insists on the unusual character of
the accident. He claims that the effect of the collision on consciousness was essentially ungraspable in order to insinuate himself into the
memory of it. Montaigne's re-creation replaces the lost scene out of a
desire to accept what he perceives as the story of his fall. This narrative projection therefore suggests that the illusion of memory is a plausible way of making sense of events, one that can be taken as "real."

This passage uncovers the tension that animates the text. Forgetting is born in a place where the identity of the injured man is mediated by the story of the wild horse. The description given by memory
seeks to determine the instant when the accident took place. However, it is fated to involve the immediate, which it constructs through
mediations such as the recasting of the injury to the body as a shock
experienced by the soul.

The symptom of trauma—"un esclair qui me frapoit l'ame" (II,
6, 377) ("a flash of lightning . . . striking my soul" [272])—generates
a train of substitutions in which the economy of energies produces the

illusion that this return from the other world (paradoxically the locus of life) supplies the occasion when that which *is* is contemplated by its other. The lightning subsequently illuminates the accident by an impression made after the fact. The subject in question appropriates this singular intensity and projects an image that conveys the reality of that which makes the impression. In navigating this passage, the concept of alterity confuses projection with perception. This scenario is therefore suggested by a rhetorical reservoir of memories that materializes after its impact.

When the injured subject regains consciousness, he paradoxically experiences the pain that had disappeared at the threshold of death:[6]

> Quand je vins à revivre et à reprendre mes forces . . . qui fut deux ou trois heures apres, je me senty tout d'un train rengager aux douleurs, ayant les membres tous moulus et froissez de ma cheute; et en fus si mal deux ou trois nuits après, que j'en cuiday remourir encore un coup, mais d'une mort plus vifve; et me sens encore de la secousse de cette froissure. (II, 6, 377)

> When I came back to life and regained my powers . . . which was two or three hours later, I felt myself all of a sudden caught up again in the pains, my limbs being all battered and bruised by my fall; and I felt so bad two or three nights after that I thought I was going to die all over again, but by a more painful death; and I still feel the effect of the shock of that collision. (272)

Ironically, the return from death snatches pleasure from life; it uncovers a self that is no longer other, floating beyond faintness in spectral longing. Instead, the refound "reality" suggests its anguish. The allusion to the possibility of "a more painful death" suggests that too strong an excitement has weakened the subject's defenses and prevented his mental faculties from overcoming the pain by opposing it. A rather curious phenomenon manifests itself here that functions thanks to a process of sublimation, in the Freudian sense of the term, involving impulses and affects. If the movement toward death paradoxically leads in the direction of a slightly sexualized "douceur" (to use Montaigne's term), the return to life requires the transposition of this sweet voluptuousness into a painful impulse. This reservoir of bodily impulses endangers the self-mastery that confronts the subject of the self-portrait. The possibility of dying a more painful death suggests that this perception threatens the conscious subject with a still more memorable fate.

The principal challenge of this essay involves the attempt to know how to taste death ("savoir" here signifying a savoring of it) through an imagination that functions independently of the body and is capable of producing a moderate degree of pleasure in a state of floating consciousness—a "very pleasant and peaceful" condition. In the context of this desire, two quotes from Tasso's *Jerusalem Delivered* occur in succession. What attracts the essayist to this work by Tasso is his treatment of mental aberration. The verses from this epic poem cited in Montaigne's text stress the contrast between the powerlessness of an injured body and the magical functioning of the mind in the same body. The first reference to Tasso is taken from canto VI and involves the story of the struggle between Tancredi and Clorinda. It tells of Tancredi's return to life after fainting:

Perhe, dubbiosa anchor del suo ritorno
Non s'assecura attonita la mente. (353)

Because the shaken soul, uncertain yet
of its return, is still not firmly set. (269)

In Montaigne's second example, taken from the same canto, a Danish knight regains life thanks to the power of a holy man:

come quel ch'or apres or chiude
Gli occhi, mezzo tra'l sonno è l'esser desto. (353)

As one 'twixt wakefulness and doze,
Whose eyes now open, now again they close. (269)

Tasso's lines are grafted onto Montaigne's text to create the possibility of going beyond them. Moreover, they allow Montaigne's thought to be profoundly altered by crossing over a textual boundary—a process that mimetically reproduces what death cannot deny the imagination in the void of aporia, namely, movement.

The two quotations from Tasso will be completely transformed and will subsequently be used to reveal the mind's ability to obliquely resuscitate a living death. As Marcel Tetel has pointed out, Montaigne's essay makes use of these textual interpolations in order to demonstrate that "the imagination remains unshakeable despite the temporary collapse of the body."[7] Plunged into the darkness of a coma, thanks to imaginative thinking the wounded essayist is still capable of awakening the force of reason due to an innate, albeit unconscious, movement:

> Ils disent que je m'advisay de commander qu'on donnast un cheval à ma femme. . . . Il semble que cette consideration deut parter d'une ame esveillée; si est-ce que je n'y estois aucunement: c'estoyent des pensemens vains, en nuë, qui estoyent esmeuz par les sens des yeux et des oreilles. (II, 6, 376)

> But also (they say) I thought of ordering them to give a horse to my wife. . . . It would seem that this consideration must have proceeded from a wide-awake soul; yet the fact is that I was not there at all. These were idle thoughts, in the clouds, set in motion by the sensations of the eyes and ears. (271)

The demand that emanated from this phantom being expresses a need that is revealed by means of the magic of the senses and points to an aporia that mechanically opens up through unconscious contact with the living world. What interests Montaigne in Tasso's work is the sensation of floating that is revealed in the indefinite space of this half-conscious state and the survival of the mind in the shadows of the unconscious during and after an experience of mental aberration. Tasso's ontological description allows Montaigne to depict the autonomy of his mind in a self-portrait that unfolds outside the constraints of temporality. The feeling of Christian guilt in Tasso's work is transformed by means of a liberating analytical process in Montaigne's essay, in which practice permits a witnessing through the absence in which it is realized. The self-generative power of the mind in Montaigne's essay functions as a vital force permitting the imagination to be trained through the clouds of introspection: "Or, comme dict Pline, chacun est à soy-mesmes une très-bonne discipline, pourveu qu'il ait la suffisance de s'espier de près" (II, 6, 377) ("Now, as Pliny says, each man is a good education to himself, provided he has the capacity to spy on himself from close up" [271–72]).

In the last part of the essay the figure of the writer engages in an attempt to justify the presumption of depicting himself on horseback—

literally of course, but also figuratively in the sense that he is astride the aporia between life and death.

> La coustume a faict le parler de soy vicieux, et le prohibe obsti-neement en hayne de la ventance qui semble tousjours estre at-tachée aux propres tesmoignages. . . . Mais, quand il seroit vray que ce fust necesserement presomption d'entretenir le peuple de soy, je ne doy pas, suivant mon general dessein, refuser une ac-tion qui publie cette maladive qualité, puis qu'elle est en moy; et ne doy cacher cette faute que j'ay non seulement en usage, mais en profession. Toutesfois, à dire ce que j'en croy, cette coustume a tort de condamner le vin, par ce que plusieurs s'y enyvrent. On ne peut abuser que des choses qui sont bonnes. (II, 6, 378)

> Custom has made speaking of oneself a vice, and obstinately for-bids it out of hatred for the boasting that seems always to ac-company it. . . . But even if it were true that it is presumptuous, no matter what the circumstances, to talk to the public about oneself, I still must not, according to my general plan, refrain from an action that openly displays this morbid quality, since it is in me; nor may I conceal this fault, which I not only practice but profess. However, to say what I think about it, custom is wrong to condemn wine because many get drunk on it. We can misuse only things which are good. (273)

Analyzing oneself has the effect of liberating speech. It is a mental habit that allows the essayist to know himself better and to draw nearer to the unknowable: "Il n'est description pareille en difficulté à la description de soy-mesmes, ny certes en utilité. Encore se faut-il testoner, encore se faut-il ordonner et renger pour sortir en place. Or je me pare sans cesse, car je me descris sans cesse" (II, 6, 378) ("There is no description equal in difficulty, or certainly in usefulness, to the description of oneself. Even so one must spruce up, even so one must present oneself in an orderly arrangement, if one would go out in public. Now, I am constantly adorning myself, for I am constantly describing myself" [273]). If he studies himself to say who he is, it is in order to enact the displacement of an intangible thought and to challenge a tradition that questions the "propriety" of speaking about oneself.

In this context the interpretive act acquires an exemplary, albeit presumptuous, value. It produces a change through an epistemological and fictive crossing in which the essayist resembles the saints in his readiness "de se jetter bien avant sur le trottoir" (II, 6, 378) ("to put [himself] prominently on display" [273]). Although his practice produces no absolute knowledge, the presumption in question, in the etymological sense of the word (from the Latin *praesumere,* to take beforehand), implies not only crossing the boundary of death but also the realization of a demise (*trépas*) in the juridical sense—a transgression arising from the presumptuousness of pretending to be able to test "death" in the fiction of the essay. This rhetorical *step* problematizes the idea of presumption as a phenomenon determinable according to the limits established by moral conventions and thus leads off into another avenue of meaning. If Montaigne goes beyond the end of life in the direction of aporia, it is ultimately so that this "possibility of the impossible" may disclose to him the emptiness of his existence and blur the boundary between presumption and nonpresumption: "Nulle particuliere qualité n'enorgeuillira celuy qui mettra quand et quand en compte tant de imparfaittes et foibles qualitez autres qui sont en luy, et, au bout, la nihilité de l'humaine condition" (II, 6, 380) ("No particular quality will make a man proud who balances it against the many weaknesses and imperfections that are also in him, and, in the end, against the nullity of man's estate" [275]).

However, to transcribe these thoughts in written form—thereby imposing a form on the formless—prevents the text from preserving the fluidity produced by indeterminate wanderings: "C'est une espineuse entreprinse, et plus qu'il ne semble, de suyvre une alleure si vagabonde que celle de nostre esprit; de penetrer les profondeurs opaques de ses replis internes; de choisir et arrester tant de menus airs de ses agitations" (II, 6, 378) ("It is a thorny undertaking, and more so than it seems, to follow a movement so wandering as that of our mind, to penetrate the opaque depths of its innermost folds, to pick out and immobilize the innumerable flutterings that agitate it" [273]). The rolling up of thoughts in a written body, or scrolled manuscript, gives birth to a textual cadaver, reflecting the root sense of the Latin word *cadere* (to fall), which realizes an unbridgeable aporia that dispels the illusion of vitality in the text: "Je m'estalle entier: c'est un SKELETOS où, d'une veue, les veines, les muscles, les tendrons paroissent, chaque piece en son siege" (II, 6, 379) ("I expose myself entire: my portrait is a *cadaver* on which the veins, the muscles, and the tendons appear

at a glance, each part in its place" [274]). Like death itself, the practice described in Montaigne's essay represents the dead matter of this
narcissistic object and thus nullifies the kinetic force of the imagination in the empty space of the text. In achieving a *mors improvisa* (an
unexpected death, prior to confession), Montaigne's essay exercises
what cannot, in fact, be exercised. The text in question thus arises
from the decomposition of thought, the immobilization of a written
body by a series of fragments encouraging a certain stasis and constituting an "arrêt de mort" (a rhetorical strategy to "immobilize the innumerable flutterings that agitate" the mind): "Ce ne sont mes gestes
que j'escris, c'est moy, c'est mon essence" (II, 6, 379) ("It is not my
deeds that I write down; it is myself, my essence" [274]). Indeed, this
sentence facilitates the final fall of the essay, namely, that of the ink
that falls on the blank page. The procreation to which the activity of
writing gives rise suffers a mortal blow: the link between body and
script is broken; the contact between the text and the person who
composes it is disrupted.

Montaigne's analysis of the consequences associated with the
anecdote of the fall generates a fiction that solicits—in the etymological sense of *sollicitare* (to totally mix together, from *sollus* ["all"]
and *ciere* ["to move"])—a figural historicization of the symptom: the
desire to transpose death to a locus of pleasure, converting it into
a malleable phenomenon. Montaigne's essay valorizes the role of a
phantasmagoric world by attributing to the simulation of death an
exemplary function as a remedy. The portrait of being-for-death
therefore becomes a supplementary representation of the aporia, a
hypothetical projection of what might happen in the future: "A toutes
avantures, je suis content qu'on sçache d'où je seray tombé" (III, 2,
817) ("In any event, I am glad to have people know whence I shall
have fallen" [621]). This process rhetorically gives voice to a soul that
magically converts a feeling both imperceptible and ungraspable into
a materialized self-referential representation: "Je n'imagine aucun estat pour moy si insupportable et horrible que d'avoir l'ame vifve et
affligée, sans moyen de se declarer" (II, 6, 375) ("I can imagine no
state so horrible and unbearable for me as to have my soul alive and
afflicted, without means to express itself" [270]). Assuming the form
of a resurrection that is not one, this rhetorical prosthesis facilitates
the simulation of an end postponed and the establishment of a paradoxical immortality in the writerly tomb where the dead matter of
Montaigne's writing rests.

THE ANXIETY OF DEATH
Narrative and Subjectivity
in "De la diversion" (III, 4)

Montaigne's "De la diversion" (III, 4) ("Of Diversion") dramatizes and exemplifies the manner in which the human subject shies away from the anxiety produced by the fear of death. The essential question raised in this essay is how one should talk about death or, rather, how one can avoid it. If diversion is an issue in this text, it is ultimately the result of the essayist's inability to become consubstantial with the object of the act of writing itself, namely, death. "Nous pensons tousjours ailleurs" (III, 4, 834) ("Our thoughts are always elsewhere" [633]) proclaims the essayist. According to Montaigne's own formulation, the human subject is always already the victim of the radical discontinuity of the self; the kinetic energy generated by the mind renders it other to itself by displacing the subject from the locus where in principle it should be. As Montaigne comments in "Du repentir" (III, 2) ("Of Repentance") in connection with the writing of the essays: "C'est un contrerolle de divers et muables accidens et d'imaginations irresoluës et, quand il y eschet, contraires: soit que je sois autre moy-mesme, soit que je saisisse les subjects par autres circonstances et considerations" (III, 2, 805) ("This is a record of various and changeable occurrences, and of irresolute and, when it so befalls, contradictory ideas: whether

I am different myself, or whether I take hold of my subjects in different circumstances and aspects" [611]).

Montaigne's "De la diversion" enacts the vain movement of diversion by mirroring the theoretical strategy that is the subject of his writing. By essaying the idea of diversion through a variety of examples of the mind's remarkable ability to redirect its own thoughts, the text becomes the symptom of the very malady that it claims to diagnose, namely, displacement and diversion. In essence, the performance of the essay becomes the object that it designates by becoming the example of that which it describes. Through the displacement of the subject of diversion, the writerly subject displaces itself in a series of fragments that emblematizes the subject's failure to become whole.

Montaigne's narrative thus produces a text not just about diversion per se but one in which a theory of the self emerges as the rhetorical effect of the subject's quest to come to terms with the idea of death. As such, it can be described as the interminable story of the difficulty of uttering the name "death." Conscious of its mortality, the human subject, as described by Montaigne, can only relieve itself through a discursive ex-centricity that leaves in its wake a lack or void that is the result of its ontological emptiness. Accordingly, the diversion before the abyss of death allows the subject to partake in the magic of its own "méconnaissance" and thereby forestall the possibility of true self-recognition. In the case of Montaigne, essaying provokes a displacement of knowledge of which it is itself the cause.

My theoretical concern in exploring the dynamics of the representation of subjectivity in this essay is threefold: to investigate the relationship of the topos of diversion to self-portraiture; to explore how the figuration of subjectivity theorizes desire and anticipates what are today considered psychoanalytic concerns; and to study how the preoccupation with death functions as the condition of narrative in its digressive movements or detours. Although the analysis presented here does not derive from the application of specific psychoanalytic models per se, my reading of "De la diversion" attempts to demonstrate how in this essay psychoanalysis supplants literature by foregrounding the rhetorical processes and topological dynamics underlying the writing of the text. Montaigne's "death sentences" in "De la diversion" reveal the implications between literature and psychoanalysis, dramatizing how the essay anticipates the preoccupations of psychoanalytic theory by speaking of itself in the language of literature. Through the fictions of desire that this essay projects, the essayist's drives emerge through a discourse contingent upon a series of identificatory representations from which the subject of enunciation is figured.

The essay is constructed around a series of displacements framed by repetitions of the diversion topos. For Montaigne death is a source of anguish. The narrative largely consists of an account of how the human subject turns away from that anxiety. By playing on the root meaning of the word "diversion" (derived from the Latin *divertere*, to turn one's attention away from), the essay literally engages in the "acting out" of diversion through the slippage of its meaning. In other words, the performative dimension of the essay identifies it with the processes of metonymy (as displacement) and repetition (as resistance to recognition) inasmuch as, through its rhetorical swerves, the diversions on "diversion" enable the essay to defer the possibility of making death a self-contained presence.

Montaigne begins his essay by recounting how he was once charged with consoling a woman who was in distress because of her inability to come to terms with the grief resulting from the loss of her husband. In this narrative the essayist assigns himself the role of physician, who renounces the possibility of a cure and instead opts for the ruse of diversion through the displacement of that malady into less anguished channels:

> Que ce plaindre n'est action ny juste ny louable, comme Chrysippus; Ny cette cy d'Epicurus, plus voisine à mon style, de transferer la pensée des choses fascheuses aux plaisantes; Ny faire une charge de tout cet amas, le dispensant par occasion, comme Cicero; mais, declinant tout mollement noz propos et les gauchissant peu à peu aus subjects plus voisins, et puis un peu plus esloingnez, selon qu'elle se prestoit plus à moy, je luy desrobay imperceptiblement cette pensée doulereuse, et la tins en bonne contenance et du tout r'apaisée autant que j'y fus. (III, 4, 831)

> That this lamenting is an action neither just nor laudable, like Chrysippus; or this one of Epicurus, closer to my style, that we should transfer our thoughts from unpleasant to pleasant things; nor did I, like Cicero, arm myself with this whole pile of cures, dispensing it according to the occasion. But, very gently deflecting our talk and diverting it bit by bit to subjects nearby, then

a little more remote, as she gave me more of her attention, I
imperceptibly stole away from her this painful thought and kept
her in good spirits and entirely soothed for as long as I was
there. (631)

The reference to the woman in pain at the beginning of the chapter will eventually have a metacritical function within the context of
the essay. To begin with, the text puts forth a topological displacement whereby rhetoric becomes a trope for psychological processes
through the assimilation of *insinuatio* to *digressio*.[1] Accordingly, the
orator-physician cares for the interlocutor-patient by engaging in a
diversionary practice—"J'usay de diversion" (III, 4, 831) ("I made
use of diversion"[631])—that releases tension through the induce-
ment of a forgetfulness that is the product of digression. What is most
striking in this context is the reference to rhetoric—conceived here
in anti-Ciceronian terms—as an antidote to the uncontrollable force
of passion. From an intersubjective standpoint, the essayist is represented as an omnipotent being whose therapeutic strategy is derived
from a form of rhetorical deception. The expression "je luy desrobay
imperceptiblement cette pensée doulereuse" ("I imperceptibly stole
away from her this painful thought") reveals the diversionary tactics
necessary for the survival of a subject who must be left unrepresented
as a lack in the manifest narrative of the dialogue. The so-called affective attunement established between the essayist and the widow
in pain is paradoxically sustained by the tension between separation
and connection.

The projection of the active forgetting of pain onto the woman ultimately becomes a figure for survival and self-definition. To be sure,
language is conceived as a form of action (*actio*) capable of regulating
affect through its persuasive force. Without the outside other, there
is indeed nothing to help the helpless subject tolerate the pain associated with internal tension. Through the subterfuge of the orator-
physician, the female figure, once viewed in Juvenal's *Satires* (VI,
272–74) as the site of simulated affect—"car la plus part de leurs
deuils sont artificiels et ceremonieux" (III, 4, 830) ("for most of their
mourning is put on and perfunctory" [630])—now becomes the locus where the rhetorician effects a simulation of change through the
power of rhetoric. The subjectivity of the woman in pain is demar-
cated as the object of rhetorical mastery whereby the representation
of the essayist's desire ostensibly motivates the desire of the other. In

order to achieve the release of tension, the subject has to take a detour, one that is motivated by the duplicitous discourse of another.

In this initial narrative Montaigne's text demonstrates how the will to say something transforms itself through the magical movement of a floating signifier; desire is figured as a detour, an imposed delay in the playing out of painful feelings. The diversion topos as used here thus demonstrates how the displacement of affect defers recognition and perpetuates nonknowledge as the defining feature of a motivated repression. The text foregrounds the importance of "rhetoric" as a bridge to the mind in order to show how life deceives us through the magic of language.

Drawing upon a military example taken from Philippe de Commines's *Mémoires* (II, iii), in a subsequent part of the essay Montaigne describes an allegory of diversion whereby the displacement of *affect* (the rage of the citizens before the possibility of surrender) short-circuits the possibility of rebellion:

> Ce fut un ingenieux destour, dequoy le Sieur de Himbercourt sauva et soy et d'autres, en la ville du Liege, où le Duc de Bourgoigne, qui la tenoit assiegée, l'avoit fait entrer pour executer les convenances de leur reddition accordée. Ce peuple . . . print à se mutiner contre ces accords passez. . . . Luy, sentant le vent de la premiere ondée de ces gens qui venoyent se ruer en son logis, lacha soudain vers eux deux des habitans de la ville . . . chargez de plus douces et nouvelles offres. . . . Ces deux arresterent la premiere tempeste, ramenant cette tourbe. . . . Somme que, par telle dispensation d'amusemens, divertissant leur furie et la dissipant en vaines consultations, il l'endormit en fin et gaigna le jour, qui estoit son principal affaire. (III, 4, 831–32)

> It was an ingenious shift by which the Sieur de Himbercourt saved both himself and others in the city of Liège, which the duke of Burgundy, who was laying siege to it, had bid him enter to carry out the terms of the surrender agreed on. These townspeople . . . broke into mutiny against the accepted agreements. . . . He, getting wind of the first wave of these people who were coming to burst into his lodgings, promptly released in their direction two of the inhabitants of the town . . . charged with new and milder offers. . . . These two stopped the first tempest, bringing this excited mob back. . . . In short, by thus dispensing pastimes,

diverting their fury, and dissipating it in empty discussions, he finally put it to sleep and got through until daylight, which was his principal task. (631)

In its reinscription of the diversion topos, this episode literalizes the previous reference to the woman in pain by demonstrating how language functions as a diversionary tactic to dissipate the irrational forces of desire. In some sense the structure of this historical example clearly reflects the structure of the human mind—its natural drive to diversion—by situating a subject within a narrative that functions as the site of a ruse. The subject's survival, endangered by the possibility of revolt, is guaranteed through a subterfuge realized within a history that allegorically represents the displacement of a threatening energy and thus quells instability. The motivation behind the citizens' vain deliberations, a form of empty discursive meandering, represents an attempt to undo their imaginary relation to the symbolic. The general's ability to manipulate and displace, to turn one thing into another (the passion of rebellion into discursive emptiness) creates a negation of reality derived from a simulation of mastery.

Montaigne's text draws on these examples of displacement to demonstrate how diversion is proposed as an ideal for survival. This idea is amplified in a subsequent passage, drawn from Ovid's *Metamorphoses* (X, 666–67), in which Atalanta is diverted by Hippomenes' apples. In that story Atalanta tried to rid herself of potential suitors by only accepting those who could race as fast at she could and punishing those who failed to keep up with the loss of their lives. Montaigne's rewriting of Ovid's narrative in this context appears to emphasize how the "goddess of this amorous ardor, calling her to his [Hippomenes'] aid," slowed Atalanta down by means of the gift of the apples that were thrown in her path. By its reference to diversion as a strategy to protect passion, the story of Hippomenes' survival is linked to the maintenance of his desire (and love) as a means of passing from the dangers of death to the pleasures of life. The goddess' gift of the apples functions as the cure that prolongs the narrative and recaptures the potentially doomed energy of passion in a life that is subject to plot.

Ironically, each repetition of the diversion topos decenters the narrative, creating new objects of observation that transform the essay into a series of detours dramatizing the imagination's psychology of displacement.

Quand les medecins ne peuvent purger le catarre, ils le diver-
tissent et le desvoyent à une autre partie moins dangereuse. Je
m'apperçoy que c'est aussi la plus ordinaire recepte aux maladies de l'ame. . . . On luy faict peu choquer les maux de droit fil;
on ne luy en faict ny soustenir ny rabatre l'ateinte, on la luy faict
decliner et gauchir. (III, 4, 832–33)

When the doctors cannot purge a catarrh, they divert it and lead
it off into some other less dangerous part. I observe that this
is also the most ordinary remedy for ailments of the soul. . . .
We rarely make the soul meet the troubles head on. We do not
make it withstand or beat down their attack, we have it avoid
and sidestep them. (632)

The "veering off" that is figured here suggests a lack or absence that
ensures the estrangement of a malaise. Diversion can thus be seen as
a means of exiling pain and discomfort and masking it through an act
of avoidance.

As the essay proceeds, providing many digressions concerning diversions both public and private, it presents an idealized self exemplified by the figure of Socrates, who is described as capable of avoiding
diversion and is thus able to confront death head on. This *exemplum*
carries a symbolic value in its representation of Socrates as a presence made perfect. What is striking in this narrative fragment is that
death is directly named ("le mourir"). In the process it constitutes
itself as an act of reference, a starting point of a narrative transference whereby the writing subject (Montaigne) acts out his own story,
which is always already articulated in the shadow of an exemplary
other (Socrates):

Il apartient à un seul Socrates d'accointer la mort d'un visage ordinaire, s'en aprivoiser et s'en jouer. Il ne cherche point de consolation hors de la chose; le mourir luy semble accident naturel
et indifferent; il fiche là justement sa veüe, et s'y resoult, sans
regarder ailleurs. (III, 4, 833)

It belongs to the one and only Socrates to become acquainted
with death with an ordinary countenance, to become familiar
with it and play with it. He seeks no consolation outside the
thing itself; dying seems to him a natural and indifferent inci-

dent. He fixes his gaze precisely on it, and makes up his mind to it, without looking elsewhere. (632)

By facing death and focusing his gaze directly upon it, Socrates finds no need for diversion (entertainment as temporal deferral) and its concomitant state of deviance (detour or spatial displacement). Socrates' psychic omnipotence, as manifested by his resolution, is represented as the counterpart to the anxiety produced by the fear of death, inasmuch as the lack of tension between inside and outside in that exemplary figure facilitates an absolute relationship of the self to itself. Montaigne's text seems to suggest that Socrates enjoys an immediate proximity to the "real." Mastery as it is depicted here is an expression of omnipotence and resolution; the object of the gaze (death) receives the energy the subject directs toward it by an unmitigated willingness to accept it for what it is, "sans regarder ailleurs" (III, 4, 833) ("without looking elsewhere" ([632]). Unlike those fearful others who use language as a form of consolation to alleviate fear, Socrates retains the Logos within the self and thereby affirms his mastery in silence.

In the context of this essay, humankind is described as anti-Socratic in its drive to avoid the infelicitous anguish provoked by the thought of death: "A ceux qui passent une profondeur effroyable, on ordonne de clorre ou destourner leurs yeux" (III, 4, 833) ("Those who are passing a fearful abyss are ordered to close or turn away their eyes" [632]). To be sure, death keeps us off balance since it constitutes an empty abyss, a center that induces anguish and that we therefore seek to avoid. The human subject, characterized as naturally drawn to diversion, inevitably becomes a subject without a center (a "vuide") whose desire is incapable of reaching a fixed point. If "our thoughts are always elsewhere," it is because the subject is made to avert the specificity of the object of loss (death) and opt instead for the condition of loss produced through the repetition of displacement.

Montaigne's text depicts the ways in which the differing symptoms of death-related anxiety are embedded in literary and cultural representations. The collective impact of these representations demonstrates how the various categories of diversion anticipate the Lacanian revision of psychoanalytic theory by rejecting the concept of a self-contained subject and instead proposing one that forever exceeds itself. From that perspective, the essay narrates an example of religious piety and transforms it into a case of psychological weakness. Given what it is—that is to say, its substantive lack of being—the human subject is bound to decenter the centrality of death by focusing on that which is external to it:

> Ces pauvres gens qu'on void sur un eschafaut . . . les yeux et les mains tendues au ciel, la voix à des prieres hautes, avec une esmotion aspre et continuelle. . . . On les doibt louer de religion, mais non proprement de constance. Ils fuyent la luicte; ils destournent de la mort leur consideration. (III, 4, 833)

> These poor people whom we see on the scaffold . . . their ears intent on the instructions that are given them, their eyes and hands on heaven, their voice on praying aloud, with a violent and continual excitement. . . . They are to be praised for piety, but not properly for constancy. They avoid the struggle; they turn their consideration away from death. [632])

By diverting their thoughts, those poor wretches not only demonstrate a lack of courage but also a logic of desire, in which the perception of lack is assuaged by the magical thinking realized through the language of prayer:

> Nous pensons tousjours ailleurs; l'esperance d'une meilleure vie nous arreste et appuye, ou l'esperance de la valeur de nos enfans, ou la gloire future de nostre nom, ou la fuite des maux de cette vie, ou la vengeance qui menasse ceux qui nous causent la mort. (III, 4, 834)

> Our thoughts are always elsewhere; the hope of a better life stays and supports us, or the hope of our children's worth, or the future glory of our name, or flight from the ills of this life, or the vengeance that threatens those who cause our death. ([633])

In this context, the essay characterizes hope, in a somewhat sacrilegious way, as a means of substituting new objects of desire for the dissatisfaction associated with the unnamed thing (death).

In the course of the essay, ontological concerns devolve to epistemological preoccupations. The language of philosophy creates confusion between sign and substance and diverts us from the possibility of isolating the meaning of the thing in itself: "Voire les arguments de la philosophie vont à tous coups costoiant et gauchissant la matiere, et à peine essuiant sa crouste" (III, 4, 834) ("Indeed the arguments of philosophy are all the time running alongside the matter and sidestepping it, and barely brushing the crust of it" [634]). In constructing its own language, the rhetoric of philosophy can never simply refer to itself; philosophy is therefore a source of diversion inasmuch as it moves elsewhere in the wake of its own pronouncements.

The familiar Montaignian topos concerning the arbitrary relationship between words and things resurfaces as the essay once again undergoes another detour. Montaigne's text relates how we can be distracted by small things that sometimes say more by simply saying less. By revealing how words can deflect the referential meaning of things while at the same time carrying within themselves the possibility of affective response, the essay demonstrates how euphemisms for death are transmitted through signifiers evoking memories of things past. Language is shown to incarnate the ghostliness of a specter capable of generating a response that stimulates grief more from the sound of words than from their content:

> Le son mesmes des noms, qui nous tintoüine aux oreilles: Mon pauvre maistre! ou, Mon grand amy! Hélas! mon cher pere! ou, Ma bonne fille! quand ces redites me pinsent et que j'y regarde de pres, je trouve que c'est une plainte grammairiene et voyelle. Le mot et le ton me blessent. Comme les exclamations des prescheurs esmouvent leur auditoire souvant plus que ne font leurs raisons et comme nous frappe la voix piteuse d'une beste qu'on tue pour nostre service. (III, 4, 837)

> The very sound of the names, which rings in our ears "My poor master!" or "My great friend!" "Alas, my dear father!" or "My sweet daughter!" when these refrains pain me and I look at them closely, I find that they are only grammatical and vocal complaints. The word and the sound hurt me, just as the exclamations of preachers move their auditors more than their reasons, and as we are struck by the piteous voice of the animal that is being killed for our use. (635)

If the human subject can be swept away by the sounds of language, it is because it is able to absorb affect representations through the sound of words. Yet this incorporation bases itself upon a partial dis-avowal of the object of grief. Through a series of linguistic turns, the subject in pain displaces the object of its loss; it focuses its attention less on the "what" of the loss than on the "who" that can now only cathect onto that other through the sound of words.

In yet other examples Montaigne's text describes the ways in which the human subject attempts to overcome death through a dis-placement that requires a form of repression engendering an other-ing of the self: "Celuy qui meurt en la meslée, les armes à la main, il n'estudie pas lors la mort, il ne la sent ny ne la considere: l'ardeur du combat l'emporte" (III, 4, 833) ("The man who dies in the melee, arms in hand, does not then study death; he neither feels it nor con-siders it; he is carried away by the heat of the battle" [633]). Viewed in these terms, diversion is represented as something heroic. The en-ergy derived from the power of battle requires the repression of the narcissism associated with fear. In essence, the denial of the possibil-ity of loss functions as a mechanism protecting the self from the real-ity of loss itself.

As the essay progresses, it demonstrates how the substitution of one passion for another enables the human subject to escape itself by allowing simulation to replace reality:

> J'ay veu aussi, pour cet effect de divertir les opinions et con-jectures du peuple et desvoyer les parleurs, des femmes couvrir leurs vrayes affections par des affections contrefaictes. Mais j'en ay veu telle qui, en se contrefaisant, s'est laissée prendre à bon escient, et a quitté la vraye et originelle affection pour la feinte. (III, 4, 836)

> I have also known women, for this purpose of diverting people's opinions and conjectures and putting the gossips off the track, to cover their true affections with counterfeit ones. But I knew one who, in counterfeiting, let herself be caught in good earnest, and abandoned the true original affection for the pretended one. (635)

The woman's "acting out" results in the forgetting of the self that be-comes the pivotal moment of exile and desire. Through the power of the imagination this diversion of affect paradoxically enables "seem-ing" to become "Being" at the very moment that the woman in ques-tion accedes to a newly born subjecthood founded on a kind of alienation. If Being attains a sense of self in this context, it is motivated by the staging of a desire derived from the image through which the self is constructed.

Throughout the essay diversion becomes the master trope that enables desire to be realized. Accordingly, Montaigne evokes the loss of his friend La Boétie as the motivation to seek refuge in distraction from the pain of his grief:

> Je fus autrefois touché d'un puissant desplaisir. . . . Je m'y fusse perdu à l'avanture si je m'en fusse simplement fié à mes forces. Ayant besoing d'une vehemente diversion pour m'en distraire, je me fis, par art, amoureux, et par estude. . . . L'amour me soulagea et retira du mal qui m'estoit causé par l'amitié. (III, 4, 835)

> I was once afflicted with an overpowering grief. . . . I might well have been destroyed by it if I had trusted simply to my own powers. Needing some violent diversion to distract me from it, by art and study I made myself fall in love, in which my youth helped me. Love solaced me and withdrew me from the affliction caused by friendship. (634)

As I have demonstrated elsewhere, the engendering of Montaigne's writing is a compensatory gesture for the loss of La Boétie; the feeling of absence and the anxiety of separation are dealt with through the essayist's endeavor to substitute his dialogic relationship with the text for the lost friend.[2] To be sure, the disappearance of the friend's gaze has resulted in the loss of the essayist's self-image and the subsequent use of language as mediator of that lack: "luy seul jouyssoit de ma vraye image, et l'emporta. C'est pourquoy je ne deschiffre moy mesme, si curousement." (983 n. 4) ("He alone enjoyed my true image, and carried it away. That is why I myself decipher myself so painstakingly" [752]).[3] Here the dissolution of the sacred bond of friendship forces the essayist to assimilate the nothingness of death; it describes his self-alienation as a phenomenon that manifests itself in the dismembered fragments of his textual corpus and his desire to see the light of day.

Lack of Being, or the perceived sense of emptiness, is thus the organizing condition of the writer's subjectivity in "De la diversion." Victim of an ontological void resulting from an encounter with death, in order to survive the writing subject must compensate for this lack through a series of references that enable self-definition to be situated elsewhere. Accordingly, the staging of desire in this essay is derived from the various narrative fragments through which the self is constructed; the text always acts as a supplement for the man who, as Richard Regosin suggests, "can never simply be."[4] The multiple references throughout the essay to displacement and deferral as a means of survival enables Montaigne to experience desire from someplace else; storytelling becomes the mechanism through which the essayist's subject-position is obliquely articulated. Subjectivity is the result of kaleidoscopic images (the widow in pain, the leader threatened by rebellion) that retrospectively build the foundation for the subject of enunciation and act as a substitute supplying the content that the subject itself lacks. Just as Montaigne explains how he was able to realize a young prince's hidden desire by turning his attention away from vengeance to ambition—"Je le destournay à l'ambition" (III, 4, 835) ("I diverted him to ambition" [634])—so the essayist's desire can be fulfilled through a displacement that liberates unconscious drives through narrative supplementation.

Although Montaigne does not endlessly draw attention to his own preoccupation with death, the form of the essay nevertheless represents it in the substitutions and recombinations through which the unconscious makes itself known. To be sure, to name directly the object of fear functions as a kind of death sentence because of the congealing of its meaning. However, to "essay" it through indirection is to make the subject of enunciation come forth by reflecting the desire for deferral that defines its subjectivity. If to write is to survive, then to live is to be caught in the signifying web of the language constituting the writing of the essay.

In this essay the writing subject therefore declares himself better able to deal with death by viewing it nonchalantly: "Je voyois nonchalamment la mort, quand je la voyois universellement, comme fin de la vie; je la gourmande en bloc; par le menu, elle me pille" (III, 4, 837) ("I saw death nonchalantly when I saw it universally, as the end of life. I dominate it in the mass; in detail it harasses me" [636]). Ironically, the essayist seeks refuge in the very details that his own desire wishes to transcend. Painful thoughts, he proclaims, can be eradicated through a fascinating tendency for diversion in anxiety, producing details that, in principle, should be subject to erasure. The memory of "la robe de Caesar" (III, 4, 837) ("Caesar's robe" [635]) is more powerful than the reality of his death:

Peu de chose nous divertit et destourne, car peu de chose nous tient. Nous ne regardons gueres les subjects en gros et seuls; ce sont des circonstances ou des images menues et superficieles qui nous frapent, et des vaines escorces qui rejalissent des subjects." (III, 4, 836)

It takes little to divert and distract us, for it takes little to hold us. We scarcely look at things in gross and alone; it is the minute and superficial circumstances and notions that strike us, and the empty husks that peel off from the things. (635)

As a corrective to the displeasure associated with powerful passions, Montaigne's text suggests the possibility of converting energy to lesser intensities as a means of dissipating drives and regulating desire:

Si vostre affection en l'amour est trop puissante, dissipez la . . . car je l'ay souvant essayé avec utilité: rompez la à divers desirs, desquels il y en ayt un regent et un maistre, si vous voulez; mais, depeur qu'il ne vous gourmande et tyrannise, affoiblissez le, sejournez le, en le divisant et divertissant. (III, 4, 835)

If your passion in love is too powerful, disperse it . . . for I have often tried it with profit. Break it up into various desires, of which one may be ruler and master, if you will; but for fear it may dominate and tyrannize you, weaken it, check it, by dividing and diverting it. (634)

The dissipation of affect prevents true re-cognition from being realized; it therefore facilitates a mollification of that which threatens the subject.

Within the logic of the essay metonymy, the trope for change, dislocates pain by forcing it elsewhere; it represents the movement by which an idea (diversion) serves as the nodal point of different associative chains:

Une aigre imagination me tient; je trouve plus court, que de la dompter, la changer; je luy en substitue, si je ne puis une contraire, aumoins un'autre. Tousjours la variation soulage, dissout et dissipe. Si je ne puis la combatre, je luy eschape, et en la fuyant je fourvoye, je ruse: muant de lieu . . . je me sauve dans la presse d'autres amusemens et pensées, où elle perd ma trace et m'esgare. (III, 4, 835–36)

A painful notion takes hold of me; I find it quicker to change it than to subdue it. I substitute a contrary one for it, or, if I cannot, at all events a different one. Variation always solaces, dissolves, and dissipates. If I cannot combat it, I escape it; and in fleeing I dodge, I am tricky. By changing place, . . . I escape into the throng of other occupations and thoughts, where it loses my trace and so loses me. (634–35)

Montaigne's attempted transcendence of pain is nothing less than a forgetting of its origins through a form of trickery ("je ruse") that provokes the dissolution of the subject.[5] The act of displacement introduces a disorganizing sense of flux whereby the loss of a painful idea originates in a process ("la variation," or variability) through which it loses its own origin by becoming subject to change. Here diversion ("la variation") simulates a partial killing of the subject of narration, but the repression that results from the ruse of rhetoric keeps it embodied in its many returns through references to associative subjects.

Although Socrates was able to resolve himself to the reality of death, Montaigne can only confront it through the diversionary process of writing, which therefore becomes a form of entertainment that acknowledges both a closeness with and a distance from death. In this way Montaigne anticipates Freud's *Beyond the Pleasure Principle* (1920), written more than three centuries later. That text foregrounds the trope of the spool in the child's game of "fort-da" (here-there); it represents the fiction describing how the child attempts to overcome separation anxiety produced by the absence of the mother. In that game the child throws a reel out of the crib and pulls it back to the alternating cries of "fort" and "da." When the child makes the toy disappear, it may be viewed symbolically as an attempted mastery of an unpleasurable situation from which the child may not escape. Like the child in Freud's study, in the writing of the text the essayist, "works out" unpleasurable experiences through active engagement with his anxiety rather than passive acceptance of it. For Montaigne displacement (diversion) is a simulation of mastery. Desire is figured in the digression of the essay, an imposed delay (deferral) in the playing out of painful feelings concerning death. The drama of salvation described in the text (the many stories about "diversion") repeats itself in the engendering of the text itself (the digressive form that the discourse on diversion takes). In a way the essayist functions in the same manner as the classical orator who, according to the narrating subject, "se laissa piper à la passion qu'il represente" (838) ("will let himself be tricked into the passion he is portraying [636]) when acting out his case. In the example of "De la diversion" the text presents itself as an imaginary space of escape where the symptomatically ridden ego attempts to replace itself with something else. By becoming other through the act of simulation (the relief produced by the essayist's vain writing), the Montaignian subject becomes, in Lacanian terms, "the playing out of his thought."[6]

Over the course of the essay Montaigne's obsession with death thus emerges as the motivating force behind the compulsion to repeat. The repetition that is actualized at the level of writing—the reinscription of the diversion topos—clearly derives from a desire to eradicate uncomfortable thoughts, thereby enabling the imagination to engage in a simulation of mastery. Ironically, this impulse to master that which is painful carries within it the radical unbinding that characterizes the rhetorical detours, pointing to the narrative subject's impulse both to approach his subject (death) and yet somehow avoid it. Changing places results when similar yet differentiated narratives are repeated as a result of what Freud described as the work of "some demoniac force."[7] The mastery that the Montaignian essay works out is linked to the desire for an end (the liquidation of the death anxiety) that paradoxically leads us back to new beginnings (the impossibility of ever truly mastering it).

By acknowledging diversion as a defense against the unknown, Montaigne's essay suggests interesting comparisons with Freud's theory of repression. Although Freud later uses a definition strikingly similar to diversion, for Freud "the essence of repression lies simply in turning something away, and keeping it at a distance from the conscious." The fundamental difference between the two processes lies in the way in which one relates to painful thoughts. In the case of repression, the individual expends the greatest mental effort to erase a painful memory. The purpose of diversion, however, is to project an illusion that allows one to cope with the infelicitous nature of death.

faict mon livre que mon livre m'a faict" (II, 18, 665) (" I have no more made my book than my book has made me" [504]). In this process the Montaignian text assimilated the knowledge that its wise progenitor was presumed to possess. By means of that symbolically nurturant act, it was able to assume a transcendence of sorts through an act of writing that projected a textual progeny more perfect than the biological workings of nature itself. For Montaigne, then, the resistance to death could only be realized through this gift of writing, the construction of a child of the mind, a textual offspring, whose being would be more perfect than life itself and would maintain the literary legacy of La Boétie (the gift of the library) through Montaigne's gift of the book, or what he termed the "monumens des muses" (II, 8, 400) ("monuments of the muses" [292]).

Literary historians Marjorie Henry Ilsley and Elayne Dezon-Jones have made us aware of the biographical dynamics concerning the relationship between Montaigne and Marie de Gournay le Jars, although they have failed to discuss it within a textual and rhetorical framework.[2] In 1595 Montaigne's adopted daughter and literary executrix, the woman he called his "fille d'alliance" (II, 17, 661) ("covenant daughter" [502]) prepared for publication a posthumous edition of the *Essays* drawn from the writer's 1588 handwritten addenda to that text. Based on the "Bordeaux Exemplar," this posthumous edition was, as Richard Regosin suggests, derived from a copy of Montaigne's original manuscript that Marie de Gournay had sent to Paris and modified to such a degree that it now included the rewriting of certain passages of the *Essays* and the excision of some archaic formulations perceived as inelegant.[3]

Being the executrix of both the paternal "will" and testament signified for Marie de Gournay bearing the burden of the writer's posterity as literary witness, a textual guardian whose function, in principle, was to maintain a subtle balance between what she knew and what she did not or could not possibly know. As daughter-secretary-successor in whose life "real" amorous relations were somewhat problematic, it could be argued that she is represented as one who is destined to be "wedded" to the Montaignian Logos: "Il ne luy en falloit, pour son bien, nul autre que moy," she declares.[4] To sustain this posture, she alludes to others who have made this literary engagement possible, such as Justus Lipsius, who opened "les portes de louange aux *Essais*" (24) and, surprisingly, Madame de Montaigne herself (Françoise de la Chassaigne). Amazingly, the essayist's wife is recuperated in a revisionist family history as the surrogate mother who makes Marie de Gournay's work as editor of the manuscript possible through "les offices d'une tres ardente amour conjugale" (25). In Marie de Gournay's narrative the essayist's wife becomes retroactively implicated in sustaining his literary legacy through what is described as the devotion of a surrogate mother-daughter relationship. Gournay enhances the glory of the name of the father through an invention of familial ties that transforms Madame de Montaigne into a benefactress of sorts who, through her magnanimity, empowers Marie to bring her husband back to life: "Que son maistre mesme n'en eust jamais eu tant de soing. . . . Chaqu'un luy doibt, sinon autant de graces, au moins autant de louanges, que je faiz: d'avoir voulu r'embrasser et r'échauffer en moy les cendres de son mary, et non pas l'espouser mais se rendre une autre luy-mesme" (25–26).

In this context, the textual addition at the end of the 1595 version of the essay "De la praesumption" (II, 17) "Of Presumption") is quite revelatory concerning the supposed genealogy of Montaigne's text. The love relations suggested in the following fragment, whether penned by Montaigne or Marie de Gournay, indicate that there are no separations from love objects in writing, and that the substance of these object-choices suggest a certain narrative presumption, an anticipatory gesture that makes possible a looking ahead to the reality of death:

J'ay pris plaisir à publier en plusieurs lieux l'esperance que j'ay de Marie de Gournay le Jars, ma fille d'alliance: et certes aymée de moy beaucoup plus que paternellement, et enveloppée en ma retraitte et solitude, comme l'une des meilleures parties de mon propre estre. Je ne regarde plus qu'elle au monde. Si l'adolescence peut donner presage, cette ame sera quelque jour capable des plus belles choses, et entre autres de la perfection de cette tres-saincte amitié où nous ne lisons point que son sexe ait peu monter encores: la sincerité et la solidité de ses mœurs y sont desjà bastantes, son affection vers moy plus que sur-abondante, et telle en somme qu'il n'y a rien à souhaiter, sinon que l'apprehension qu'elle a de ma fin, par les cinquante et cinq ans ausquels elle m'a rencontré, la travaillast moins cruellement. Le jugement qu'elle fit des premiers Essays, et femme, et en ce siecle, et si jeune, et seule en son quartier, et la vehemence fameuse dont elle m'ayma et me desira long temps sur la seule estime qu'elle en print de moy, avant m'avoir veu, c'est un accident de tres-digne consideration. (II, 17, 661–62)

I have taken pleasure in making public in several places the hopes I have for Marie de Gournay le Jars, my covenant daughter, whom I love indeed more than a daughter of my own, and cherish in my retirement and solitude as one of the best parts of my own being. She is the only person I still think about in the world. If youthful promise means anything, her soul will some day be capable of the finest things, among others of perfection in that most sacred kind of friendship which, so we read, her sex has not yet been able to attain. The sincerity and firmness of her character are already sufficient, her affection for me more than superabundant, and such, in short, that it leaves nothing to be desired, unless that her apprehension about my end, in view of my fifty-five years when I met her, would not torment her so cruelly. The judgment she made of the first Essays, she a woman, and in this age, and so young, and alone in her district, and the remarkable eagerness with which she loved me and wanted my friendship for a long time, simply through the esteem she formed for me before she had seen me, is a phenomenon very worthy of consideration. (502)

If Montaigne is indeed the author of this passage, he gives himself the pleasure of enjoying the fantasy of being the father of a daughter onto whom he projects a fictional symbiosis—"comme l'une des meilleures parties de mon propre estre"; "as one of the best parts of my own being"—that functions as the emblem of his desire to invent one whom he calls "ma fille d'alliance" (my covenant daughter). Desire as it is represented here is inextricably linked to a "family romance" that transcends the boundaries and limitations of biological relationships; it is more an invention of the imagination than anything else. The natural daughter Léonor and the authentic mother Madame de Montaigne are replaced by a love object derived from a narcissistic model capable of nurturing the self and equal in quality to the greatest minds of the times. In a way, mothers and natural children appear to disappoint Montaigne to such an extent that what he discovers in the surrogate-child relationship is described as potentially superior to the child he has biologically fathered. The "invention" of the surrogate daughter functions as an anticipatory omen of the joys the future will bestow upon his literary legacy: "Si l'adolescence peut donner presage, cette ame sera quelque jour capable des plus belles choses, et entre autres de la perfection de cette tres-saincte amitié où nous ne lisons point que son sexe ait peu monter encores") ("If youthful promise means anything, her soul will some day be capable of the finest things, among others of perfection in that most sacred kind of friendship which, so we read, her sex has not yet been able to attain.") In a sense, Montaigne discovers in the young girl what he fearfully described in the 1588 edition of "De la vanité" (III, 9) ("Of Vanity") as being potentially impossible, namely, the existence of a sponsor or a "respondant" to execute his "will" and testament: "Je scay bien que je ne lairray apres moy aucun respondant si affectionné bien loing. . . . Il n'y a personne à qui je vousisse pleinement compromettre de ma peinture" (III, 9, 983, n. 4) ("I know well that I will leave behind no sponsor anywhere near as affectionate. . . . There is no one to whom I would be willing to entrust myself fully for a portrait" ([752 n. 14]). However, the potential sponsorship of Marie de Gournay—who, in a way, turns out to be more like a man in her ability to transcend the limitations of the sacred bonds of friendship from which women are traditionally excluded—offers the essayist the hope of escaping entrapment within the infelicitous commentaries of the less gifted readers of the *Essays*. As he suggests in "De l'amitié" (I, 28) ("Of Friendship") concerning friendship with women: "D'y comparer l'affection envers les femmes, quoy qu'elle naisse de nostre choix, on ne peut, ny la loger en ce rolle" (I, 28, 185) ("To compare this brotherly affection with affection for women, even though it is the result of our choice—it cannot be done; nor can we put the love of women in the same category" [137]).

In a way, Marie de Gournay is represented as being more perfect than a woman might ever possibly become, the "perfection de cette tres-saincte amitié où nous ne lisons point que son sexe ait peu monter encores" ("perfection in that most sacred kind of friendship which, so we read, her sex has not yet been able to attain"). The father's partial disassociation from the women in his family and his continuing desire to establish differences between women and man make it difficult for him to recognize his adoptive daughter in terms of her gender. He therefore obliquely makes her portrayal, as it is embodied in the book, more closely aligned with that of a surrogate son, one in whom he discovers a potentially nascent amorous relationship, "beaucoup plus que paternellement" ("more than a daughter of my own"). Moreover, Marie de Gournay's exemplarity stems from a remarkable cognitive ability to read and interpret the *Essays,* which therefore raises her above the deficiencies usually accorded to those of her own sex: "le jugement qu'elle fit des premiers Essays, et femme, et en ce siecle, et si jeune, et seule en son quartier" ("the judgment she made of the first Essays, she a woman, and in this age, and so young, and alone in her district"). This rhetorical cross-dressing obliges the female voice to engage in a symbolic masquerade; it defines the daughter negatively as she is mediated by the image of a masculine ideal traditionally associated with judgment and virtue.

Montaigne attributes a kind of omnipotence to the magical daughter with whom he identifies; she is meant to represent his being beyond death, a role that he had previously attributed to himself in terms of preserving La Boétie's literary fortune following his friend's demise:

> Privé de l'ami le plus doux, le plus cher et le plus intime, et tel que notre siècle n'en a vu de meilleur, de plus docte, de plus agréable et plus parfait, Michel de Montaigne, voulant consacrer le souvenir de ce mutuel amour par un témoignage unique de sa reconnaissance, et ne pouvant le faire de manière qui l'exprimat mieux a voué à cette mémoire ce studieux appareil dont il fait ses délices.[5]

In a way, the memory of La Boétie is meant not only to invoke the continuity of lost friendship but also a striving for survival ("survie") associated with an identificatory drive that functions as the sign of mutual attraction ("certes aymée de moy beaucoup plus paternellement" and "la vehemence fameuse dont elle m'ayma et me desira long temps"; "whom I love indeed more than a daughter of my own" and "the remarkable eagerness with which she loved me and wanted my friendship for a long time"). The representation of this attraction, however, is not without its paradoxes and ambiguities. Unlike Montaigne's perfect friend, with whom he maintained a seamless bond of communication, a perfect symbiosis or interchangeability of souls, the woman who is represented here is yet to have a voice of her own; by accepting the "name of the daughter," she must relinquish her entitlement to desire and preserve the essayist's omnipotence. Instead of recognizing the female other as different, the father identifies her only to disidentify her as an imperfect copy of the same. If she is to speak as she finally crosses the threshold into the realm of womanhood, her coming into language can only be a simulacrum of the power and desire that she aspires to, which is ultimately possessed by the man whom she idealizes.

What if Marie de Gournay is the author of the passage near the close of "De la praesumption"? In that case the muted voice described by Montaigne abandons the proleptic dream of maturity for the daughter and produces a narrative segment that leads us back to a future already inscribed in the editing of the text's present. By inverting the narrative point of view previously articulated, one now encounters a different perspective that can be shown to unsettle the first reading by projecting a future that is already now. No longer portrayed as a mere representation of what she might one day become as the result of the surrogate father's naming her daughter by covenant, Marie de Gournay now becomes an authorizing force entitling herself to speak. She engages in a pseudoprocess of individuation whose idealism is subverted by the writing of a family history which identifies the female voice with the likeness of the father: "J'estois toute semblable à mon Pere, je ne puis faire un pas, soit escrivant ou parlant, que je ne me trouve sur ses traces" (45). Assuming the other's position and imaginatively perceiving the father's needs enables her to lose herself in the other. This lack of mutual recognition creates the gender polarity underlying the self-other relationship between Montaigne and Marie de Gournay. The inscription of the female figure as dutiful daughter is less the result of her being engendered by the substitute father inscribed in the text than a consequence of Marie de Gournay's "fathering" of her desire to write. I insist on the issue of "fathering" here because the perceived image of and identification with the male writer engenders her desire to seek entry into writing through the pleasure of taking hold of the body, or corpus, constituting the *Essays*. The recognition of the other as textual strategy enables Marie de Gournay to engage in a process of differentiation by simultaneously maintaining separateness and connection. The ideal of autonomy is held hostage to a discourse that "others" the desiring subject and ultimately distances her from the project of becoming.

Marie de Gournay's role as textual editor of the Montaignian corpus is clearly associated with a process of mourning that sustains itself through a carthetic relationship to the lost object. Ironically, the plenitude of affection can only be realized phantasmically since the ideal union only comes into being because of a feeling of deprivation.

"Etre seul," declares Marie de Gournay, "c'est n'estre que demy" (47). Unquestionably, the mourning topos inscribes the female subject in a quasi-libidinal relationship (involving questions of attachment and loss) through which the female subject is protected against the libidinal expenditure associated with mourning and the erotic drives that it motivates: "Mais combien est encore plus miserable celuy qui demeure demy soy-mesme, pour avoir perdu l'autre part, qu'à faute de l'avoir rencontré!" (47). The death of the surrogate father enables the living book to appropriate the remains of the dead textual corpus. However, the discourse embodying Montaigne is retained as representative of the symbolic capital of sociopaternal power.

In examining the writerly relationship between Marie de Gournay and Montaigne, what I am particularly interested in is not the authenticity of the literary performance attributed to either one of the possible narrative voices. Rather, I am drawn to the ways in which amorous figurations are sustained in the text by what is unquestionably a series of object relations. In any event, the authenticity of authorship is less important than its figurative dynamics and the ways in which representation constructs itself as literary myth. In this context, one must therefore ask the following questions: What narrative function is Marie de Gournay assuming in her role as literary executrix? Where do her commentaries on Montaigne end and where does her self-assertion as authorizing subject begin? To be sure, as one scans Marie de Gournay's "Préface" to the 1595 edition of the *Essays* and her textual addenda—such as the possibly counterfeit addition to the chapter "De la praesumption"—what emerges is the representation of a female subject who is both primary and secondary to textual production, one who is both central and marginal to the engendering of the text. In a way, the figure of Marie de Gournay emerges as an authorizing agent: the excluded female presence alluded to in the preface of 1595 may be regarded as the condition of both the enabling and disabling factors in representing her identity. Marie de Gournay describes herself as being in a rather paradoxical situation: having become daughter by social covenant and as the result of magical thinking, she owes more to the rhetorical construction of an artificially conceived nature ("nature m'ayant faict tant d'honneur" [45]) than she does to the workings of biological relations. She is a specially chosen friend in a world where female friendship with men appears to be something of a social anomaly. Authorship, taken in its etymological sense of *auctoritas,* or authority, thus becomes a process that seeks its own justification. Accordingly, when discussing the essayist's position on religious matters, she proclaims the value of her judgments concerning Montaigne: "C'est à moy d'en parler; car moy seulle avois la parfaicte cognoissance de cette grande ame, et c'est à moy d'en estre creue de bonne foy, quand ce livre l'esclairciroit pas. . . . Je dis doncq avec verité certaine" (34).

In the context of the 1595 preface, Montaigne becomes for Marie de Gournay the prototype of intellectual exemplarity, one in whom the author finds an ideal image of the self. In confronting the reality of paternal loss, the female subject finds comfort in her fictional role as mediator of paternal omnipotence. In terms of fatherly relations, Marie de Gournay comes to terms with the power of her own desire and elaborates it through the projection of an internally constructed ideal: "Lecteur, l'appeller autrement; car je ne suis moymesme que par où je suis sa fille" (25). Ironically, the daughter-father relation is based on a preexisting affective model involving two men, Montaigne and La Boétie, who are engaged in a sublimated homoerotic relationship. As in both cases, the figuration of object relations is the result of paternal loss, for which ideal love becomes the only source of salvation.

In its most rudimentary form, Marie de Gournay's story is a narrative of paternal legitimation; it is enacted through a rhetorical performance whose potency is realized by means of a mimetic reproduction of the other that enables the textual editor to lose herself in him:[6] "Je ne suis moy-mesme que par où que je suis sa fille" (25). Marie de Gournay's "performance" functions, in part, as a textual prosthesis of fragments of Montaigne's literary corpus. In adopting the name of the father she assumes a position that enables her to transcend what might in psychoanalytic terms be called her "narcissistic black hole." By becoming Montaigne's double she permits herself to engage in a rhetorical transvestism that manifests itself as a hermeneutic fetishism in terms of its relationship with the master's text: "Je te dirois qu'il a pensé . . . je te diray que la faveur publicque dont il parle n'est pas celle qu'il cuidoit" (23–24). The legitimation of the name of the father is based not only on the desire to protect his name but is sustained according to the exigencies of an editorial project previously protected against the infelicities of "la miserable incorrection" by "quelque bon Ange" but now guaranteed by someone described as being greater than heaven itself, the dutiful daughter: "J'ose me vanter qu'il ne luy en falloit, pour son bien, nul autre que moy, mon affection suppleant à mon incapacité" (53).

At the beginning of the 1595 preface Marie de Gournay conceives of her writing strategy as a defensive posture whose line of articulation is one of excess: "Tu devines ja, Lecteur, que je me veux plaindre du froid recueil, que nos hommes ont fait aux *Essais:* et cuydes peult-estre avoir suject d'accuser ma querimonie, en ce que leur ouvrier mesme dit que l'approbation publicque l'encouragea d'amplifier les premiers" (23). To be sure, the lost object of desire (Montaigne) is gradually absorbed by the desiring daughter; the female subject retains the imprint of the lost object such that mourning becomes a process through which gender is inscribed on the female body (or the textual corpus) and thereby mirrors the father's perceived desire as "truth." The paternal word therefore carries within it the law of the father, which is passed on to the surrogate daughter: "soubs ceste seulle consideration que celuy qui le voulut ainsin estoit Pere, et qu'estoit Montaigne" (53).

Following the 1595 preface Marie de Gournay's writings on Montaigne take on a more ambivalent and slightly measured perspective that signifies the conditional rather than the absolute nature of Montaigne's literary fatherhood. As Adam Phillips has pointed out, "children," in Freud's view, "realize desire but without possibility," whereas D. W. Winnicot suggests "they are all dressed up with no place to go."[7] Like the desiring child implicated in the oedipal romance, Marie de Gournay was the victim of a literary seduction that left her imprisoned in an unproductive passion. The origin of desire as represented in the language of the preface of 1595 was the result of a literary seduction to be understood in its etymological sense as meaning a leading away from.[8] Marie de Gournay reveals how her first encounter with Montaigne's text stimulated her to such a degree that she was given the sedative hellebore to assuage her anxiety: "On estoit prest à me donner de l'hellebore lors que comme ils me furent fortuitement mis en main au sortir de l'enfance, ils me transsissoient d'admiration" (24). Beyond the obvious references to figures of metamorphosis associated with the Neoplatonic tradition, for Marie de Gournay the act of reading Montaigne's *Essays* provoked a spontaneous reaction, a transfiguration of sorts, that produced a kind of metaphorical death for the female writer.[9] If anxiety replaces pleasure at this originary act of desire, its ultimate effect is to make the female subject incapable of realizing her autonomy before this encounter with a seductively powerful text. Incited by the perception of the father and the magnetic force of his knowledge, the female subject assimilates the substance of his writerly being and makes it her own: "Les grands esprits sont desireux, amoureux, et affolez des grands esprits: comme tenans leur estre du mouvement, et leur prime mouvement de la rencontre d'un pareil" (47). Ultimately the phallic identification with the father, as described in the preface, disinclines the female subject from engaging in a symbolic performance on the level of language. Nevertheless, Marie de Gournay paradoxically appropriates a kind of authority by situating herself among "the happy few," those intellectually gifted readers capable of recognizing the value of Montaigne's discourse: "C'est de telles ames qu'il fault souhaitter la ressemblance et la bonne opinion" (25).

Underlying Marie de Gournay's "malady of the soul"[10] is, metaphorically speaking, a rhetorical perversion, defined as behavior that deviates from the norm, in this case manifesting itself as the desire to write in a vaguely counterpatriarchal tradition. As she states in a letter to Justus Lipsius dated November 1596 concerning the preface (composed just one year earlier): "Que je lui laissois couler en saison où ma douleur ne me permettoit ni de bien faire ni de sentir que je faisois mal."[11] The abandonment of the 1595 preface can thus be interpreted as a taking possession of her female subjectivity, a decision by means of which the woman writer can become the subject of her own writing, albeit this time more on her own terms. This movement away from dependency allows for the almost impossible act of self-inscription. It enables Marie de Gournay to give shape to her repressed rhetorical corpus, whose initial nonexistence is the result of her inability to transcend the implicit paralysis produced by Montaigne's disabling death.

It is thus not surprising to recall that in one of his early essays entitled "Que le goust des biens et des maux depend en bonne partie de l'opinion que nous en avons" (I, 14) ("That the Taste of Good and Evil Depends in Large Part on the Opinion We Have of Them"), Montaigne draws our attention to the fact that "il est ordinaire à beaucoup de nations de nostre temps de se blesser à escient, pour donner foy à leur parole" (I, 14, 60) ("It is a common practice in many nations of our time for people to wound themselves intentionally to give credit to their word" [41]). Among the examples the essayist draws upon is that of a young girl who disfigures herself in

order to maintain the constancy of her word: "J'ay veu une fille, pour
tesmoigner l'ardeur de ses promesses, et aussi sa constance, se donner du poinçon qu'elle portoit en son poil, quatre ou cinq bons coups
dans le bras, qui luy faisoient craquetter la peau, et la saignoient bien
en son escient" (I, 14, 60) ("I have seen a girl, to show the ardor of
her promises, and also her constancy, strike herself, with the bodkin
she wore in her hair, four or five lusty stabs in the arm, which broke
the skin and made her bleed in good earnest" [41]). In examining
the 1595 edition of the Essays established by Marie de Gournay, one
discovers that this passage has been rewritten in a most revelatory
manner. Specifically, she substitutes the formulation "J'ay veu une
fille" ("I have seen a girl") by "Quand je veins de ces fameux Estats
de Blois, j'avois veu peu auparavant une fille de Picardie" (I, 14, 60,
n. 6). The reference is definitely to Marie de Gournay. According to
Donald Frame's biography, Montaigne had visited the young woman
in Picardy in 1588 while attending the Estates General at Blois.[12]

The variant of this text conceals more than first meets the eye.
The metaphoric reference to the disfiguring of the female body
takes on an even greater significance within the allegorical dynamics involved in the daughter-father relationship and the previously
articulated unconditionally laudatory references to the Montaignian
corpus. There are those who choose to read this passage as a somewhat literal affirmation of the female writer's coming into being.[13]
Yet one could even go a step further by suggesting that this image of
the wound or representation of martyrdom, traditionally viewed as
a metaphoric means of transcendence, here represents the literal violence done to the female body. However, one must remember to read
this passage in an allegorical fashion. It is not simply about violence
inflicted on a female body destined for marriage. Rather, it represents
the passage of violence through language itself (from "to force," one
of the root meanings of this word), an attempt to ascribe an oppositional tone to a literary performance by replacing the pleasure of Marie de Gournay's prefatory statements with a new introduction that
paradoxically gives voice to what was previously silent. The various
writings and rewritings alluded to by Alan Boase (reprinted in the
editions published between 1598 and 1617) attest to Marie de Gournay's "double-talk." Her revisionist history assured her the possibility of dissociating the name of the father from the production of a
revisionist literary culture: "LECTEUR, si je ne suis assez forte pour
escrire sur les Essais, aumoins suis-je bien genereuse pour advouër

ma foiblesse, et te confesse que je me retracte de cette Preface que l'aveuglement de mon aage et d'une violente fievre d'ame me laissa n'aguere eschaper des mains."[14] If guilt is an issue here, as it has been suggested by Regosin, it does not stem from the "writer's guilt of having spoken at all."[15] Rather, it takes the form of a muted yet powerful rhetoric constituting a drama realized at the level of the Logos. As a result of this corporeal albeit textual excision, Marie de Gournay is motivated to act. The narrative disfiguration alluded to here undoes the privileged and identificatory position with the father. Ironically, it devalues the initial female position by representing Marie de Gournay as a rather puerile being; her unresolved tension serves to justify her seeking refuge within the very problem that her own desire has engendered. Although the removal of the daughter's illusion of paternal omnipotence ironically liberates her, it transforms her rhetorical performance into a simulacrum of a partially realized autonomy that reestablishes the discourse of this "newly born woman" and enables her to represent her being through a distancing from the master narrative: "C'est une femme qui parle."[16] By withdrawing unconditional support of the name of the father, Marie de Gournay engages in a discourse where the newly excluded material is now seen as the narrative symptom of the wound or gap created by the excision of her prefatory corpus. No longer described as "un semblable" who bore witness to the exemplarity of Montaigne's writing, her word now begins to emerge from the wound inflicted on the representation of the paternal body, the literary corpus of which now only the ashes remain and from which the surrogate daughter can no longer rekindle her originary desire in the name of the father.

PART III

Philosophical Impostures

THE SOCRATIC MAKEOVER

The Ethics of the Impossible
in "De la phisionomie" (III, 12)

 In "De la phisionomie" (III, 12) ("Of Physiog-nomy") Montaigne makes the topos of vision cen-tral to the understanding of the essay.[1] From the outset the essayist engages in an epistemological critique that draws attention to our inability to see things as they are:

Nous n'apercevons les graces que pointues, bouffies et enflées d'artifice. Celles qui coulent soubs la nayfveté et la simplicité eschapent ayséement à une veue grossiere comme est la nostre: elles ont une beauté delicate et cachée; il faut la veue nette et bien purgée pour descouvrir cette secrete lumiere. (III, 12, 1037)

We perceive no charms that are not sharpened, puffed out, and inflated by artifice. Those which glide along naturally and simply easily escape a sight so gross as ours. They have a delicate and hidden beauty; we need a clear and well-purged sight to discover their secret light. (793)

For Montaigne the appearance of a thing always already constitutes its otherness since our perception constrains us and allows what is seen to be viewed equivocally. According to this logic, once we see something, the *aporia* between seeming and being is foregrounded to such an extent that we can no longer distinguish between reality and fiction.

Montaigne's essay draws on the popular treatises of the day, according to which a person's external facial features reflected his or her inner moral character. The text's conceptual framework is organized around a debate concerning the relationship between inner and outer spheres and how one might inform the other: "Il n'est rien plus vraysemblable que la conformité et relation du corps à l'esprit" (III, 12, 1057) ("There is nothing more likely than the conformity and relation of the body to the spirit" [809]). Within this context, the essay's focus on the physical act of seeing and the psychic process of visualization leads to an investigation of the validity of the science of physiognomy.

Etymologically physiognomy conjoins the concepts of nature (*physis*) and knowledge (*gnos*). From Barthélemy Coclès to Jean d'Indagine, it was thought that for the specialist of this science Being could be made to surface through the image of the face.[2] This engagement with the world of phenomenal forms identified the face as the privileged locus for the unveiling of Being and the gateway to one's character. The physiognomic unity upon which this science insists is one of analogy between the parts. Yet the outward face of things is far from transparent, and vision is often overdetermined, based as it is on the limitations of spatial perspective.

The most striking problem that physiognomy encounters, according to Montaigne, concerns the counterexample represented by the discrepancy between the grotesque features of Socrates' face and the beauty of his soul: "Socrates, qui a esté un exemplaire parfaict en toutes grandes qualitez, j'ay despit qu'il eust rencontré un corps et un visage si vilain, comme ils disent, et disconvenable à la beauté de son ame, luy si amoureux et si affolé de la beauté (III, 12, 1057) (About Socrates, who was a perfect model in all great qualities, it vexes me that he hit on a body and face so ugly as they say he had, and so incongruous with the beauty of his soul, he who was so madly in love with beauty" [809]).

One glimpse of Socrates reveals him in all his ugliness. In this context, vision fails to account for the "beauté de son ame" ("beauty of his soul"). Nevertheless, initially the representation of Socrates draws on the Silenic image found in Plato's *Symposium*. According to Alcibiades, this image underscores the necessity of looking beyond the philosopher's grotesque image, his "si vile forme" (III, 12, 1037) ("so mean a form" [793]), in order to discover the beauty within. To be sure, the phenomenon of the Silenic Socrates puts into question physiognomy itself. However, this project can only be realized with a "veue nette et bien purgée" (III, 12, 1037) ("a clear and well-purged sight" [793]), which paradoxically replaces the phenomenon of sight with the imagination's power of visualization. Montaigne assigns to the mind's eye the ability to imagine a virtual reality that paradoxically enables us to see more accurately things as they are. Reality thus becomes that which is not grasped with the eyes but rather with the intellect.

The language of credit and borrowing is a central motif in "De la phisionomie." The opening line of this essay substantiates this fact: "Quasi toutes les opinions que nous avons sont prinses par authorité et à credit" (III, 12, 1037) ("Almost all the opinions we have are taken on authority and on credit" [792]). However, this emphasis on "otherness" is quickly put into question by a reference to the figure of Socrates, who in his individuality acquires exemplarity: " Vrayment il est bien plus aisé de parler comme Aristote et vivre comme Caesar, qu'il n'est aisé de parler et vivre comme Socrates. Là loge l'extreme degré de perfection: l'art n'y peut joindre" (III, 12, 1055) ("Truly it is much easier to talk like Aristotle and live like Caesar than it is to talk and live like Socrates. There lies the extreme degree of perfection and difficulty; art cannot reach it." [808]). In many ways Socrates embodies the Montaignian ideals of learned ignorance and authenticity as manifested in his engagement with academic skepticism. As a paragon of human virtue in following nature's example, Socrates exemplifies the model of proper living in his understanding of the infelicitous consequences of not knowing limits:. "Il a faict grand faveur à l'humaine nature de montrer combien elle peut d'elle mesme. Nous sommes chacun plus riche que nous ne pensons; mais on nous dresse à l'emprunt et à la queste: on nous duict à nous servir plus de l'autruy que du nostre" (III, 12, 1038) ("He did a great favor to human nature by showing how much it can do by itself. We are each richer than we think, but we are trained to borrow and beg; we are taught to use the resources of others more than our own" [794]). Philosophical dogma, that malady produced by those engaged in "excez fievreux" (III, 12, 1039) ("feverish excesses" [794]), is little more than vanity, "cette complaisance voluptueuse qui nous chatouille par l'opinion de science" (III, 12, 1039) ("that voluptuous complacency which tickles us with the notion of being learned" [794]). The value of Socrates' teaching suggests that by borrowing or buying on credit one risks occluding the authenticity of the self. In criticizing the phenomenon of borrowing, Montaigne appears to suggest that our very own nature can be a source of true wealth. Socratic humility is therefore praised for its ability to discover wisdom in the activities of everyday life: "C'est luy qui ramena du ciel, où elle perdoit son temps, la sagesse humaine" (III, 12, 1038) ("It is he who brought human wisdom back down from heaven, where she was wasting her time" [793]).

How does Montaigne get us to know Socrates, and how can the essayist represent this most natural of men? The figure of Socrates, a man of unpretentious verbal expression, is transmitted through texts that mediate his very being and allow us to visualize who he is. Interestingly, as the text unfolds it introduces the question of "phisionomie," which acts as a trope for the hermeneutic practices of reading and writing that permit us to visualize instead of simply to see:

Sans peine et sans suffisance, ayant mille volumes de livres autour de moy en ce lieu où j'escris, j'emprunteray presentement s'il me plaist d'une douzaine de tels ravaudeurs, gens que je ne feuillette guiere, de quoy esmailler le traicté de la phisionomie. Il ne faut que l'espitre liminaire d'un alemand pour me farcir d'allegations. (III, 12, 1056)

Without trouble and without competence, having a library of a thousand volumes around me in this place where I write, I will presently borrow, if I please, from a dozen such patch-makers, people whom I do not often leaf through, enough to bedeck this treatise on physiognomy. I need only the preliminary epistle of some German to stuff me with quotations. (808)

The figure of Socrates permeates Montaigne's essay. He is revealed through references to the writings of various figures of antiquity, such as Cicero, whom the essayist criticized for his rigidity and the artificiality of his rhetorical praxis: "Fussé je mort moins allegrement avant qu'avoir veu les Tusculanes? J'estime que non" (III, 12, 1039) ("Should I have died less cheerfully before having read the Tusculans? I think not" [794]). The philosopher in the text becomes a copy of the "déjà lu," for the authenticity of his image is conceived as a simulation predicated on the authority of borrowing on credit. " Il est bien advenu que le plus digne homme d'estre cogneu et d'estre presenté au monde pour exemple, ce soit celuy duquel nous ayons plus certaine cognoissance. Il a esté esclairé par les plus clair voyans hommes qui furent onques: les tesmoins que nous avons de luy sont admirables en fidelité et en suffisance" (III, 12, 1038) ("It happened fortunately that the man most worthy to be known and to be presented to the world as an example should be the one of whom we have most certain knowledge. We have light on him from the most clear-sighted men who ever lived; the witnesses we have of him are wonderful in fidelity and competence" [793]). In spite of this praise, the philosopher who rejected bookish knowledge for lived experience can only be transcribed in that which is otherwise than Being: "En toutes choses les hommes se jettent aux appuis estrangers pour espargner les propres, seuls certains et seuls puissans, qui sçait s'en armer. (III, 12, 1045) ("In all things men cast themselves on the resources of others to spare their own, which alone are sure and alone powerful, if we know how to arm ourselves with them" [799]). If nature is to become visible it can only be seen from the paradoxical effects of the art of reading.

Montaigne is able to see Socrates through the act of reading classical texts inherited from antiquity: "cette image des discours de Socrates que ses amys nous ont laissée" (III, 12, 1037) ("the version of the sayings of Socrates that his friends have left us" [792]). Through the process of contemplation, the mind's eye is able to visualize what it has read and transform it into a series of differentiations. The singularity of Socrates thus becomes multiple and consequently renders his image subject to change. With this in mind, Raymond La Charité has noticed that the essayist's textual borrowings act as "a kind of facial binding for the book, and it is in this way . . . that writing and book [function] as faces to be read."[3] Writing, however, can never be transparent since the image in the text represents an untranslatable reality articulated in improper terms. This mediation renders visible the image of Socrates in the only form in which he can possibly emerge, namely, the realm of appearances.

The ghost of Socrates acts as a powerful figure in this essay, and this phenomenon permits the future to have an existence in Montaigne's text:

Socrates faict mouvoir son ame d'un mouvement naturel et commun. Ainsi dict un paysan, ainsi dict une femme. Il n'a jamais en la bouche que cochers, menuisiers, savetiers et maçons. Ce sont inductions et similitudes tirées des plus vulgaires et cogneues actions des hommes!; chacun l'entend. Soubs une si vile forme nous n'eussions jamais choisi la noblesse et splendeur de ses conceptions admirables, nous, qui estimons plates et basses toutes celles que la doctrine ne releve, qui n'apercevons la richesse qu'en montre et en pompe. Nostre monde n'est formé qu'à l'ostentation: les hommes ne s'enflent que de vent, et se manient à bonds, comme les balons. Cettuy-cy ne se propose point des vaines fantasies: sa fin fut nous fournir de choses et de preceptes qui reelement et plus jointement servent à la vie, servare modum, finemque tenere, naturamque sequi. Il fut aussi tousjours un? et pareil, et se monta, non par saillies mais par complexion, au dernier poinct de vigueur. Ou, pour mieux dire, il ne monta rien, mais ravala plustost et ramena à son point originel et naturel, et lui soubmit la vigueur, les aspretez et les difficultez. Car, en Caton, on void bien à clair que c'est une alleure tendue bien loing au dessus des communes: aux braves exploits de sa vie, et en sa mort, on le sent tousjours monté sur ses grands chevaux. Cettuy-cy ralle à terre, et d'un pas mol et ordinaire traicte les plus utiles discours; et se conduict et à la mort et aux plus espineuses traverses qui se puissent presenter au trein de la vie humaine. Il est bien advenu que le plus digne homme d'estre cogneu et d'estre presenté au monde pour exemple, ce soit celuy duquel nous ayons plus certaine cognoissance. Il a esté esclairé par les plus clair voyans hommes qui furent onques: les tesmoins que nous avons de luy sont admirables en fidelité et en suffisance. C'est grand cas d'avoir peu donner tel ordre aux pures imaginations d'un enfant, que, sans les alterer ou estirer, il en ait produict les plus beaux effects de nostre ame. Il ne la represente ny eslevée ny riche; il ne la represente que saine, mais certes d'une bien allegre et nette santé. Par ces vulgaires ressorts et naturels, par ces fantasies ordinaires et communes, sans s'esmouvoir et sans se piquer, il dressa non seulement les plus reglées, mais les plus hautes et vigoreuses creances, actions et meurs qui furent onques. C'est luy qui ramena du ciel, où elle perdoit son temps, la sagesse humaine, pour la rendre à l'homme, où est sa plus juste et plus laborieuse besoigne, et plus utile. Voyez le plaider devant ses juges, voyez par qu-elles raisons il esveille

son courage aux hazards de la guerre, quels arguments forti-
fient sa patience contre la calomnie, la tyrannie, la mort et contre la teste de sa femme: il n'y a rien d'emprunté de l'art et des
sciences; les plus simples y recognoissent leurs moyens et leur
force; il n'est possible d'aller plus arriere et plus bas. Il a faict
grand faveur à l'humaine nature de montrer combien elle peut
d'elle mesme. Nous sommes chacun plus riche que nous ne pensons; mais on nous dresse à l'emprunt et à la queste: on nous
duict à nous servir plus de l'autruy que du nostre. (III, 12,
1037–38)

Socrates makes his soul move with a natural and common motion. So says a peasant, so says a woman. His mouth is full of
nothing but carters, joiners, cobblers, and masons. His are inductions and similes drawn from the commonest and best-known
actions of men; everyone understands him. Under so mean a
form we should never have picked out the nobility and splendor
of his admirable ideas, we who consider flat and low all ideas
that are not raised up by learning, and who perceive richness
only in pomp and show. Our world is formed only for ostentation; men inflate themselves only with wind, and go bouncing
around like balls. This man did not propose to himself any idle
fancies: his aim was to furnish us with things and precepts that
serve life really and more closely:

> To keep the mean, to hold our aim in view,
> And follow nature.

LUCAN

He was also always one and the same, and raised himself,
not by sallies but by disposition, to the utmost point of vigor.
Or, to speak more exactly, he raised nothing, but rather brought
vigor, hardships, and difficulties down and back to his own natural and original level, and subjected them to it. For in Cato we
see very clearly that his is a pace strained far above the ordinary;
in the brave exploits of his life and in his death we feel that he
is always mounted on his high horse. The other walks close to
the ground, and at a gentle and ordinary pace treats the most

useful subjects; and behaves, both in the face of death and in the thorniest trials that can confront us, in the ordinary way of human life.

It happened fortunately that the man most worthy to be known and to be presented to the world as an example should be the one of whom we have most certain knowledge. We have light on him from the most clear-sighted men who ever lived; the witnesses we have of him are wonderful in fidelity and competence.

It is a great thing to have been able to impart such order to the pure and simple notions of a child that, without altering or stretching them, he produced from them the most beautiful achievements of our soul. He shows it as neither elevated nor rich; he shows it only as healthy, but assuredly with a very blithe and clear health. By these vulgar and natural motives, by these ordinary and common ideas, without excitement or fuss, he constructed not only the best regulated but the loftiest and most vigorous beliefs, actions, and morals that ever were. It is he who brought human wisdom back down from heaven, where she was wasting her time, and restored her to man, with whom lies her most proper and laborious and useful business. See him plead before his judges, see by what reasonings he rouses his courage in the hazards of war, what arguments fortify his patience against calumny, tyranny, death, and his wife's bad temper. There is nothing borrowed from art and the sciences; even the simplest can recognize in him their means and their strength; it is impossible to go back further and lower. He did a great favor to human nature by showing how much it can do by itself. (743–44)

Ironically Socrates incarnates a figure that is both real and unreal, which is to say that for Montaigne he is real in his mind's eye despite the fact that he no longer exists to be seen. To be sure, the spectrality of Socrates in this essay forces us to question what it means to exist and what may be perceived as natural.

Near the end of the essay Montaigne becomes his own double, juxtaposing the narrator's perspective in relation to the character in the narrative. Moreover, he relates the question of physiognomy to his own experience, recounting how the openness of his face saved him from highwaymen, who tried to rob him. In the process, he is able to distinguish himself from Socrates: "J'ay un port favorable et en forme et en interpretation . . . et qui faict une contraire montre à celuy de Socrates" (III, 12, 1059–60) ("I have a favorable bearing, both in itself and in others'interpretation . . . one very unlike that of Socrates" [811]). In the two tales that follow Montaigne engages in storytelling in such a way that his experience is transformed into a drama that becomes a metacommentary on the limits of knowledge. Here the text examines the capabilities of the look and how we bring things to light by looking. Montaigne wishes to explore the conditions of phenomenalism by exploring its limits.

The first tale involves a deceptive neighbor who attempted to profit from Montaigne's apparent naïveté in order to gain entry into his house and occupy it. This aggressive neighbor, who also happens to be a marital relation, invents a tale of attack and escape, a narrative that prefigures the story that he and his troops are in the process of staging. As the intruder enters, he is accompanied by several soldiers who wish to seize Montaigne's property. They are succeeded by a band of twenty-five or thirty men whom Montaigne admits by seemingly following his natural inclinations: "Je me laissay aller au party le plus naturel et le plus simple" (III, 12, 1060) ("I abandoned myself to the most natural and simple course" [812]). In reacting to this intrusion, Montaigne engages in what David Quint has called "conscious simplicity."[4] Despite appearances, however, Montaigne realizes the evil intentions of his neighbors and profits from their perception, which functions as the threshold to a calculated strategy for survival in the worst of times (the treacherous religious wars): "Je n'ignorois pas en quel siecle je vivois" (III, 12, 1060) ("I was not unaware in what sort of an age I was living" [812]). He therefore hides his true awareness of the situation and greets his guests as a proper host in an utterly improper situation:

> Tant y a que, trouvant qu'il n'y avoit point d'acquest d'avoir commencé à faire plaisir si je n'achevois, et ne pouvant me desfaire sans tout rompre, je me laissay aller au party le plus naturel et le plus simple, comme je faicts tousjours, commendant qu'ils entrassent. (III, 12, 1060)

> However, feeling that there was nothing to be gained by having begun to be pleasant if I did not go through with it, and being unable to get rid of them without ruining everything, I aban-

doned myself to the most natural and simple course, as I always do, and gave orders for them to come in. (812)

Ironically, it was the intruder's misapprehension of the essayist's *parrhesia* that foreclosed the possibility of subsequent aggression. Montaigne's engagement in a form of theatricality results from his recognition of the facial qualities nature has made available to him: "Il m'est souvant advenu que, sur le simple credit de ma presence et de mon air, des personnes qui n'avoyent aucune cognoissance de moy s'y sont grandement fiées" (III, 12, 1066) ("It has often happened that on the mere credit of my presence and manner, persons who had no knowledge of me have placed great trust in me" [811–12]). The scene of judgment enacted here creates a spatial distance between the one who judges and the one who is being judged. Montaigne's staging of what appears to be natural bears witness to the strategic function of dissimulation. What matters above all else is the way in which the gaze of the intruder falls on the object of aggression. The enemy's reading of the face overdetermines his subsequent inaction. To complicate things ever further, Montaigne renders the moral of this story other than itself: "Je penche volontiers vers l'excuse et interpretation plus douce. . . . Et suis homme en outre qui me commets volontiers à la fortune et me laisse aller" (III, 12, 1060–61) ("I am apt to lean toward the milder excuse and interpretation. . . . And besides, I am the sort of man who readily commits himself to Fortune and abandons himself bodily into her arms" [812]).

By engaging in this strategy of self-preservation—an activity foreign to the behavior of Socrates at his trial—Montaigne attributes to the other a kind a myopia that makes him the victim of the referential fallacy. Believing that the gaze of Montaigne could not possibly be denatured, the naïve enemy falls victim to the illusion that equates his look with Being itself. In this context surface appearance assumes its perceived function as signifier of the soul. Vision paradoxically produces misrecognition. Like Socrates, Montaigne demonstrates fearlessness when encountering the threat of death, except that here the essayist is able to survive by modulating his desire and submitting to power while maintaining the sense of honor that binds aristocrats together.

The first adventure suggests that the enemy's perception of Montaigne's face ultimately "saves his hide." As in the case of the psychoanalytic encounter, Montaigne's face constitutes a disturbance in the visual field of the other. Confronted with an image, the aggressor is positioned before a gaze that compels him to reverse previously conceived imperatives.

In the second story Montaigne is attacked and robbed by a band of armed masked men while journeying through a forest. His life having been threatened, the essayist's fate depends on the presentation of a ransom payment. Instead of succumbing to the threat, he remains steadfast. This demonstration of courage, as it is perceived by the attacker, motivates the latter to abandon his aggression: "Je vis revenir à moy le chef avec parolles plus douces, se mettant en peine de recercher en la troupe mes hardes escartées, et m'en faisant rendre selon qu'il s'en pouvoit recouvrer, jusques à ma boyte" (III, 12, 1062) ("I saw the leader return to me with gentler words, taking pains to search for my belongings scattered among the troop, and having them returned to me as far as they could be recovered, even including my money box" [813]). Interestingly, the steadfast heroism of Montaigne, his "liberté indiscrete" (III, 12, 1062) ("indiscreet freedom" [814]), enabled him to preserve his honor when confronted with a dangerous situation.

The Montaignian self is represented here within the context of an address in which meaning is comprised of contingencies otherwise unavailable to desire. According to Adam Phillips, "accidents became in Freud's vision ways of securing unconscious gratification."[5] However, what one discovers in Montaigne's text are desires revealed by contingencies instructive to the self. Unlike Freud, for whom finding is the result of looking, Montaigne foregrounds what we find when we are not focused on looking, namely, the opportunity to appear courageous. Beyond that, Montaigne's personal story brings the events of the past into the present. These events are placed within a new context so that they may be seen in a different light as they are narrated. Such a representation has been affected by the imagination—by the act of telling, as well as by the influence of what has been read as its affects the memory and the use of language in the self-portrait.

As in the first story, Montaigne here suggests that the cause of his freedom remains somewhat undetermined. The verbal text challenges the actual situation by mystifying the scopic relations in which we are held:

La vraye cause d'un changement si nouveau et de ce ravisement, sans aucune impulsion apparente, et d'un repentir si miraculeux,

en tel temps, en une entreprinse pourpensée et deliberée, et deve-
nue juste par l'usage . . . certes je ne sçay pas bien encores quelle
elle est. (III, 12, 1062)

The true cause of so unusual an about-face and change of mind,
without any apparent motivation, and of such a miraculous repentance, at such a time, in a premeditated and deliberate enter-
prise which had been made lawful by custom . . . I truly do not
even now well know. (813–14)

The inability of the story's denouement to engender certainty
functions as an affirmation and abnegation that cannot simply be
considered in an oppositional way. Instead, the story's success may
be found in its failure to produce absolute meaning, which must be
viewed in that word's etymological sense as a phenomenon that ab-
solves itself of all objects and ends. Although sight discerns and concerns a situation and a place, it knows no bounds since contingency
renders meaning equivocal. Montaigne's text makes mobile and ten-
tative what physiognomists might consider determinable: "C'est une
foible garantie que la mine; toutesfois elle a quelque consideration"
(III, 12, 1059) ("The face is a weak guarantee; yet it deserves some
consideration" [811]).

In both stories Being cannot necessarily be equated with truth and
perception; it cannot be reduced to pure receptivity since it is subject
to interpretation and change. Although Montaigne admires fortitude,
as others admire it in him, ultimately he cannot remain entirely reso-
lute in his actions: "Comme aux actions legitimes je me fasche de
m'y employer quand c'est envers ceux qui s'en desplaisent, aussi, à
dire verité, aux illegitimes je ne fay pas assez de conscience de m'y
employer quand c'est envers ceux qui y consentent" (III, 12, 1063)
("As I do not like to take a hand in legitimate actions against people
who resent them, so, to tell the truth, I am not scrupulous enough to
refrain from taking a hand in illegitimate actions against people who
consent to them" [814]). As Montaigne discovers as spectator of the
rhetoric of self-portraiture, writing can never be transparent. According to Slavoj Zizek, "self-consciousness is founded upon the non-
transparency of the subject to itself."[6] The writer once again discovers that he is a man just like all men, "merveilleusement vain, divers,
et ondoyant" (I, 1, 9) ("marvelously vain, diverse, and undulating"

[5]), an "escuyer de trefles" (III, 12, 1063) ("jack of clubs" [814]), signifying a character without importance. Nevertheless, the motif of specular identification in Montaigne's essay eventually succeeds through the ability to assume, as part of his cultural memory, what he considers to be the Socratic failures of the past: the inability to adapt to the trajectory of life's contingencies. In juxtaposing Socrates' story with his own, Montaigne discovers a new emphasis on action as either creative or adaptive—and perhaps even contingent.

Montaigne's text compares the essayist to Socrates, who defends himself before his Athenian judges. By referring to Socrates' trial and martyrdom as his "loftiest essay," and considering his trials and tribulations in a similar light, Montaigne describes himself as strikingly un-Socratic in his ability to adapt to the vicissitudes of human existence. In the essay the figure of Socrates—historically regarded as a morally accessible being who followed the course of nature—paradoxically appears as the one who is paralyzed, the victim of a lofty ideal. Engaged in a form of moral narcissism, Socrates' clarity of mind vanishes before his judges. His self-imposed blindness and rigidity lead him down the path of immoderate desire. For Socrates the inability to see seemingly functions as a way of avoiding the gaze of the other. Yet this illusion of autonomy paradoxically prevents him from recognizing that he has already unwittingly situated himself before an imagined gaze against which he measures his perception of moral purity. The human wisdom that Socrates had once brought down to earth now finds itself compromised as a result of the philosopher's obstinacy. In his arrogance (lit. "talking from a high standpoint" in Greek) Socrates made the immoderate decision to choose death over life and refuse the defense that Lysias had prepared on his behalf. This act put an end to the future once and for all; it eradicated it in a present without difference. By deciding to become a martyr in the name of justice, Socrates' act of resistance, his rigidity when confronted with an ideal, was perceived as disdainful conduct. Furthermore, it was Socrates' speech, as recounted in the Apology, that led to his demise:. "Eust-on ouy de la bouche de Socrates une voix suppliante" (III, 12, 1054) ("Should people have heard a supplicating voice from the mouth of Socrates?" [807]). Montaigne was able to succeed where Socrates could only fail: "Les plus belles vies sont, à mon gré, celles qui se rangent au modelle commun et humain, avec ordre, mais sans miracle et sans extravagance" (III, 13, 1116) ("The most beautiful lives, to my mind, are those that conform to the common human pattern, with order, but without miracle and without eccentricity" [857]).

The Socrates described by Montaigne in the text appears to follow Xenophon's version of the trial, which reflects the presumption of the unrepentant philosopher, who vainly asserts his wisdom in the name of philosophical dogma.[7] By failing to be flexible, Socrates posits a continuity between past and present that must be distinguished from the nonpositing representations of the imagination. His refusal to appeal to the pity of his judges by projecting "laches contenances" transforms him into a stoic hero exiled from nature's realm.

From a tropological perspective Socrates' unreasonable reason undermines his quest to be unequivocally natural: "Je n'ay pas corrigé, comme Socrates par force de la raison mes complexions naturelles. . . . Je me laisse aller, comme je suis venu" (III, 12, 1059) ("I have not, like Socrates, corrected my natural disposition by force of reason. . . . I let myself go as I have come" [811]). Unlike Montaigne, who has the good fortune to possess a "port favorable" (III, 12, 1059) ("favorable bearing" [811]), a sign of virtue, Socrates had to overcome the grotesque face that nature had given him through the lessons of philosophy. What implicitly emerges here is the suggestion that Montaigne is closer to nature than Socrates.

Montaigne's makeover of the Socratic model suggests that in order to survive nature sometimes needs to be supplemented by art: "Si mon visage ne respondoit pour moy, si on ne lisoit en mes yeux et en ma voix la simplicité de mon intention, je n'eusse pas duré sans querelle et sans offence si long temps" (III, 12, 1062) (" If my face did not answer for me, if people did not read in my eyes and my voice the innocence of my intentions, I would not have lasted so long without quarrel and without harm" [814]). Credit and the possibility of illusion produce a misrecognition that might have actually saved Montaigne from impending death. In a sense reading replaces seeing, according to which the essay becomes an allegory about how to read Montaigne. Physiognomy reveals itself as a trope for the role assigned to us as readers. The image inscribed in Montaigne's essay enables us to assess the value of his face and decipher him as a text.

The defacement of Socrates undoes the factitious unity of the ego and dissolves the possibility of projecting a monolithic self-identity. The repositioning of Socrates into a contemporary context allows Montaigne to discover the impossibility of being unequivocally Socratic. His engagement in the two encounters undermines the possibility of consubstantiality with the Socratic model. Just as Socrates' *parrhesiastic* speech makes him the agent of his own demise, Montaigne's staging of firmness in physiognomy and in speech ultimately proves that artifice might ultimately enable one to escape the threat of a hostile other. Within the recounting of his personal history, Montaigne's de-formation of nature suddenly acquires a curative effect. In the course of the essay, the evocation of nature suggests an *aporia* of the proper in representation: "Les paroles redictes ont, comme autre son, autre sens" (III, 12, 1063) ("Words when reported have a different sense, as they have a different sound" [814]). The self-presence of nature is perhaps only something than can be an ideality, for nature and the proper depend on an experience of the impossible.

It is through his experiences, however, that Montaigne is able to question the Socratic model, imitate it, and try to make it his own. The specularity and identification offered through the example of Socrates are internalized by the essayist, with the end result being represented as cognitively different: "Il ne nous faut guiere de doctrine pour vivre à nostre aise. Et Socrates nous aprend qu'elle est en nous, et la manière de l'y trouver et de s'en ayder. . . . Recueillez vous; vous trouverez en vous les arguments de la nature contre la mort" (III, 12, 1039) ("We need hardly any learning to live at ease. And Socrates teaches us that it is in us, and the way to find it and help ourselves with it. . . . Collect yourself: you will find in yourself Nature's arguments against death" [795]).

The Socratic model paradoxically leaves itself open to change by challenging the very idea of authority. The action of the mind's eye testifies to the subjectivity of the "I" by recognizing the discrepancy between an immoderate ideal and the exigencies of reality. By revising the Socratic model, Montaigne's self-portrait becomes a work in progress that simultaneously questions our understanding of Socrates: "Il n'importe pas seulement qu'on voye la chose, mais comment on la voye" (I, 14, 67) ("What matters is not merely that we see the thing, but how we see it" [47]).

The essayist's reading of Socrates foregrounds the inability of the so-called pure Being of nature to simply let itself be. In a way, the surface of Montaigne's text disfigures as it rewrites and scars the face of Socrates. Montaigne positions himself as the narrator. His relationship to Socrates thus transcends the spatial and temporal boundaries of the Socratic intertexts and incarnates a sphere of desire. In the process Montaigne's text transforms the homogeneity of the Socratic antimodel into one that is not. Socrates therefore serves as a kind of mirror that blurs the essayist's self-image and deflects it in a series of splintered perspectives.

Montaigne's essay calls into question the norms that establish regimes of truth underlying ontology. From this emerges an interiority that cannot be subsumed by an other; it produces a radical form of individuation that resists philosophy's desire to normalize and transform the kinetic energy of becoming into the monumental qualities of a static form of Being. As a narrative event, the essay on physiognomy becomes one of defacement: "Je ne veux donc pas oublier encor cette cicatrice, bien mal propre à produire, en public: c'est l'irresolution" (II, 17, 654–55) ("So I do not want to forget this further scar, very unfit to produce in public: irresolution" [496]). For Montaigne, to turn around the wound is to turn around one's self, which paradoxically projects an image that resists representation.

Montaigne's story begins belatedly or in medias res since the capacity for self-reflection can only take shape once he has retold his stories in a new narrative frame. Just as the image of Socrates is mediated by other narratives in order that it might be understood, so Montaigne's self-portrait contributes to his life story through its oblique references to Socrates. However, as Montaigne assumes the position of the narrator, he comes to infiltrate the textual space left vacant by Socrates.[8] The Socratic makeover provides a perspectival structure, a haunting, that at best provides a partial account of a self divided from within and for whom there is no final story. In rereading his two stories Montaigne as narrator witnesses a double whose story could only begin to take place in the future. The essayist's revisiting of the past enables him to see his double in a transformative light rather than in a state of self-constitution, for it is the narrator's thinking that literally becomes act by making itself into acting: "Les livres m'ont servi non tant d'instruction que d'exercitation" (III, 12, 1039) ("Books have served me not so much for instruction as for exercise" [795]). The essayist's story of survival becomes a trope for his ability to live on in his writerly quest to escape the transcendent appeal of the Socratic model.

By measuring himself, albeit obliquely, against Socrates, Montaigne succeeds in projecting an ethos (in its fifth-century B.C.E meaning as character) derived from the rhetoric of self-portraiture. However, as Tobin Siebers has suggested, one must also consider the Homeric meaning of "ethos," which signifies a place or a haunt where language becomes habitual.[9] Accordingly, one might consider the mosaic of texts constituting the image of Socrates as forming a literary commonplace or accepted topos against which the essayist reveals his own "hauntology." This process requires that ethics transcend a limited monological notion of morality based on contractually regulated commonplaces, whether literary or otherwise, appearing to have universal validity. In this context ethics, conceived as a process of critique, acquires a performative function and emerges as a strategy that blocks all attempts to govern ontology in a totalized way.[10] What releases us from the enslavement to an idea (as in the tragic fate of Socrates) is an ethical act that suspends our adherence to the exigencies of the Law and the forced choice imposed by an imaginary superego. Montaigne's essay challenges the imposition of categorical principles in the representation both of self and of other; his text performs a veritable spectacle that one can only begin to envision: the revelation of a face through the process of rereading. In the end, the rhetoric of Montaigne's essay projects exemplarity in the anti-exemplum of a self-portrait; it multiplies physiognomies and therefore refuses to eradicate difference.

8
ROMANCING THE STONE
"De l'experience" (III, 13)

The real voyage of discovery consists not in seeking
new landscapes but in having new eyes.
MARCEL PROUST

Tout autre est tout autre.
JACQUES DERRIDA, "DONNER LA MORT"

 For decades we have upheld the illusion of a logo-
centric ontology underlying the *Essays*. Nowhere
do critics experience that idealized moment of ju-
bilation of the oneness of Montaigne with his text
more than in "De l'experience" (III, 13) ("Of Experience"). More often than not, the critical literature on Montaigne (from Frame to Friedrich to Defaux) adheres to a
Neoplatonic concept of mimesis realized through the voice of a subject bound to a preexistent idea.[1] These readers, often following in
the tradition of Sainte-Beuve and Thibaudet,[2] ascribe to the text an
ontological priority, a resolution according to which self-reflexivity
is anchored in a textual production that, they claim, reflects being
in the present or what might be described as the ideality of the word
become flesh. In short, they engage in a simulation that makes the
real empirically apprehensible based on a claim to mastery of knowledge. By engaging in such a hermeneutic practice, these readers of
the *Essays* attempt to render the impropriety of Montaigne proper
and thus, through the imposition of a "romantic" rhetoric, ironically
engage in what they accuse others of doing, namely, providing anachronistic readings of the text.

EXPERIENCE AND IDENTIFICATORY MODALITIES

To be sure, experience, here figured as a "condition mixte," must be seen as the result of the reading process implicated in life's journey, as a bridge or crossing, for it is in that process that hermeneutic meta-narratives are disassembled and master terms are challenged. Ironically, etymologically the word "essai," which means both "balance" (as in the scales of justice) and "trial," suspends any absolute rule of law in the very process of writing. In other words, the quest for knowledge resists totalization: "Je prononce ma sentence par articles descousus, ainsi que de chose qui ne se peut dire à la fois et en bloc" (III, 13, 1076) ("I speak my meaning in disjointed parts, as something that cannot be said all at once and in a lump" [824]). Accordingly, it is paramount that one realizes the impossibility of the text fulfilling itself through the internal construction of identity. Indeed, identity can never be made essential so that it can attain the false euphoria that plenitude is supposed to provide. Rather, temporality renders the representation of the self unstable, for it is modulated by sensations and mediated by the rhetorical dynamics of the imagination: "J'ay un dictionnaire tout à part moy: je passe le temps, quand il est mauvais et incommode: quand il est bon, je ne le veux pas passer, je le retaste, je m'y tiens" (III, 13, 1111) ("I have a vocabulary all my own. I 'pass the time,' when it is rainy and disagreeable; when it is good, I do not want to pass it; I savor it, I cling to it" [853]). In this essay what we call identity is represented as a dynamic phenomenon resisting the establishment of forced boundaries. It is the product of experience, conceived as textual commentary, which confronts the figure of the writer with alterity, according to which the self is formed through a series of identificatory modalities. "Combien souvent et sottement à l'avanture ay-je estandu mon livre à parler de soy?" (III, 13, 1069) ("How often and perhaps how stupidly have I extended my book to make it speak of itself!" [818]) These modalities of perspective represent multiples axes of vision that demarcate a fragmented narrative, carrying the subject across a series of borders. Subject and object of narration are dislocated from one another and subsequently shatter the ideality of oneness associated with consubstantiality: "J'ordonne à mon ame de regarder et la douleur et la volupté de veuë pareillement . . . ferme, mais gayement l'une, l'autre severement, et selon ce qu'elle y peut aporter, autant songneuse d'en esteindre l'une que d'estendre l'autre" (III, 13, 1110–11) ("I order my soul to look upon both pain and pleasure with a gaze equally . . . firm, but gaily at the one, at the other severely, and, according to its ability, as anxious to extinguish the one as to extend the other" [853]).

For Montaigne experience is the result of encounters with otherness: "Cette longue attention que j'employe à me considerer me dresse à juger aussi passablement des autres: (III, 13, 1076) "This long attention that I devote to studying myself trains me also to judge passably of others" [824]). What Montaigne sees in the essay is always already something else: "Nostre vie est composée, comme l'armonie du monde, de choses contraires" (III, 13, 1068) ("Our life is composed, like the harmony of the world, of contrary things" [835]). Alterity is engendered in the act of writing and temporality subverts the consubstantiality that is the stated desire of self-portraiture: "Je fons et eschape à moy" (III, 13, 1101) ("Thus do I melt and slip away from myself" [845]). The horizon of knowledge is thus not fixed in any of its forms. The indistinctness of the world in its infinite movement in time and space creates *aporias* of cognition betraying what may otherwise be perceived as unproblematic.

The act of essaying is a process of exteriorization; it opens the desire that binds the narrative and opens the self-portrait as much to the past as to the future. The process whereby the past never stops passing through represents an archaeology of the self, as depicted in the essayist's narrative of interrupted sleep: "A celle fin que le dormir mesme ne m'eschapat ainsi stupidement, j'ay autresfois trouvé bon qu'on me le troublat pour que je l'entrevisse" (III, 13, 1112) ("To the end that sleep itself should not escape me thus stupidly, at one time I saw fit to have mine disturbed, so that I might gain a glimpse of it" [854]). To experience sleep one must interrupt the very experience, for neither experience nor authorship can partake fully of the plenitude of the self in the specificity of the moment: "Nous cherchons d'autres conditions, pour n'entendre l'usage des nostres, et sortons hors de nous, pour ne sçavoir quel il y fait" (III, 13, ("We seek other conditions because we do not understand the use of our own, and go outside of ourselves because we do not know what it is like inside" [857]).

What emerges in the writing of the essay is an aporetic self; its representation demonstrates the inadequacy of the example and, ultimately, the inability to fix the present: "J'ay des portraits de ma forme de vingt et cinq et trente cinq ans; je les compare avec celuy d'asteure: combien de fois ce n'est plus moy" (III, 13, 1102) ("I have portraits of myself at twenty-five and thirty-five; I compare them with one of the present: how irrevocably it is no longer myself!" [846]). The *aporia* is thus not a dead end, but it engenders the movement that is inherent to the essaying process, for it results in the noncoincidence of Being. "Nostre vie n'est que mouvement" (III, 13, 1095) ("Our life is nothing but movement" [840]). If, as Richard Regosin has suggested, in the essay "judgment is a surrogate of memory, the memory-duration of experience can never reconstitute the wholeness of its interiority":[3] "A faute de memoire naturelle j'en forge de papier, et comme quelque nouveau symptome survient à mon mal, je l'escris" (III, 13, 1092) ("For lack of a natural memory I make one of paper, and as some new symptom occurs in my disease, I write it down" 837–38).

Experience, as textual practice, can thus never be made essential, for the very notion of essaying is opposed to essentialism and the absolute singularity of the instant:

> Combien de fois changeons-nous nos fantaisies? Ce que je tiens aujourd'huy et ce que je croy, je le tiens et le croy de toute ma croyance. . . . Mais ne m'est-il pas advenu, non une fois, mais cent, mais mille, et tous les jours, d'avoir ambrassé quelque autre chose à tout ces mesmes instrumens, en cette mesme condition, que depuis j'aye jugée fauce? (II, 12, 563)

> How many times we change our notions! What I hold today and what I believe, I hold and believe it with all my belief. . . . But has it not happened to me, not once, but a hundred times, a thousand times, and every day, to have embraced with these same instruments, in this same condition, something else that I have since judged false? (423)

Thinking, as it is figured in the tropes constituting the text, stands as a challenge to science and calculation. In the Montaignian essay experience has no horizon if one conceives of it as its name signifies: the idea of a limit. In epistemological terms, *aporia* underscores the very idea of the signifying process constituting experience as commentary. The work of the essay goes beyond that which is considered essential

or proper, and this process demystifies the very idea of the presence
of the present:

> Et quand à ces mots: present, instant, maintenant, par lesquels
> il semble que principalement nous soustenons et fondons
> l'intelligence du temps, la raison le descouvrant le destruit tout
> sur le champ: car elle le fend incontinent et le part en futur et en
> passé comme le voulant voir necessairement desparty en deux.
> (II, 12, 603)

> And as for these words, present, immediate, now, on which it
> seems that we chiefly found and support our understanding of
> time, reason discovering this immediately destroys it; for she at
> once splits and divides it into future and past, as though wanting
> to see it necessarily divided in two. (456)

The practice of essaying produces fragments, textual particles
fuctioning as part-objects, whose resonances are displayed in the tensions between Eros and Thanatos and the desire for wisdom:

> Je la [life] jouys au double des autres, car la mesure en la jouys-
> sance depend du plus ou moins d'application que nous y prestons.
> Principallement à cette heure que j'apercoy la mienne si briefve en
> temps, je la veux estendre en pois; je veux arrester la promptitude
> de sa fuite par la promptitude de ma sesie. (III, 13, 1111)

> I enjoy it twice as much as others, for the measure of enjoyment
> depends on the greater or lesser attention that we lend it. Espe-
> cially at this moment, when I perceive that mine is so brief in
> time, I try to increase it in weight; I try to arrest the speed of its
> flight by the speed with which I grasp it. (853)

Never fully accessible, the fragment produces cuts in what would be
the text's recording energy of inscription, which negotiates between
presence and absence and represents the potentially present and almost lost erotic perigrinations of the psyche. In the sphere of vision,
the emergence and the fading of the "I" produces a fragmentation
between Being and becoming. The *aporia* between the "I" and the
objects of observation and desire simultaneously conceals and reveals
the psychic drama in the scopic field.

The so-called confessional nature of this essay functions meta-phorically as a kind of "striptease" whose partial exposure attains a quasi-erotic quality by transcending the regime of vision based on the rapport between seeing and being seen. Montaigne's "De l'experience" presents us with the immodest offering of the tropologi-cal representation of the essayist's body and a taxonomy of the highly personal yet banal aspects of everyday life: teeth, radishes, defeca-tion. Montaigne's entire body comes under the gaze of the reader as an exposed piece of flesh in the corpus constituting the text. Yet this very act of exposure does not unveil that which is hidden, for the representation of the body paradoxically renders it somewhat imper-ceptible in its nakedness and state of abandonment, leaving the eyes with nothing to focus on.

In "De mesnager sa volonté" (III, 10) ("Of Husbanding Your Will") the text presents an ideality that is foregrounded by the dis-tinction made between natural desire and the "desreiglement de nostre fantasie" (III, 10, 1009) ("the disorder of our imagination" [771]), which seemingly is disavowed. If desire is to be tamed at all, it can only be realized through a process of domestication achieved by circumscribing it:

> La carriere de nos desirs doit estre circonscripte et restraincte à un court limite des commoditez les plus proches et contigues; et doit en outre leur course se manier, non en ligne droite qui face bout ailleurs, mais en rond, duquel les deux pointes se tiennent et terminent en nous par un brief contour. (III, 10, 1011)

> The range of our desires should be circumscribed and restrained to a narrow limit of the nearest and most contiguous good things; and moreover their course should be directed not in a straight line that ends up elsewhere, but in a circle whose two extremities by a short sweep meet and terminate in ourselves. (773)

When it is salubrious, it seems that desire follows the parameters of nature's gait; otherwise it risks getting lost in the vertiginous laby-rinth of the imagination. It is here suggested that proper desire has its limits in the laws of nature, whose order is guaranteed by what can only be characterized as an "esprit de géometrie": "Ceux desquels on voit le bout sont siens, ceux qui fuient devant nous et desquels nous ne pouvons joindre la fin sont nostres" (III, 10, 1009) ("Those whose limits we can see are hers, those that flee before us and whose end we cannot reach are ours" [771]). This mathematical reasoning rejects the lawlessness associated with the Greek concept of *paranomos,* suggesting that unruly desire can be governed by the power of the law.

Yet the parameters of desire depicted in "De l'experience" represent a series of modalities of perspective, motivated by the love of wisdom, in which the multiple axes of vision partake of a narrative line that carries the represented subject across a series of thresholds. By becoming other as a result of the undoing of singularity and the vicissitudes of desire that the essaying process puts into practice, both subject and object of the narrative are occluded from one another and thereby shatter the symmetry of the mirror vision.

"THE EPISTEMOLOGY THAT IS NOT ONE"

The opening of Montaigne's essay is based on a paraphrase of the first line of Aristotle's *Metaphysics,* a text in which the latter declares that by nature all men desire to know. Aristotle's epistemology was conceived as a theoretical science that could delineate the causes and principles of what one can know. From this perspective, metaphysics may be viewed as the science of Being, the study of things as they are; objects are elucidated through the establishment of totalized meaning, which guarantees truth.

However, in Montaigne's text Aristotle's incipit "Omnes homines natura scire desiderant" ("All men desire by nature to know") rather curiously changes its focus by turning attention away from knowledge to desire through the restrictive force of a syntactic negation: "Il n'est desir plus naturel que le desir de connoissance" (III, 13, 1065) ("There is no desire more natural than the desire for knowledge" [815]). Montaigne has taken Aristotle's "desiderant" (a verb in the third-person plural), nominalized it, and made it multiple, implying that there are many different types of desire and reinforcing the sense of difference as derived from the repetiton of the same. For Montaigne thought becomes instrinsic to the drive associated with desire, and the latter, as it manifests itself in the performance of the essay, transcribes the errancy of being. In a way desire suggests what is to come and thereby collapses into the deceptive phenomenon of self-identity. As a result, the essaying process suspends the teleological thrust of Aristotelian metaphysics and its doctrine of ethics based on a principle of totalization. Like the lover's quest for an impossible erotic object, the passion for transgression and for trespassing the boundary of possibility alluded to here refers to a thinking process beyond knowledge or a naming beyond ordinary nomination. Desire thus simultaneously functions as a promise and divestment of wholeness.

Montaigne's text sugggests the impossibility of maintaining the self-identity of knowledge. "Nous ouvrons la matiere et l'espandons en la destrempant; d'un subject nous en faisons mille, et retombons, en multipliant et subdivisant, à l'infinité des atomes d'Epicurus" (III, 13, 1067) ("By diluting the substance we allow it to escape and spill it all over the place; of one subject we make a thousand, and, multiplying and subdividing, fall back into Epicurus'infinity of atoms" [817]). Montaigne's text clearly parallels Aristotle's in the belief that sensory experience—particularly sight—enables us to delineate similarities of "the same thing." Whereas Aristotle's epistemology proceeds from the projection of inductive generalizations in order to construct universals from the study of particulars, Montaigne discovers in the vicissitudes of experience a challenge to the infelicitious consequences of the rule of law. Beyond that, the passion for truth produces the cognitive equivalent of manifest destiny, a phenomenon that trespasses the possibility of closure by engaging the desiring subject in the seductive power of the imagination: "Il pense remarquer de loing je ne sçay quelle apparence de clarté et verité imaginaire; mais, pendant qu'il y court, tant de difficultez luy traversent la voye, d'empeschemens et de nouvelles questes, qu'elles l'esgarent et l'enyvrent" (III, 13, 1068) "It thinks it notices from a distance some sort of glimmer of imaginary light and truth; but while running toward it, it is crossed by so many difficulties and obstacles, and diverted by so many new quests, that it strays from the road, bewildered" [817]).

At the heart of Montaigne's epistemological critique is the belief that difference cannot be absolutized:

> La consequence que nous voulons tirer de la ressemblance des evenemens est mal seure, d'autant qu'ils sont tousjours dissemblables; il n'est aucune qualité si universelle en cette image des choses que la diversité et varieté. . . . La dissimilitude s'ingere

d'elle-mesme en nos ouvrages; nul art ne peut arriver à la simili-
tude. . . . La ressemblance ne faict pas tant un comme la difference fait autre. Nature s'est obligée à ne rien faire autre, qui ne
fust dissemblable. (III, 13, 1065)

The inference that we try to draw from the resemblance of events
is uncertain, because they are always dissimilar: there is no quality so universal in this aspect of things as diversity and variety. . . .
Dissimilarity necessarily intrudes into our works; no art can attain similarity. . . . Resemblance does not make things so much
alike as difference makes them unlike. Nature has committed
herself to make nothing separate that was not different. (815)

By avoiding the establishment of identity without difference, Montaigne's text presents a more radical approach that resists teleological
or dialectically grounded considerations. Difference is that which prevents knowledge from the paralysis of indifference. If truth becomes
little more than an illusion due to the impossibility of rendering
knowledge subject to the false logic of indifference, any attempt to
establish the essence of things can only fail, for it ignores the alterity
that subscribes to the work of difference.

In a sense, Montaigne's text produces an epistemology that is not
entirely one. Resemblance enables signification to transcend undiffer-
entiated sameness. What this epistemology suggests is that the cornucopia of possibilities produced by the differences within the same
cannot be contained. To live with possibility is to live with difference and to accept a certain epistemological anxiety resulting from
the inability to live with indifference. Only then can one confront the
vicissitudes of knowledge and life and the impossible situation that
difference opens up. Paradoxically ignorance remains the only un-
questionable truth of human knowledge.

The oxymoronic reference to "universal diversity" constitutes a
paradox since the very idea of diversity undercuts universality. It is
this figure which disables the establishment of a topology of knowledge and the parameters defining it. Montaigne's epistemology reveals a structure of exemplarity; the interplay between resemblance
and difference in terms of the discussion of the "event" destabilizes
identity in the very process of iterability. What may be truly singular
about diversity is that it is always ready to open itself up to the alterity of another experience through the writing of the essay.

The play of difference as it is presented in this essay reveals, by means of a reference to Apollo, how philosophical language can become poetic by going beyond the boundaries of the perceptible and not in representing it as truth. The pursuits of a probing mind are boundless, translating what Lacan has described as libidinal energy in the continual process of symbolization.

> Ce que declaroit assez Appollo, parlant tousjours à nous doublement, obscurement et obliquement, ne nous repaissant pas, mais nous amusant et embesongnant. C'est un mouvement irregulier, perpetuel, sans patron, et sans but. Ses inventions s'eschauffent, se suyvent, et s'entreproduisent l'une l'autre. (III, 13, 1068)

> Apollo revealed this clearly enough, always speaking to us equivocally, obscurely, and obliquely, not satisfying us, but keeping our minds interested and busy. It is an irregular, perpetual motion, without model and without aim. Its inventions excite, pursue, and produce one another. (818)

The poetic gait of critical thinking produces a sense of indeterminancy that keeps desire alive. As in the disjunctive rhetoric of the essay, the language of poetry translates the impossibility of producing a proper term. Apollo's language violates the logic of reason and foregrounds ambiguity rather than a reduction of meaning.

A bit farther along in the text Montaigne advances the idea that the lack of a universal language makes the possibility of justice virtually impossible. For Montaigne our disputes are essentially linguistic controversies that cannot offer any determinate or real content for the realization of justice: "Nostre contestation est verbale. . . . La question est de parolles, et se paye de mesme" (III, 13, 1069) ("Our disputes are purely verbal. . . . The question is one of words, and is answered in the same way" [818]). The interpretation of laws produces even more laws, which proliferate meaning in a vertiginous hermenutic maze that mimetically represents one of the etymological meanings of the word "essai," namely, *experiri*, to try something out: "Nous ouvrons la matiere et l'espandons en la destrempant; d'un subject nous en faisons mille, et retombons, en multipliant et subdivisant, à l'infinité des atomes d'Epicurus" (III, 13, 1067) ("By diluting the substance we allow it to escape and spill it all over the place;

of one subject we make a thousand, and, multiplying and subdividing, fall back into Epicurus'infinity of atoms" [817]).

Montaigne, like Derrida, views the nature of the force of law as a phenomenon tied to its potentially deceptive quality and its status as an absolute entity:[4] "Or les loix se maintiennent en credit, non par ce qu'elles sont justes, mais par ce qu'elles sont loix. C'est le fondement mystique de leur authorité; elles n'en ont poinct d'autre" (III, 13, 1072) ("Now laws remain in credit not because they are just, but because they are laws. That is the mystic foundation of their authority" [821]). The imposition of the law through acts of judgment, paradoxically subsumes difference in the name of justice. Far from being transcendent, the law must be thought of as something that cannot take *place* since in its practice the law is ultimately not a judgment but a *non-lieu*.

Montaigne's essay foregrounds the disjunction between the singularity of a case and a principle of law:

> Qu'ont gaigné nos legislateurs à choisir cent mille especes et faicts particuliers, et y attacher cent mille loix? Ce nombre n'a aucune proportion avec l'infinie diversité des actions humaines. La multiplication de nos inventions n'arrivera pas à la variation des exemples. Adjoustez y en cent fois autant: il n'adviendra pas pourtant que, des evenemens à venir, il s'en trouve aucun qui, en tout ce grand nombre de milliers d'evenemens choisis et enregistrez, en rencontre un auquel il se puisse joindre et apparier si exactement, qu'il n'y reste quelque circonstance et diversité qui requiere diverse consideration de jugement. (III, 13, 1066)

> What have our legislators gained by selecting a hundred thousand particular cases and actions, and applying a hundred thousand laws to them? This number bears no proportion to the infinite diversity of human actions. Multiplication of our imaginary cases will never equal the variety of the real examples. Add to them a hundred times as many more: and still no future event will be found to correspond so exactly to any one of all the many, many thousands of selected and recorded events that there will not remain some circumstance, some difference, that will require separate consideration in forming a judgment. (815–16)

To be sure, the multiplicity of situations in which to judge forecloses the possibility of establishing a legal syntax that would always result in a justifiable end. If a judgment is to be equitable, it cannot be derived from the application of a universal metanarrative since a just judgment must foreground the singularity of what is being judged.

> On donne authorité de loy à infinis docteurs, infinis arrests, et à autant d'interpretations. Trouvons nous pourtant quelque fin au besoin d'interpreter. . . . Nous obscurcissons et ensevelissons "intelligence"; nous ne la descouvrons plus qu'à la mercy de tant de clostures et barrieres. (III, 13, 1068)

> We give legal authority to numberless doctors, numberless decisions, and as many interpretations. Do we therefore find any end to the need of interpreting? . . . We obscure and bury the meaning; we no longer find it except hidden by so many enclosures and barriers. (817)

If, as Montaigne suggests, there is little interrelation among the variety of our actions, it is because the event through which a law is "read" is always unanticipated. From a legal standpoint the singularity of an event cannot be subjected to a horizon of intelligibility. No event is identical to another; the law cannot foresee the virtualities of that which is yet to come.

In Montaigne's critique, the law is never quite transparent and the fulfillment of its claims—are not universal. According to the essayist, if the application of the law subjects itself to web of differences it is because the universalizing imperative of the law imposes totalizing effects that preclude singularities:

> Pourquoy est-ce que nostre langage commun, si aisé à tout autre usage, devient obscur et non intelligible en contract et testament? . . . Car, en subdivisant ces subtilitez, on apprend aux hommes d'accroistre les doubtes; on nous met en trein d'estendre et diversifier les difficultez, on les alonge, on les disperse. (III, 13, 1115)

> Why is it that our common language, so easy for any other use, becomes obscure and unintelligible in contracts and wills, . . . For by subdividing these subtleties they teach men to increase their doubts; they start us extending and diversifying the difficulties, they lengthen them, they scatter them. (816)

No longer regarded as that which clarifies, the application of the law is seen as a practice which engenders difference and produces doubt.

If, as has been suggested, justice is a discursive issue, Montaigne's text foregrounds the arbitrary nature of the law and suggests that justice as law cannot be justice at all. To be sure, no longer viewing the law as a phenomenon founded on the power of reason, it ultimately finds itself subject to questions open to the interpretation of its meaning. Experience, predicated on the act of "essaying," necessitates the questioning of the law's validity; it engenders an encounter with alterity and produces an aporia between law and its so-called promise. The result ultimately undercuts the possibility of the law's legitimation. The *aporia* of the law appears in the impossibility of writing a narrative that can account for what is to come since experience shares with the law the improprieties of chance. Despite the desire to differentiate, the law can never account for all eventualities.

The scopic and oral parameters of desire are represented in an anecdotal fragment drawn from Aesop that dramatizes the fatal attraction resulting from the pursuit of desire.[5] In this story a pack of dogs desires to reach the body of a dead man on the other side of the shore. They consume the body of water that separates them from the corpse, thereby bringing about their demise. The desire of these canines can be read as a libidinal impulse that reveals itself as a paradoxical phenomenon. The energy produced by the need to satisfy desire brings about desire's end. Might the very presence of the tale in this essay suggest that an excess of desire may lead to a loss of being, whereby desire ultimately erases the subject and marks a limit?

Montaigne's epistemological critque has ontological consequences. The performative function of the essay is to question the artificial boundaries between inside and outside, as well as the authorizing modalities of the proper and the improper. As in my discussion of the quest for knowledge, experience as a textual practice cannot be guaranteed by a body of prescriptions: "La raison a tant de formes, que nous ne sçavons à laquelle nous prendre; l'experience n'en a pas moins" (III, 13, 1065) "Reason has so many shapes that we know not which to lay hold of; experience has no fewer" [815]). The very drive that constitutes desire precludes the possibility of imposing limits on knowledge, making the experience of being in the "here and now," as Heidegger once claimed, completely ineffable. The result of this phenomenon suggests that there is no moment when we properly are:

> Moy qui me vente d'embrasser si curieusement les commoditez de la vie, et si particulierement, n'y trouve, quand j'y regarde ainsi finement, à peu pres que du vent. Mais quoy, nous sommes par tout vent. Et le vent encore, plus sagement que nous, s'ayme à bruire, à s'agiter, et se contente en ses propres offices, sans desirer la stabilité, la solidité, qualitez non siennes. (III, 13, 1106–7)

> I, who boast of embracing the pleasures of life so assiduously and so particularly, find in them, when I look at them thus minutely, virtually nothing but wind. But what of it? We are all wind. And even the wind, more wisely than we, loves to make a noise and move about, and is content with its own functions, without wishing for stability and solidity, qualities that do not belong to it. (849)

Yet this very deficiency acquires a certain degree of exemplarity since it paradoxically transforms nothing into something, which suggests the symptom of our own vanity. Our faulty imagination creates the illusion that we are able to escape the ontological void of existence and pursue the impossible essence of things: "C'est signe de racourciment d'esprit quand il se contente, ou de lasseté. Nul esprit genereux ne s'arreste en soy: il pretend tousjours et va outre ses forces; il a des eslans au delà de ses effects; . . . son aliment c'est admiration, chasse, ambiguité" (III, 13, 1068) ("It is a sign of contraction of the mind when it is content, or of weariness. A spirited mind never stops within itself; it is always aspiring and going beyond its strength. . . . Its pursuits are boundless and without form; its food is wonder, the chase, ambiguity" [817–18]). There is indeed an impulse within the mind's "I" that seeks to transcend the void that is synonymous with the ontological condition of humankind. This passion for transgression enables the mind to nurture itself on the very emptinees it seeks to escape. Truth is something one can never arrive at; it never presents itself absolutely since it belongs to a domain beyond the provisional nature of knowledge. However, in the quest for truth one can still apprehend singular experiences: "Je ne sçay qu'en dire, mais il se sent par experience que tant d'interprétations dissipent la verité et la rompent" (III, 13, 1067) ("I do not know what to say about it, but it is evident from experience that so many interpretations disperse the truth and shatter it" [817]).

BODIES OF EXPERIENCE: MEDICINE AND THE LAW

In "De l'experience" knowledge based on experience renders scientific knowledge inadequate as a measure of "truth" in matters of the body. The specialized medical arts are divested of authority and treated with suspicion:

> Les arts qui promettent de nous tenir le corps en santé et l'ame en santé, nous promettent beaucoup, mais aussi n'en est il point qui tiennent moins ce qu'elles promettent. . . . On peut dire d'eus pour le plus, qu'ils vendent les drogues medecinales; mais qu'ils soyent medecins, cela ne peut on dire. (III, 13, 1079)

> The arts that promise to keep our body in health and our soul in health promise us much; but at the same time there are none that keep their promise less. . . . The most you can say for them is that they sell medicinal drugs; but that they are doctors you cannot say. (p. 827)]

Conceived as an overdetermined and formulaic science, medical discourse uncritically imposes definitions of health as disciplinary tools to which the body must conform. Instead of adhering to a system of medical taxonomies, the speaking body engages empirically with the passage of life, acquiring an exemplary value in its confrontation with self-knowledge: "Mon mestier et mon art, c'est vivre" (II, 6, 379) ("My trade and my art is living" [274]). A bad liturgical bedtime story of absolute health, medical science promises a cure based on the messianic advent of a scientific truth realized through nothing more than magical thinking. This infelicitous use of the imagination proposes general rules as a panecea for all cases of physical illness.

In opposition to doctrinal knowledge, which prescribes and rationalizes human biology through the invention of an abstract medical grammar, the experience of the body must be conceived of as a heuristic phenomenon capable of translating and measuring the vicissitudes of human health based on corporeal sensation: "Je ne me juge que par vray sentiment, non par discours" (III, 13, 1095) ("I judge myself only by actual sensation, not by reasoning" [840]). This experiential process transforms the body into a subject of knowledge functioning independently of scientific fact. As Judith Butler would later suggest in her reading of Freud, the body is interchangeable with the ego[6]

> Ainsi Platon avoit raison de dire que pour estre vray medecin, il seroit necessaire que celuy qui l'entreprendroit eust passé par toutes les maladies qu'il veut guarir et par tous les accidens et circonstances dequoy il doit juger. C'est raison qu'ils prennent la verole s'ils la veulent sçavoir penser. (III, 13, 1079)

> So Plato was right in saying that to become a true doctor, the candidate must have passed through all the illnesses that he wants to cure and all the accidents and circumstances that he is to diagnose. It is reasonable that he should catch the pox if he wants to know how to treat it. (827)

For Montaigne it is necessary to think with the body in order to apprehend illness. Appearing to represent more authentic proximity to Being, the body also represents the possibility of the impossible: a thinking body whose signifying powers project an ontology of the corporeal. As it is transcribed by language, the body functions as a vital force that serves as a mediating ground. It is not an object of observation to be considered in relation to the formulas proposed by science; rather, it becomes the object of self-knowledge and the matter of experience itself.

As with Montaigne's critique of the law, which foregrounds the disjunction between itself and its promise, medical discourse announces a determinism that cannot guaranteed the coincidence of the theoretical with its corporeal manifestations. Through its production of symptoms, the body detaches the name of an illness from what it is supposed to designate. Instead of confirming a universal medical principle, the symptom testifies to the singularity of the illness. In so doing, every symptom confirms the unrepeatablity of a corporeal experience, thereby excluding the body from categorization.

Nevertheless the body is not as autonomous as one might be led to believe. In a number of essays in the first book custom and habit foreground the body's overdetermined character, suggesting that it is a socially constructed entity bearing the mark of culture. The body is modified both physically and within the imagination by such external forces.

For Montaigne the very idea of physical health is similarly a relative phenomenon. In "De l'experience" the discourse of anality—which I have described elsewhere as "excremental writing"[7]—constitutes the fetishized object of health par excellence, in which the body metonymically represents the passage that is life. The alterity of the undissolved kidney stone translates in narrative form the decomposition that subsumes the body. It is played out metaphorically as an interior perception, a threat whose effect is corporeal pain: "C'est quelque grosse pierre qui foule et consomme la substance de mes roignons, et ma vie que je vuide peu à peu, non sans quelque naturelle douceur, comme un excrement hormais superflu et empeschant" (III, 13, 1095) ("It is some big stone that is crushing and consuming the substance of my kidneys, and my life that I am letting out little by little, not without some natural pleasure, as an excrement that is henceforth superfluous and a nuisance" [840]). By means of a curious reversal, the corporeal excretion of dead matter enables the human subject to give birth to a self that is no longer itself, for the emptying out of the other within the same enables the subject to speak. This self, which is constructed in what Montaigne calls "la matiere de mon livre" ("Au lecteur") "the matter of my book" [2]), is but "des excremens d'un vieil esprit" (III, 9, 946) ("some excrements of an aged mind" [721]).

Although the body becomes the lens through which modalities of identification are viewed, the body in the text can only be mediated through language. The language in question, however, does not conceive of the body as a mirror. Ironically, language produces the body that it subsequently claims to find prior to the constitution of signification. Accordingly, the identification given to the subject through the sensations of the body is linguistically fleshed out. Blurring the distinction between the biological and the psychological, the entry into poetic language precipitates a "fading of Being," suggesting that the embodiment of flesh is a tropological construction and not "natural" in any way. The represented body in this essay becomes a theater of passage, a space through which viscous liquids flow in the minutely depicted acts of urinating, defecating, and sweating. The speaking body dismembers itself in the act of essaying. Digestion and incorporation construct the self as a performative body that is the effect of the fiction of the digestive process as played out in the text.

The romance of the stone, the story of the passing of Montaigne's kidney stone, constitutes a fusion of the aggressive and erotic satisfaction experience in the act of emptying out. The metaphor of the corporeal evacuation of the kidney stone resurfaces in "De l'experience" and functions as a commentary on that same topos in "De la ressemblance des enfans aux peres" (II, 37) ("Of the Resemblance of Children to Fathers"). In the latter the biological body functions as a symbol of the fatal attachment to the father and the impetus to transcend it. Indeed, Pierre Eyquem has been marked by the illness of kidney stones and Michel, diminished by it, suffers as a victim of heredity. The real challenge will be to go beyond this "qualité pierreuse" (II, 37, 763) ("petrifying quality" [592]) and disengage from the figure of the paternal body. Antoine Compagnon has suggested that Montaigne's text envelops the name "Pierre" with symbolic mystery through homophonic and metaphoric iteration.[8] It is this process that allows the figure of the son to partake in a family romance liberated from the biological constraints produced by heredity—beyond, that is, such a "qualité pierreuse": "Il semble y avoir en la genealogie des Princes certains noms fatalement affectez" (I, 46, 276) ("Item, in the genealogy of princes there seem to be certain names earmarked by fate" [201]). By rendering an ontological matter a question of heredity and conceiving of it from a temporal perspective, the Montaignian text projects a geneological fatality and becomes the target of what might be described today as an oedipal drama:

> Quel monstre est-ce, que cette goute de semence dequoy nous sommes produits, porte en soy les impressions, non de la forme corporelle seulement, mais des pensemens et des inclinations de nos peres? Cette goute d'eau, où loge elle ce nombre infiny de formes? Et comme portent-elles ces ressemblances, d'un progrez si temeraire et si desreglé que l'arriere fils respondra à son bisayeul, le neveu à l'oncle. (II, 37, 763)

What a prodigy it is that the drop of seed from which we are produced bears in itself the impressions not only of the bodily form but of the thoughts and inclinations of our fathers! Where does that drop of fluid lodge this infinite number of forms? And how do they convey these resemblances with so heedless and irregular a course that the great-grandson will correspond to his great-grandfather, the nephew to the uncle? (578)

The challenge to the fatality of heredity is here unmistakable: "Mon pere haïssoit toute sorte de sauces; je les aime toutes" (III, 13, 1102) ("My father hated all kinds of sauces; I love them all" [846]).

The experience of the body suggests the necessary relationship between suffering and pleasure as a phenomenon reflecting the fundamentally complex nature of human experience. The essay itself surpasses the empirical, for the representation of the self in its dynamic and contradictory energy can only be realized through the power of the imaginary as an "acte à un seul personnage" (III, 9, 979) ("an act for one single character" [748]), who processes and reconfigures the sensations of the body. As a writerly practice, experience marks the link between the body and the imagination; it enables the desire for knowledge to function as an opening for something to come, "quelque chose se passera." This fable of omnipotence is one in which the physicality of the body, mediated by the figure of the stone, extends itself beyond the limits of its spatial constraints. What emerges in the essay is a rhetoric of empowerment based on the mode of the virtual as it is projected by the imagination: "Or je trete mon imagination le plus doucement que je puis et la deschargerois, si je pouvois, de toute peine et contestation. Il la faut secourir et flatter, et piper qui peut" (III, 13, 1090) ("Now I treat my imagination as gently as I can, and would relieve it, if I could, of all trouble and conflict. We must help it and flatter it, and fool it if we can" [836]). In this figural encounter the mind dispossesses the body. The care of the body becomes one of concern for the soul by allowing nature to partake of old age: "Il [the mind] dict que c'est pour mon mieux que j'ay la gravele: que les bastimens de mon aage ont naturellement à souffrir quelque goutiere" (III, 13, 1090) ("It tells me that it is for my own good that I have the stone; that buildings of my age must naturally suffer some leakage" [836]). Through the search for family resemblances between the body and a building of the same age, the mind's eye conflates the contingency of the kidney stone with the necessity of a general law of aging. The imaginary associates the meaning of bodily decline with a highly aestheticized identification. In this manner, the material of bodily experience becomes locked in a crypt that transforms the human psyche, and ultimately immobilizes the body, as in sleep: "Par tels argumens, et forts et foibles, comme Cicero le mal de sa vieillesse, j'essaye d'endormir et amuser mon imagination et gresser ses playes. Si elles s'empirent demain, demain nous y pourvoyerons d'autres eschapatoires" (III, 13, 1095) ("By such arguments, both strong and weak, I try to lull and beguile my imagination and salve its wounds. If they get worse tomorrow, tomorrow we shall provide other ways of escape" [839])

The project of Montaigne's narrative takes shape in the romance of the stone, whose reflexivity projects itself outside itself. The "gravelle" (kidney stone) representing the spectrality of the Father, problematizes the ontological status of the self. In this context, the essayist enters into a relationship with death and mourning through a metaphor that motivates the return of the repressed. If psychanalytically inspired identification operates according to the exigencies of incorporation and introjection, then the image of the kidney stone as blockage is a metaphor of what is killing the essayist within.

The passage of what might be termed "the phallic stone" becomes the necessary movement for a renewed sense of tranquillity. The consequences of corporeal blockage challenge the natural inclinations of libidinal energy and multiply the threat of disengagement from objects of desire. The possible eclipse of the desiring subject is forestalled by a strategic move that disembodies the pain and engages in an agonistic relationship with the figure of the disease itself:

Je donne grande authorité à mes desirs et propensions. Je n'ayme point à guarir le mal par le mal; je hay les remedes qui importunent plus que la maladie. D'estre subject à la cholique et subject à m'abstenir du plaisir de manger des huitres, ce sont deux maux pour un. Le mal nous pinse d'un costé, la regle de l'autre. Puisque on est au hazard de se mesconter, hazardons nous plustost à la suitte du plaisir. (III, 13, 1086)

I give great authority to my desires and inclinations. I do not like to cure trouble by trouble; I hate remedies that are more nuisance than the disease. To be subjected to the stone and subjected to abstaining from the pleasure of eating oysters, those are two troubles for one. The disease pinches us on one side, the rule on the other. Since there is a risk of making a mistake, let us risk it rather in pursuit of pleasure. (832)

The refusal to inhibit the appetite that is desire facilitates the acceptance of the natural voluptuousness of life: "Pour moy donc, j'ayme la vie et la cultive telle qu'il a pleu à Dieu nous l'octroier. . . . On fait tort à ce grand et tout puissant donneur de refuser son don, l'annuller et desfigurer" (I, 13, 1113) ("As for me, then, I love life and cultivate it just as God has been pleased to grant it to us. . . . We wrong that great and all-powerful Giver by refusing his gift, nullifying it, and disfiguring it" 854–55]). By evacuating the figure of the Father, the figure of the son may once again find satisfaction in the harmonious balance of body and mind and the cultivation of pleasure. The passage of the stone suggests an anteriority purged through the process of evacuation. It acquires an ethical dimension ironically consecrated by a Heavenly Father who has bequeathed life to us and who is perfection and fullness. The figure of the son can therefore eliminate the discomfort produced by the trace of the biological father.

Montaigne's description of this drama furnishes a poetic compensation for loss whereby art regulates the infelicities of nature. Interestingly, this text, which represents the imagination's drama, enables the body's degeneration to overcome its discomfort as a result of the kidney stone and, through this projection, to engender a poetry of epic proportions. The text presents a stoic drama that makes thinking the impossible "real" through the imaginary work of the body:

On te voit suer d'ahan, pallir, rougir, trembler, vomir jusques au sang, souffrir des contractions et convulsions estranges, degouter par foys de grosses larmes des yeux, rendre les urines espesses, noires, et effroyables, ou les avoir arrestées par quelque pierre espineuse et herissée qui te pouinct et escorche cruellement le col de la verge. (III, 13, 1091)

They see you sweat in agony, turn pale, turn red, tremble, vomit your very blood, suffer strange contractions and convulsions, sometimes shed great tears from your eyes, discharge thick, black, and frightful urine, or have it stopped up by some sharp rough stone that cruelly pricks and flays the neck of your penis. (836–37)

The desire to engage in magical thinking through the power of the imagination creates an exceptional situation in which the figure of thought transcends the constraints of life's limitations: "Mon esprit est propre à ce service: il n'a point faute d'apparences par tout; s'il persuadoit comme il presche, il me secourroit heureusement" (III, 13, 1090) "My mind is suited to this service; it has no lack of plausible reasons for all things. If it could persuade as well as it preaches, it would help me out very happily" [836]).

The text produces a drama in which the subject is represented through a dialogic interplay between second- and third-person discourse that translates showing through saying. Implicated in this drama is a reader-spectator whose gaze bears witness to the theatrical performance that is played out by the essayist as "metteur en scène." Here the figure of the essayist acquires a kind of omnipotence through the "playing out" of multiple roles. With this strategy of magical thinking, one may conceive of this rhetorical drama as the coming into being of contingency. Despite the multiple references the text makes to the ontological void within the self, this rhetorical maneuver permits the figure of the essayist—at least momentarily—to enjoy the illusory plenitude resulting from this sense of omnipotence.

In this passage the doubling of the self—the relation between the figure of the essayist and his other—enables the human body to attain a heroic level. Through this rhetorical mise-en-scène a simulation of the self emerges, predicated on forgetting that may be the result of learning to live with what one cannot avoid: "Il faut apprendre à souffrir ce qu'on ne peut eviter" (III, 13, 1089) ("We must learn to endure what we cannot avoid" [835]). The double represents what Freud once described as "an insurance against the destructon of the ego."[9]

If the drama of the passage of the stone is to be successful and offer a sense of peace, the representation of the self must, through the process of prosopopoeia, engage in a dialogic process that paradoxically foregrounds the imagination and functions as a textual conceit. In the following passage prosopopoeia gives a human voice to that which does not have one and suggests, through this image, how the subject puts into question the "I" as a self-identical entity:

Or je trete mon imagination le plus doucement que je puis et la deschargerois, si je pouvois, de toute peine et contestation. Il la faut secourir et flatter, et piper qui peut. Mon esprit est propre

à ce service: il n'a point faute d'apparences par tout; s'il persuadoit comme il presche, il me secourroit heureusement. (III, 13,
1090)

Now I treat my imagination as gently as I can, and would relieve
it, if I could, of all trouble and conflict. We must help it and
flatter it, and fool it if we can. My mind is suited to this service;
it has no lack of plausible reasons for all things. If it could persuade as well as it preaches, it would help me out very happily.
(836)

This anthropomorphic representation allows fear to foreclose on affect's movement, permitting the desiring albeit mortal subject to attain the state it needs: "Je la [life] jouys au double . . . du plus ou
moins d'application que nous y prestons" (III, 13, 1111) ("I enjoy it
twice as much as others, for the measure of enjoyment depends on
the greater or lesser attention that we lend it" [853]).

In order to recover the pleasure threatened by the unassimilable
difference that is the kidney stone, the subject in pain must excrete
the foreign matter through the imagination's ability to bring desire to
fruition. The narration of corporeal pain gives birth to the felicitous
consequences of a fabulous imagination:

Mais est-il rien doux au pris de cette soudaine mutation, quand
d'une douleur extreme je viens, par le vuidange de ma pierre, à
recouvrer comme d'un esclair la belle lumiere de la santé, si libre
et si pleine, comme il advient en nos soudaines et plus aspres
choliques? Y a il rien en cette douleur soufferte qu'on puisse con-
trepoiser au plaisir d'un si prompt amandement? De combien la
santé me semble plus belle apres la maladie, si voisine et si con-
tigue que je les puis recognoistre en presence l'une de l'autre en
leur plus haut appareil, où elles se mettent à l'envy, comme pour
se faire teste et contrecarre! (III, 13, 1093)

But is there anything so sweet as that sudden change, when from
extreme pain, by the voiding of my stone, I come to recover as
if by lightning the beautiful light of health, so free and so full,
as happens in our sudden and sharpest attacks of colic? Is there
anything in this pain we suffer that can be said to counterbal-

ance the pleasure of such sudden improvement? How much more beautiful health seems to me after the illness, when they are so near and contiguous that I can recognize them in each other's presence in their proudest array, when they vie with each other, as if to oppose each other squarely! (838)

In the context of this drama, Montaigne's essay blurs the parameters of the pleasure-pain opposition, a metamorphosis of pain into pleasure, and vice versa. The excitement elicited by pain in the romance of the stone functions in the service of an evacuatory "end pleasure" that leads Montaigne from evacuation to ejaculation. By conjoining the metaphor of light with pleasure, the text demonstrates how vision becomes a trope for good health. Accordingly, light acquires a privileged status as a signifier of the soul.

In the romance of the stone one witnesses the sexualization of pain through the power of the imagination. The representation of pleasure in the practice of the self-portraiture translates the experience of the body's vulnerability. Nevertheless, the trope of the stoic mask, inscribed in this rhetorical drama, suggests how imagination, far beyond the power of reason, can construct an image of the body as the signifier of desire: "Et puis, combien est-ce de contenter la fantasie! A mon opinion cette piece là importe de tout, aumoins au delà de toute autre. Les plus griefs et ordinaires maux sont ceux que la fantasie nous charge" (III, 13, 1087) "And then how much it is to satisfy the imagination! In my opinion that faculty is all-important, at least more important than any other. The most grievous and ordinary troubles are those that fancy loads upon us" [833]).

The drama of the kidney stone creates a crossing over of aggressive and erotic satisfaction in the act of emptying out, such that a continuity is established between pain and the body's libidinal energy. The body, represented as engaged in a performative function, dismembers itself in the act of narration and engages in a process that challenges the limit between inside and outside. The language of the text mirrors an ontological possibility that the writing subject wishes to enact. In the syntax of the fable, pain is metonymically related to masochistic pleasure through a reference to Socrates' itchy legs:

Lors que Socrates, apres qu'on l'eust deschargé de ses fers, sentit la friandise de cette demangeson que leur pesanteur avoit causé

en ses jambes, il se resjouyt à considerer l'estroitte alliance de
la douleur à la volupté, comme elles sont associées d'une liai-
son necessaire, si qu'à tours elles se suyvent et s'entr-engendrent.
(III, 13, 1093)

When Socrates, after being relieved of his irons, felt the relish of
the itching that their weight had caused in his legs, he rejoiced
to consider the close alliance between pain and pleasure, how
they are associated by a necessary link, so that they follow and
engender each other in turn. (838)

Like the relationship of the stone to Montaigne's aging body, the removal of the chains in which Socrates was imprisoned suggests that
submission to the infelicities of corporeal decline eventually produces
erotic delight. In this context, sexuality is depicted as the effect of
the body's exercise in power over the imagination and the paradoxical logic behind the act of writing. Medically speaking the "gravelle"
can produce impotence, but the passage of the stone imparts to the
desiring subject a second life and a transcendence of "la maladie
pierreuse."

In passing from what Jules Brody has described as the "degree
zero" of pain to the relief produced by the removal of the chains, the
text suggests the pleasure associated with masochism and the narcissistic delight derived from displeasure.[10] The emergence of pleasure
results from a certain fragmentation of the imaginary coherence of
the body and a challenging of its boundaries. Montaigne's text creates a paradoxical relationship between pain and pleasure and the
realization of fuller vitality. The way toward a greater access to desire
passes by way of the de-sedimentation of the body, which ascribes
to the illness an exemplary function. Like the sex act itself, the passage of the stone dramatizes a deathlike experience involving the loss
of self, whereby the symbolic expenditure of dead matter paradoxically leads to a continuation of life. The logic of what the French call
"le petit mort" recapitulates the previously discussed excremental
logic.

The romance of the stone thus encapsulates a certain ironic burden toward change and a call to live on the edge, to will a little pain
in order to encounter pleasure: " Mes reins ont duré un aage sans
alteration; il y en a tantost un autre qu'ils ont changé d'estat. Les
maux ont leur periode comme les biens; à l'avanture est cet accident

à sa fin" (III, 13, 1093) ("My kidneys lasted an age without weakening; it will soon be another age since their condition changed. Evils have their period like good things; perhaps this ailment is coming to an end" [838]). Viewed as an allegory, the text depicts a way of confronting life so that it can support the most extreme intensities as a hankering to taste ("essay") the diversity of the human experience.

It is interesting to consider the romance of the stone in what might be described as one of a series of details regarding Montaigne's daily life. In the narrative of the fallen tooth, realized through the topos of the *disjecta membra,* the present is fractured as it is described metaphorically in the testimony of the remainder. The writer is put in the position of a fallen present and removed from the illusory fullness of the past: "Voilà une dent qui me vient de choir, sans douleur, sans effort: c'estoit le terme naturel de sa durée. Et cette partie de mon estre et plusieurs autres sont desjà mortes, . . . des plus actives et qui tenoient le premier rang pendant la vigueur de mon aage" (III, 13, 1101) ("Here is a tooth that has just fallen out, without pain, without effort; that was the natural term of its duration. Both that part of my being and several others are already dead, others half dead, even some of the most active, which held the highest rank in my vigorous prime" [845]). The extruded kidney stones, like the fallen tooth, function as emblems of the reality of death. The body in decomposition paradoxically becomes a life-giving force in the very process of decline. The spectrality of the figure of the corpse projects itself onto the trope of the body and thus enables life and death to intersect and dissipate simultaneously: "La mort se mesle et confond par tout à nostre vie" (III, 13, 1102) ("Death mingles and fuses with our life throughout" [846]). Haunted by the impersonality of death, the "I" had been contaminated by the impurity of the excremental matter. The narrative of the fallen tooth can only be realized within a context that restricts the impact of loss and reconceives it as a synecdochic process: "Quelle bestise sera-ce à mon entendement de sentir le saut de cette cheute, desjà si avancée, comme si elle estoit entiere? Je ne l'espere pas" (III, 13, 1101–2) ("How stupid it would be of my mind if it were to feel the last leap of this decline, which is already so far advanced, as acutely as if it were the whole fall. I hope this will not happen" [845]). Here, somewhat magically, the imagination triumphs, This narrative puts death in its place and rescues it from indifference.

The poetry of difference through which the romance of the stone is transcribed suggests that the desire to accept life as it is in each separate but discrete moment as it is represented in the disjunctive nature of Montaigne's life narrative. The ontological impossibility of plenitude maintains the energy of desire and permits a coming to terms with the oxymoronic and fractured nature of existence. Desire, exercised through the power of the imagination, enables the reinvigoration of life, with enjoyment depending on the attention we lend to it. If pleasure is something that is allowed to take shape freely, it is because desire inhabits a space that prevents satisfaction from bringing the self into its own. "Les autres sentent la douceur d'un contentement et de la prosperité; je la sens ainsi qu'eux, mais ce n'est pas en passant et glissant" (III, 13, 1112) ("Others feel the sweetness of some satisfaction and of prosperity; I feel it as they do, but it is not in passing and slipping by" [854]).

THE SOCRATIC OTHER

Why does Montaigne's essay conclude with a critique of Socrates? To be sure, in Plato's *Symposium* Socrates is an enigma in matters of love.[11] He is angered by Alcibiade's homoerotic behavior yet admits that he is attracted to him. In his *Memorabilia* Xenophon, who claims to possess a certain degree of intimacy with Socrates, insists that this satyrlike creature was conflicted and accordingly was forced to choose celibacy.[12] He not only exercised strict self-control where libidinal drives were concerned but also demanded that absolute restraint be observed with respect to the pleasure he experienced with "the Beautiful Ones." Socrates is here depicted as an enemy of sexual pleasure who appropriates for himself a particularly atypical Hellenic stance in matters of love.

Socrates chooses to become the victim of a self-imposed sexual blindness by subscribing to the logic of reason self. However, it is the very force of reason and the abstinence before the menacing power of libidinal drives that ultimately lead to the negation of desire. Montaigne's text suggests that Socrates' demon functions as the figure of an unhappy consciousness that undercuts the pleasure principle and suppresses libidinal impulses:

C'est folie!: au lieu de se transformer en anges, ils se transforment en bestes; au lieu de se hausser, ils s'abattent. Ces humeurs

transcendentes m'effrayent, comme les lieux hautains et inacces-
sibles; et rien ne m'est à digerer fascheux en la vie de Socrates
que ses ecstases et ses demoneries, rien si humain en Platon que
ce pourquoy ils disent qu'on l'appelle divin. (III, 13, 1115)

That is madness: instead of changing into angels, they change
into beasts; instead of raising themselves, they lower themselves.
These transcendental humors frighten me, like lofty and inacces-
sible places; and nothing is so hard for me to stomach in the life
of Socrates as his ecstasies and possessions by his daemon, nothing is so human in Plato as the qualities for which they say he is
called divine. (856)

Throughout this essay desire is represented by tropes of appetite,
by analogy with hunger and thirst. In this respect, like the ancient
Athenians it depicts a longing for a desired object. What Socrates
experiences, according to Montaigne, is *eros* and not *philia.*, The
paralyzing effect of Socrates's inner voice forecloses the possibility of
erotic engagement.

Montaigne's description of Socrates'denial stands in contradistinc-
tion to the choreographics of desire depicted in this essay, where the
body's needs are represented as succumbing to the magical thinking of
the mind's desire. Here Socrates' resistance to eroticism excludes him
from the community of lovers. Adherence to a higher principle ironically transforms the quest for perfection into the possibility of corporeal pleasure and the suppression of the human. Montaigne's text
suggests that the acceptance of the instinctive drives within the self,
through the process of experience, might erase the distinction between
the divine and its diametrical opposite. Socrates'attempt to reject the
human allows him to believe that he can contain within the self what
he perceives as menacing. Once Socrates has constructed an image
of an ethical life, he remains imprisoned within a fantasy that leads
him astray. Montaigne's reference to Socrates's dilemma enables us to
see that if we are able to go beyond the boundaries of self-imposed
limitations, through the coming to terms with self-knowledge, we
might in fact achieve a sense of tranquillity in accepting the contingencies of life.

By granting access to the erotic, Montaigne's text foregrounds
the hospitality that Plato considers the soul of philosophical engage-

ment. Recall that the oracle at Delphi named Socrates the wisest of men to the extent that he knew the nature of his ignorance. In a way, Montaigne anticipates Nietzsche, who describes how morality turns against us and redirects it against ourselves. Within this context, the constitution of the Socratic subject is realized in terms of regulation. However, this ethical regulation of bodily impulse, motivated by the power of the demonic, is itself a desiring activity. In order to engage in the miscognition of self-knowledge, the Socratic subject sublates difference into sameness. This ontological move is regarded as a denial of difference. Transcendence as a strategy of concealment projects a fictive self-identifical subject that becomes, in fact, other than itself. Perhaps the Montaignian commentary on the inner voice of Socrates is meant to demystify the role of his personal demons as a measure of truth warning against an improper act. This critique of Socrates' demons enables the discovery of a possibility, an openness to the corporeal pleasures of life. They are motivated from within the mind's deeper strata, which is so far from reason that it might paradoxically constitute sanity itself.

Unlike Socrates, who performs sublation before all earthly forms in the name of an abstract ideal, the essayist appropriates the positon of Alcibiades as a counterexample in his refusal to look away from the world and reject the metaphysical explanation concerning the death of desire: "J'en suis là comme Alcibiades, que je ne me representeray jamais, que je puisse, à homme qui decide de ma teste, où mon honneur et ma vie depende de l'industrie et soing de mon procureur plus que de mon innocence" (III, 13, 1071) ("My position, like that of Alcibiades, is this: I shall never turn myself over, if I can help it, to a man who can dispose of my head, where my honor and my life depend on the skill and diligence of my attorney more than on my innocence" [820]). The implied reference here is to Socrates's trial, where the philosopher chose imprisonment and death in the name of a higher form of virtue before the accusation of having corrupted youth. Alcibiades, known for his insolent behavior and lawlessness, conversely finds liberty in transgressive behavior. Accused of a plan to overthrow Athenian democracy, he surreptitiously escaped judgment and fled to Sparta, where he betrayed Athens'military secrets and was tried in absentia. Montaigne's trial ("essai") becomes the work of the essay, whereby the essayist shall become Socrates perfected.

As Kaja Silverman has suggested in her analysis of Plato's *Symposium*, the experience of the lover, as exemplified by the figure of Socrates, undergoes a process of "deindividuation" whereby the "non-sensory spectacle of the Beautiful subjects" commits desire to plenitude by the "negation of phenomenal forms."[13] Socrates' self-imprisonment is the result of becoming one with an ideal that he describes as "wholly perfect and free of all troubles." Unlike Socrates, Alcibiades takes pleasure in not satisfying the desire Plato described in the *Republic* as a boundless ambition to manage affairs and Thucydides referred to as an insatiable need for prestige. Ironically, the essayist who describes himself as "encore vierge de procés" (III, 10, 1017) ("till virgin of lawsuits" [779]) remains committed to the trial that is the essay and yet paradoxically passes judgment on Socrates of what must be: "Ce que Socrates feit sur sa fin, d'estimer une sentence d'exil pire qu'une sentence de mort, contre soy, je ne seray, à mon advis, jamais ny si cassé ny si estroitement habitué en mon païs et je le feisse" (III, 9, 973) ("What Socrates did near the end of his life, in considering a sentence of exile against him worse than a sentence of death, I shall never, I think, be so broken or so strictly attached to my own country as to do" [743]). For the claustrophobia derived from the imprisonment in a place that is one—"tant de gens clouez à un quartier de ce royaume" (III, 13, 1072) ("so many people, nailed down to one section of this kingdom" [821])—motivates the desire to effect a distanciation and foreclose on the possibility of a rule of law declaring what we "properly" are. Like Alcibiades, the figure of the essayist engages in an openness of being: "Si celles [the laws] que je sers me menassoient seulement le bout du doigt, je m'en irois incontinent en trouver d'autres, où que ce fut" (III, 13, 1072) ("If those that I serve threatened even the tip of my finger, I should instantly go and find others, wherever it might be" [821]). Interestingly, being unable to reject the cultivation of the body, the Montaignian subject engages in a more exemplary wisdom than that of Socrates: "Moy, qui ne manie que terre à terre, hay cette inhumaine sapience qui nous veut rendre desdaigneux et ennemis de la culture du corps" (III, 13, 1106) ("I, who operate only close to the ground, hate that inhuman wisdom that would make us disdainful enemies of the cultivation of the body" [849]).

To be sure, the essay suggests that nature is anything but normative. By welcoming the irregularities of the rhythm of life, Montaigne is able to be "at home" in difference. The essayist shows us that the impossibility of life follows the impossible logic of hospitality, becoming both "hote" (host) and "hote" (guest). Montaigne nevertheless shows us that by accepting this impossible logic, one is able to imagine the experience of life:

> J'ay pris, comme j'ay dict ailleurs, bien simplement et cruement pour mon regard ce precepte ancien: que nous ne sçaurions faillir à suivre nature, que le souverain precepte c'est de se conformer à elle. Je n'ay pas corrigé, comme Socrates, par force de la raison mes complexions naturelles, et n'ay aucunement troublé par art mon inclination. Je me laisse aller, comme je suis venu. (III, 12, 1059)

> As I have said elsewhere, I have very simply and crudely adopted for my own sake this ancient precept: that we cannot go wrong by following Nature, that the sovereign precept is to conform to her. I have not, like Socrates, corrected my natural disposition by force of reason, and have not troubled my inclination at all by art. I let myself go as I have come. (811)

By interrogating the truths of Socrates, Montaigne's text opts for the nobler engagement with the human in place of the divine. In Plato's *Republic* those who engage in the quest for pleasure inhabit the so-called city of pigs, and in the *Symposium* bodily pleasure is described by Socrates as animalistic and "of no account." On the contrary, for Montaigne the physical side of existence, based on the sensations of experiential knowledge, derives from the desire to "know thyself" even in what may be perceived as the most unappealing of bodily functions: "Et au plus eslevé throne du monde si ne sommes assis que sus nostre cul" (III, 13, 1115) ("And on the loftiest throne in the world we are still sitting only on our own rump" [857]). In this essay the corporeal and the spiritual converge and demonstrate that pleasure—"intellectuellement sensible et sensiblement intellectuel" (III, 13, 1107)("intellectually sensual, sensually intellectual" [850]) —can permeate all aspects of life as it warns against ignoring the stirrings of the body: "Je hay qu'on nous ordonne d'avoir l'esprit aus nues, pendant que nous avons le corps à table" (III, 13, 1107) ("I hate to have people order us to keep our minds in the clouds while our bodies are at table" [850]).

In the course of the essay a particularly pertinent reference is made in which the essayist compares himself to the character Quartillia in Petronius's *Satyricon*.[14] Here the text brings Montaigne into contact with an earlier self for whom desire is the result of a fatal attraction:

> Et me suis jeune . . . presté autant licentieusement et inconsiderée-ment qu'autre au desir qui me tenoit saisi. . . . Il y a du malheur certes, et du miracle, à confesser en quelle foiblesse d'ans je me rencontray premierement en sa subjection. Ce fut bien rencontre, car ce fut long temps avant l'aage de choix et de cognoissance. Il ne me souvient point de moy de si loing. Et peut on marier ma fortune à celle de Quartilla, qui n'avoit point memoire de son fillage. (III, 13, 1087)

> I lent myself as licentiously and thoughtlessly as any other man to the desire that held me in its grip. . . . It is certainly dis-tressing and miraculous to confess at what a tender age I first chanced to fall under its subjection. It was indeed by chance, for it was long before the age of choice and knowledge. I do not remember about myself so far back. And my lot may be cou-pled with that of Quartilla, who had no memory of her maiden-hood. (833)

Priestess of Priapus, the phallic god, Quartilla had an erotic appetite so unlimited that she could not remember a time when she had been a virgin. In the section of the *Satyricon* that deals with the exploits of Quartilla one learns that Encolpius and his companions are accused by Quartilla of illegally observing the rites of Priapus. The temple of Priapus, where Quartilla reigns, is the place where such violent sexual rituals as sodomy are performed. Ironically, the punishment of the two young protagonists makes them become the object of what they had secretly observed. Anally raped by a Priapus figure, they find pleasure in their pain only when the object of aggression is with-drawn just prior to sexual climax, thereby frustrating the Priapus fig-ure and the boys alike.

What emerges in Petronius's tales is the manner in which sexual-ity is controlled by a dominant female figure whose insatiable desire is projected onto effeminate men and the Priapus figure alike. As in Plato's *Symposium,* the Quartilla episode in the *Satyricon* is organized around a banqueting scene. In the context of the latter, a male prostitute enters the house and chants:

> Come hither, come hither, you faggots so frisky,
> Come running, come prancing, come skipping here briskly;
> Come bring your soft thighs, agile bottoms, lewd hands,
> Your flaccid old eunuch from Delian land.

Inhabiting the island of Delos, Apollo is here associated with castration because of his support of doctors. Under Apollo's guidance, it is suggested, a male subject emerges who is impaired, and viewed as other. Dating back to Assyrian law (1300–1100 B.C.E.), the sodomized male was often associated with eunuchs. The sodomite's sexuality, was punished by castration, thereby rendering subjectivity as the consequence of a missing part.

The figure of Quartilla acts as a reference point whereby male sexuality and passivity conjoin with an omnipotent female, who herself becomes a phallic other. Quartilla may lack the penis, but she is indeed in possession of the phallus, both figuratively and literally. Quartilla's signature is imprinted on the male body and functions as a coitus interuptus that cannot be forgotten. This is achieved not through fulfillment but rather through interruption, of lack of fulfillment. The incompletion of the corporeal act might be conceived as haunting the body with a promise of a new sexual image. Beginning not with plenitude but with loss, fantasy, which Jean Laplanche and J. B. Pontalis describe as an "imaginary scene [. . .] representing the fulfillment of a wish,"[15] offers the promise of an other that one might become. However, the sacrifice of male sexuality here is one that cannot be mourned; it precludes subject formation and leaves an indelible corporeal scar.

In order to disavow the loss of passionate attachments, the subject is constituted by a free-floating desire that is destined never to be fulfilled. The Priapus figure as well as these victims of homoerotic violence are psychically subjugated as a result of loss. The loss of the same-sex object precludes the very possibility of overcoming mourning. By averting the danger of sustained sexual experience, the coitus interruptus in Petronius's narrative defers the satisfaction of the desiring subject. The present absence of the love object is paradoxically necessary for keeping desire in play.

Through its rhetorical acrobatics Montaigne's text engages in modalities of identification in which sexuality is figured as a phenomenon whose borders remain in flux. The mobility of desire produces a series of identifications that undermine the possibility of assigning definition to questions of gender. Through the reference to Quartillia there is an identification with the figure of a non-identical subject. In a way, by marrying his fortune to that of Quartilla Montaigne, like Aristophanes in the *Symposium,* foregrounds the myth that humans were composed of three sexes: male, female, and male-female. Acccording to Aristophanes, humans were split into halves; for him eros reflected the desire to reconstitute that broken whole. For Aristophanes, however, if this longing were to be satisfied, the erotic would disappear. Eros, therefore, is the desire for what we lack.

In the Quartilla narrative Montaigne suggests a manner of being in which alterity cannot be domesticated. In linking his fate to that of Quartilla, the essayist identifies with a woman who acts like a man and is responsible for the deflowering of young men. Having situated himself under the sign of female desire, he also places himself in an endless quest of it. Quartilla's insatiable desire is projected onto these young men, who become subjugated to a sexuality that is motivated as much by excess as it is by lack. Quartilla represents sexual difference, which males both lack and possess; she is capable of inflicting a punishment whose term knows no end. In assuming the function of a feminized phallus, Quartilla acts for the essayist as the signifier of a fatal attraction.

Interestingly, the Quartilla reference in Montaigne's text is followed by a quote from an epigram by the Latin poet Martial that relates some homoerotic fantasies: "Hence goatish smells, precocious hair / A beard to make my mother stare." The Martial quote is transcribed with an important modification; a significant portion of the epigram is truncated when it is inscribed in the essay. In transposing these lines from Martial's epigram, Montaigne adds the personal pronoun "mae," which Floyd Gray sees as "diverting it from its original homosexual content . . . to refer to his own sexual, presumably heterosexual precociousness."[16]

The beard that makes the mother marvel—presumably Montaigne's, since there is a shift in the use of the personal pronoun in the essay—points to the consequences of a fatal act, like the one imposed on Quartilla and which she subsequently inflicted on adolescents. The truncated quote from Martial's epigram in Montaigne's essay circumscribes the question of homoerotic desire. In the case of the Quartilla narrative and in the truncated epigram from Martial masculinity is not defined in opposition to heterosexual love. On the contrary, the boy described in Martial's text realizes his manhood, a difference within the order of the same, as the result of the touch of another man's hand. Manliness is not necessarily an outgrowth of heterosexual desire and it is not something that is overdetermined by sexual preference:

> That you rub snow-white Galaesus's soft skin with your hard mouth, that you lie with naked Ganymede—it's too much, who denies it? But let it be enough. Refrain at least from stirring their groins with your fornicating hand. Where smooth boys are concerned, the hand is a worse offender than the cock; fingers make and precipitate manhood. Hence come the goat and rapid hairs and a beard to make a mother marvel, hence baths in broad daylight displease. Nature divided the male: one part was created for girls, one part for men. Use your part.[17]

If manhood (figured in the images of a goatlike odor and facial hair) can be viewed as the consequence of touching, it is because it represents the possibility of a different relation to sameness. The ellipses in Montaigne's text suggest that homoerotic desire can acquire equanimity with heteroeroticism. Martial's text suggests an otherness that cannot be reduced to the alterity of another person. Nature may have "divided the male," but it has done so by challenging the distinction between sameness and difference. Accordingly, by inscribing homoerotic desire within the order of nature, what might be perceived as the realm of the improper becomes utterly proper. To be sure, sexual preference is more than a social differential: "Je la sçauray assez quand je la sentiray." (III, 13, 1073) "I shall know it well enough when I feel it" [821]). As in Montaigne's text, an image emerges in which the imagination allows the body to speak desire and in the process reveal both the collapse and the maintenance of distinctions.

In a way both Petronius's and Martial's texts mirror Montaigne's in its disavowal of the absoluteness of identity. It acknowledges, through suggestion, the ability of the mind to imagine other forms of pleasure by transforming how sexuality has been known. Through these intertextual references, categories such as man, woman, male, and female, are destabilized. This process suggests that the relationship between sexual preference and gender has no permanent ground. The signs of gender cannot be constrained by the imposition of convention. Beyond that, through these references Montaigne's text reveals how in the course of the essay sex and gender are discursively constructed and challenge the idea of manliness. As in the case of the rhetorical drama constituting the romance of the stone, identity is contingent and subject to the discursive performance that challenges ontologically petrified representations of the self: "La plus part de nos vacations sont farcesques. 'Mundus universus exercet histrionam' Il faut jouer deuement nostre rolle, mais comme rolle d'un personnage emprunté (III, 10, 1011) ("Most of our occupations are low comedy. The whole world plays a part [Petronius]. We must play our part duly, but as the part of a borrowed character" [773]).

To be sure, the essay on experience is about eroticism and narcissistic delight in the abandonment of the self to life as it unravels in all its inconsistencies. The Horatian text that signals the end of the essay is a prayer to the god Apollo that seeks comfort in the language of poetry. Apollo, god of music, poetry, science and philosophy, also has a role as the god of healing. In Greek culture Sophia (wisdom) refers to rhetorical skill; for the sophist, wisdom was associated with poetry, and it was separate from what Montaigne later referred to as science. In Plato's *Republic* the notion of *philos eros,* unlike erotic pursuit and capture, includes intellectual intercourse to produce "intelligence and truth." However, the truth that the intelligence puts in play in Montaigne's essay suggests that the imagination lies at the heart of human experience and that the body enables the human subject to give birth to sensations upon which the drives of the imagination may work. Moreover, the language of poetry reflects its inability to formulate the proper; it points to an ungroundedness whereby a subject can only become a subject through the alterity that sets desire in motion. The language of poetry referred to in this essay constitutes what Philippe Lacoue-Labarthe has described as an "an upsetting relation to what is upset, in being, in the direction of no-thingness."[18] Montaigne writes: "Le poete, dict Platon, assis sur le trepied des Muses, verse de furie tout ce qui luy vient en la bouche . . . et luy eschappe des choses de diverse couleur, de contraire substance et d'un cours rompu" (III, 9, 995) ("The poet, says Plato, seated on the tripod of the Muses, pours out in a frenzy whatever comes into his mouth, . . . and from him escape things of different colors and contradictory substance in an intermittent flow" [761]). Montaigne's essay engenders a poetry of everyday life even in its banalities that seeks to find pleasure in the art of experience.

If, as has been suggested, the essay reflects an entry into poetic language, it is because the rhythm of the text precipitates a "fading of being" described earlier by Montaigne as a "condition mixte": "C'est une absolue perfection, et comme divine, de scavoyr jouyr loiallement de son estre" (III, 13, 1115) ("It is an absolute perfection and virtually divine to know how to enjoy our being rightfully" [857]). Could the desire to accept life in the singularity of each moment be an oblique reference to the need to transcend absolutism in order to come to terms with the oxymoronic nature of human existence?

> Je ne vay pas desirant qu'elle eust à dire la necessité de boire et de manger, et me sembleroit faillir non moins excusablement de desirer qu'elle l'eut double ("sapiens divitiarum naturalium quaesitor acerrimus"), ny que nous nous sustentissions mettant seulement en la bouche un peu de cette drogue par laquelle Epimenides se privoit d'appetit et se maintenoit, ny qu'on produisit stupidement des enfans par les doigts ou par les talons, ains, parlant en reverence, plus tost qu'on les produise encore voluptueusement par les doigts et par les talons, ny que le corps fut sans desir et sans chatouillement. Ce sont plaintes ingrates et iniques. J'accepte de bon coeur, et recognoissant, ce que nature a faict pour moy, et m'en agrée et m'en loue. (III, 13, 1113)

I do not go about wishing that it should lack the need to eat and drink, and it would seem to me no less excusable a failing to wish that need to be doubled. The wise man is the keenest searcher for natural treasures [Seneca]. Nor do I wish that we should sustain ourselves by merely putting into our mouths a little of that drug by which Epimenides took away his appetite and kept himself alive; nor that we should beget children insensibly with our fingers or our heels, but rather, with due respect, that we could also beget them voluptuously with our fingers and heels; nor that the body should be without desire and without titillation. Those are ungrateful and unfair complaints. I accept with all my heart and with gratitude what nature has done for me, and I am pleased with myself and proud of myself that I do. (854–55)

To be sure, to follow what nature has given us is to taste the variety of life by engaging in the art of experience. The symptom of what was previously described as "universal diversity" may be found in the differences within the self, which in the practice of the essay acquires a certain exemplarity.

At the end of *Seminar VII* Lacan proposes an ethics contrary to what has traditionally been thought of as the moral life, one that was anticipated by Montaigne. Like the essayist, Lacan suggests that it is through desire rather than its denial that humans may acquire virtue by conjoining the erotic with the ethical: "The only thing of which one can be guilty is having given ground relative to one's desire".[19]

Montaigne's text suggests that access to the so-called authenticity of being is an impossibility. Since the self is always already in the process of becoming, it remains diametrically opposed to Platonic metaphysics. In this context, wisdom can only be derived from the variety of experiences and the multiple ways in which we conduct our lives: "Composer nos meurs est nostre office, non pas composer des livres, et gaigner, non pas des batailles et provinces, mais l'ordre et tranquillité à notre conduite" (III, 13, 1108) ("To compose our character is our duty, not to compose books, and to win, not battles and provinces, but order and tranquillity in our conduct" [850–51]).

As in the practice of the essay itself, Montaigne's text foregrounds the corporeal metaphor of taste, a synecdochic representation of bodily functions, which acts as an invitation to partake of the banquet that is the instability of life: "J'ay assez vescu, pour mettre en compte l'usage qui m'a conduict si loing. Pour qui en voudra gouster, j'en ay faict l'essay, son eschançon (III, 13, 1080) ("I have lived long enough to give an account of the practice that has guided me so far. For anyone who wants to try it I have tasted it like his cupbearer" [827]). To be sure, the archaeology of the text shapes "experience" as a multiplicity of textual commentaries that are repeated and turned against themselves in much the same way that the multiple "Socrates" figures in Plato's texts move through a variety of sites that ultimately undercut the logic of institutionalized "Platonism." The act of essaying thus paradoxically de-subjugates subjectivity and in the process transcribes an alterity in which the so-called singularity of the natural is overcome. In the writing of the essay the text engages with the philosophical, which in the end becomes a responsibility exceeding the constraints of scientific knowledge.

NOTES

INTRODUCTION

1. Michel de Montaigne, *Les Essais,* 2 vols., ed. Pierre Villey (Paris: Presses Universitaires de France, 1965); Michel de Montaigne, *Complete Works,* trans. Donald M. Frame (Stanford, Calif.: Stanford University Press, 1957). Henceforth all parenthetical text references will be to these editions.

2. Michel Foucault, "Theatrum Philosophicum," *Critique* 282 (November 1970): 908. On the relationship of the visual to theory, see Rodolphe Gasché, "Theatrum Thorecticum," in *The Honor of Thinking: Critique, Theory, Philosophy* (Stanford, Calif.: Stanford University Press, 2007), 188–208.

3. Edmond Huguet, *Dictionnaire de la langue française du seizième siècle,* 7 vols. (Paris: Librairie Arienne Edouard Champion, 1925–67), available online at http://www.champion-electronique.net.

4. On Montaigne and the imagination, see the following: Tom Conley, "An Allegory of Prudence," *Montaigne Studies* 4 (1992): 156–79; idem, "Montaigne Moqueur: 'Virgile' and Its Geographies of Gender," in *High Anxiety: Masculinity in Crisis in Early Modern France,* ed. Kathleen P. Long (Kirksville, Mo.: Truman State University Press, 2001), 93–106; Claude-Gilbert Dubois, *L'Imaginaire de la Renaissance* (Paris: Presses Universitaires de France, 1985); Ann Hartle, *Michel de Montaigne: Accidental*

Philosopher (Cambridge: Cambridge University Press, 2003); John D. Lyons, "Ethics, Imagination, and Surprise," *Montaigne Studies* 14 (2002): 95–204; Glyn Norton, *Montaigne and the Introspective Mind* (The Hague, Neth.: Mouton, 1975); John O'Brien, "Reasoning with the Senses: The Humanist Imagination," *South Central Review* 10, no. 2 (1993): 3–20; Dora E. Polachek, "Montaigne and the Imagination: The Dynamics of Power and Control," *Le Parcours des "Essais": Montaigne, 1588–1988*, ed. Marcel Tetel and G. Mallary Masters (Paris: Aux Amateurs de Livres, 1989), 135–45; Jean Starobinski, "Imagination," in *Actes de l'association de littérature comparée*, ed. François Jost (The Hague, Neth.: Mouton, 1966), 952–63. On the concept of the imagination in the Renaissance, see Gianfrancesco Pico della Mirandola, *De Imaginatione* (Venice, 1501; Strasbourg, 1507); trans. Antoine de Baif as *Traité de l'imagination* (Paris: Weschel, 1557).

5. Randle Cotgrave, *A Dictionarie of the French and English Tongues* (1611; reprint, Columbia: University of South Carolina Press, 1968).

6. Richard Regosin, *Montaigne's Unruly Brood: Textual Engendering and the Challenge to Paternal Authority* (Berkeley: University of California Press, 1996), p. 84.

7. See Murray Wright Bundy, *The Theory of the Imagination in Classical and Medieval Thought*, University of Illinois Studies in Language and Literature, 12 (Urbana: University of Illinois Press, 1927).

8. See Aristotle, "On the Soul," in *The Complete Works of Aristotle*, Bollingen Series, 71, ed. Jonathan Barnes (Princeton, N.J.: Princeton University Press, 1984), 641–92. See also Malcolm Schofield, "Aristotle on the Imagination," in *Essays on Aristotle's "De Anima,"* ed. Martha C. Nussbaum and Amélie Oksenberg Rorty (Oxford: Oxford University Press, 1992), 641–92.

9. Pierre de La Primaudaye regards the imagination from an anti-Aristotelian perspective. See *Suite de l'Académie Française* (Paris: Guillaume Chaudière, 1580).

10. John Lyons, *Before Imagination* (Stanford, Calif.: Stanford University Press, 2005).

11. On the themes of metamorphosis and motion, see the following: Jean Starobinski, *Montaigne en mouvement* (Paris: Gallimard, 1982); François Rigolot, *Les Métamorphoses de Montaigne* (Paris: Presses Universitaires de France, 1988); Michel Jeanneret, *Perpetuum Mobile: Métamorphoses des corps et des œuvres, de Vinci à Montaigne* (Paris: Macula, 1997) [English: *Perpetuel Motion: Transformative Shapes in the Renaissance from da Vinci to Montaigne*, trans. Nina Pollen (Baltimore: Johns Hopkins University Press, 2001)]. One of the most compelling analyses of the kinetic nature of the *Essays* is presented by Tom Conley: "Poetic fragments of a 'primary' process of association break the finished look of a prose into arcane figures, or miniature 'testes' letters that jumble and move indiscriminately or atom-

istically about the essays. An unconscious is glimpsed through the gaps and crannies opened by the visible art of writing." *The Graphic Unconscious in Early Modern French Writing* (Cambridge: Cambridge University Press, 1992), 119.

12. See Lawrence D. Kritzman, *The Rhetoric of Sexuality and the Literature of the French Renaissance* (Cambridge: Cambridge University Press, 1991).

13. Jacques Derrida, *Mémoires—for Paul de Man,* trans. Cecile Lindsay, Jonathan Culler and Eduardo Cadava (New York: Columbia University Press, 1989), 34.

14. John O'Brien, "Seeing the Dead: The Gaze as Commemoration," *Montaigne Studies* 4 (Sept. 1992): 97–110.

15. Jacques Derrida, "Roland Barthes," in *The Work of Mourning,* ed. Pascale-Anne Brault and Michael Naas (Chicago: University of Chicago Press, 2001), 36.

16. Harold Bloom, "Introduction," in *Michel de Montaigne: Modern Critical Views,* ed. Harold Bloom (New York: Chelsea House, 1987), 5.

CHAPTER 1. MONTAIGNE'S FANTASTIC MONSTERS AND THE CONSTRUCTION OF GENDER

1. See the entry *"chimeres"* in Randle Cotgrave, *A Dictionarie of the French and English Tongues* (1611; reprint, Columbia: University of South Carolina Press, 1968). Mary B. McKinley discusses the agonistic encounter between Montaigne's essay on idleness and Epistle 2 of Horace's *Ars poetica* in *Words in a Corner: Studies in Montaigne's Latin Quotations,* French Forum Monographs, 26 (Lexington, Ky.: French Forum, 1981). By focusing on the Latin quotation *"velut aegri somnia, / vanae Finguntur species,"* she suggests that Montaigne violates Horace's warning against trying to combine "the wild with the tame" in a work of art (37–40). Michel Jeanneret's commentary concerning the excessive nature of Rabelais's writing is in some ways applicable to Montaigne as well: "Il [l'excès] parasite les grilles interprétatives étroites, il déstabilise la lecture et, du même coup, la stimule. Se joue ainsi le devenir de l'œuvre. L'excédent des sens possibles fait de la lecture une opération sans fin—recherche d'une totalisation irréalisable, défi permanent qui maintient vivante la productivité du texte." Michel Jeanneret, "Débordements rabelaisiens," *Nouvelle Revue de Psychanalyse* 43 (1991): 123.

2. Lawrence D. Kritzman, "Montaigne's Family Romance," in *The Rhetoric of Sexuality and the Literature of the French Renaissance* (Cambridge: Cambridge University Press, 1991), 73–92. See also Glyn P. Norton, *Montaigne and the Introspective Mind* (The Hague, Neth.: Mouton, 1975), 28–32.

196 CHAPTER 1. MONTAIGNE'S FANTASTIC MONSTERS

3. According to Robert D. Cottrell, "*Desreglement* is the menace of emasculation, the threat of irresolution that is an ever-present danger and that signals the dissolution of the only thing 'really in our power'— our will—and thus, to the extent that being is identified with manliness and steadfastness, the dissolution of being itself." *Sexuality/Textuality: A Study of the Fabric of Montaigne's "Essais"* (Columbus: Ohio State University Press, 1981), 25. Cottrell sees in Montaigne's text a binary tension between "the masculine ethics of stiffness and the feminine ethics of laxness" (39).

4. Richard L. Regosin has stated: "Montaigne's monster is that which is shown and which shows itself, that which shows what it is, *that* it is." "Montaigne's Monstrous Confession," *Montaigne Studies* 1 (1989): 77. While Regosin's analysis deals with the "play of language," I have chosen to focus on the issue of gender representation. In the chapter "L'Essai, corps monstrueux" (in *Montaigne: l'écriture de l'essai* [Paris: Presses Universitaires de France, 1988] 221–40) Gisèle Mathieu-Castellani examines Montaigne's text as an emblem for the multilayered form the essay takes. She pays particular attention to narrative structure and intertextuality and the function of quotation. See also Fausta Garavini, "La Présence des 'monstres' dans l'élaboration des *Essais:* A propos de I, iii, 'Nos affections s'emportent au-delà de nous,'" in *Le Parcours des "Essais": Montaigne, 1588–1988,* ed. Marcel Tetel and G. Mallary Masters (Paris: Aux Amateurs de Livres, 1989), 33–46; *Qu'est-ce qu'un monstre,* ed. Annie Ibrahim (Paris: Presses Universitaires de France, 2005).

5. According to John D. Lyons, "Difference is here converted into an effect of distance. Life becomes a kind of gigantic anamorphic painting that we can never see from the proper distance." *Exemplum: The Rhetoric of Example in Early Modern France and Italy* (Princeton, N.J.: Princeton University Press, 1989), 137.

6. For a thematic approach to the imagination, see Dora Pollachek, "Montaigne and Imagination: The Dynamics of Power and Control," in *Le Parcours des "Essais",* 135–45.

7. In Foucault's late work sexuality is conceived as a work of art. See, e.g., *Le Souci de soi* (Paris: Gallimard, 1984).

8. Ovid, *Metamorphoses,* trans. A. D. Melville (Oxford: Oxford University Press, 1986), 224.

9. Ambroise Paré, *On Monsters and Marvels,* trans. Janis L. Pallister (Chicago: University of Chicago Press, 1982), 32.

10. My analyses here differ from those found in Thomas Laqueur's *Making Sex: Body and Gender from the Greeks to Freud* (Cambridge, Mass.: Harvard University Press, 1990), which focuses on the concept of the "one-sex model" in early modern texts. Laqueur tends to read Montaigne's al-

legorical examples in a somewhat literal fashion. In an otherwise remarkable study, I find some indecision in his movement between the real and the representational. Montaigne may well "refuse to come to rest on the question of what is imaginative and what is real" (128), but isn't the representation of the "real" in the essay just another level of the fiction-making process or what might be termed an allegory of the essayist's own gender quest?

11. Paré, *On Monsters and Marvels*, 38.

12. Ibid., 39.

13. According to Jacques Lacan, "the phallus is a signifier . . . whose function in the intra-subjective economy of the analysis lifts the veil, perhaps from the function it performed in the mysteries. For it is the signifier destined to designate as a whole the effects of the signified, in that the signifier conditions them by its presence as a signifier." "The Signification of the Phallus," in *Ecrits: A Selection,* trans. Alan Sheridan (New York: Norton, 1977), 285.

14. For a discussion of the impotence topos within the context of cultural history, see Lee R. Entin-Bates, "Montaigne's Remarks on Impotence," *Modern Language Notes* 91 (1976): 640–54.

15. Henri Gelin, "Les Noueries d'aiguillette en Poitou," *Revue des Etudes Rabelaisiennes* 8 (1910): 122. For the physician Paré impotence could have demonological roots: "Nouer l'esguillette, et les paroles ne font rien, mais c'est l'austuce du diable. Et ceulx qui la nouent ne le peuvent faire sans avoir eu convention avec le diable, qui est une meschancé damnable." "Des Noueurs d'esguillette," quoted in *Des monstres et des prodiges,* ed. Jean Céard (Geneva: Droz, 1971), 100.

16. Lyons, *Exemplum*, 141.

17. Elsewhere I have discussed other aspects of manliness in Montaigne's *Essays.* See the chapter "Pedagogical Graffiti and the Rhetoric of Conceit," in *The Rhetoric of Sexuality and the Literature of the French Renaissance (Cambridge: Cambridge University Press, 1991),* 57–72. See also Todd W. Reeser, *Moderating Masculinity in Early Modern Culture,* North Carolina Studies in Romance Languages, no. 283 (Chapel Hill: University of North Carolina Press, 2006).

CHAPTER 2. REPRESENTING THE MONSTER

1. "Elle [la correction du Calendrier] ne fut non plus miracle . . . combien que beaucoup de simples gens l'estiment fort merveilleuse." Louis Richeome, *Trois discours pour la religion catholique, des miracles, des saincts & des images* (Bordeaux: S. Millanges, 1597), 41. See R. M. Calder, "Montaigne,

'Des Boyteux' and the Question of Causality," *Bibliothèque d'humanisme et Renaissance* 45 (1983): 446 n. 4.

2. On the intersection of the miracle-monster *topoi,* I have benefited greatly from Richard L. Regosin's analyses in "Montaigne's Monstrous Confession," *Montaigne Studies* 1 (1989): 73–87. For Regosin "this is an essay about seeing, about witnessing and bearing witness to phenomena which are often characterized as miracles and which the essayist, against the pressure of common opinion, would reinscribe in the domain of nature or on which he would reserve judgment altogether" (78).

3. Ibid., 77.

4. See chapter 1 of the present study. In *Des monstres, des prodiges, des voyages* (Paris: Livre Club du Libraire, 1964), the sixteenth-century French physician Ambroise Paré proclaims: "Monstres sont choses qui apparaissent outre le cours de Nature (& sont le plus souvent signes de quelque malheur à venir" (181). On the use of the monster metaphor in Montaigne's *Essays,* see the following: Mary B. McKinley, *Words in a Corner: Studies in Montaigne's Latin Quotations, French Forum Monographs,* 26 (Lexington, Ky.: French Forum, 1981); Gisèle Mathieu-Castellani, *Montaigne: De l'écriture de l'essai* (Paris: Presses Universitaires de France, 1988); Fausta Garavini, "La Présence des monstres dans l'élaboration des *Essais* à propos de I, iii, 'Nos affections s'emportent au-dela de nous,'" in *Le Parcours des "Essais": Montaigne, 1588–1988,* ed. Marcel Tetel and G. Mallary Masters (Paris: Aux Amateurs de Livres, 1989), 33–46. John D. Lyons has treated the question of the exemplary value of monstrosity in Montaigne's essays in *Exemplum: The Rhetoric of Example in Early Modern France and Italy* (Princeton, N.J.: Princeton University Press, 1989). For a general discussion of the monster in literary production, see Marie-Hélène Huet, *Monstrous Imagination* (Cambridge, Mass.: Harvard University Press, 1993). The most important book on the concept of the monster in the Renaissance is Jean Céard's *La Nature et les prodiges* (Geneva: Droz, 1977). See also Katharine Park and Lorraine J. Daston, "Unnatural Conceptions: The Study of Monsters in Sixteenth- and Seventeenth-Century France and England," *Past and Present* 92 (1981): 20–54.

5. See Calder, "Montaigne," 452–54.

6. Jean Bodin, *De la demonomanie des sourciers* (Paris: Jacques du Puys, 1580).

7. Richard A. Sayce, *The Essays of Montaigne: A Critical Exploration* (Evanston, Ill.: Northwestern University Press, 1972), 248.

8. According to Marianne S. Meijer, "It is not so much the poor witches who go beyond the natural, as the learned among us. . . . Through science, man goes beyond the natural and becomes unwise." "Guesswork or Facts: Connection between Montaigne's Last Three Chapters (III:11, 12 and 13)," *Yale French Studies* 64 (1983): 177.

9. Floyd F. Gray comments: "Le vrai monstre, c'est l'oeuvre qu'il sort de lui-même qui contemple cette oeuvre, née comme hors de lui, en dépit de son désir de modération et d'ordre." *La Balance de Montaigne: Exagium, essai* (Paris: Nizet, 1982), 50.

10. Natalie Zemon Davis, *The Return of Martin Guerre* (Cambridge, Mass.: Harvard University Press, 1983), 19. On Montaigne's testimony at the Martin Guerre trial in Toulouse, see Emile V. Telle, "Montaigne et le procès Martin Guerre," *Bibliothèque d'humanisme et Renaissance* 37 (1975): 387–419.

11. Davis notes: "For a while Martin and his family might have hoped the impotence would pass. . . . Still nothing happened. Bertrande's family was pressing her to separate from Martin; since the marriage was unconsummated, it could be dissolved after three years and she would be free by canon law to marry again. It was humiliating, and the village surely let them know about it." *The Return of Martin Guerre,* 20.

12. According to Tom Conley, "In 'Des boyteux' [Of cripples] Montaigne chooses III, xi to classify the chapter on sorcery. It happens that eleven is the digit of the devil because the integer 1 is doubled into 11; but when the author remarks that 10 days have been added to the Gregorian calendar in October 1582, the numerical count can be as much as 10 or 11 days, the number matching the 'bissextile' tension of the chapter." *The Graphic Unconscious in Early Modern Writing* (Cambridge: Cambridge University Press, 1992), 118–19.

13. Todd W. Reeser, *Moderating Masculinity in Early Modern Culture,* North Carolina Studies in Romance Languages, 283 (Chapel Hill: University of North Carolina Press, 2006).

14. Sextus Empiricus, *Outlines of Scepticism,* trans. Julia Annas and Jonathan Barnes (Cambridge: Cambridge University Press, 1994).Todd Reeser

15. Stephen Greenblatt, "Limping Examples: Exemplarity, the New Historicism, and Psychoanalysis," in *Creative Imitation: New Essays on Renaissance Literature in Honor of Thomas M. Greene,* ed. David Quint et al. (Binghamton, N.Y.: Medieval and Renaissance Texts and Studies, 1992), 281–95. See also Carla Freccero, "Psychoanalysis, Montaigne and the Melancholic Subject of Humanism," *Montaigne Studies* 9 (1997): 17–34; and my essay "Montaigne et la psychanalyse, in *Dictionnaire Montaigne,* ed. Philippe Desan (Paris: Champion, 2004). On the question of ethics in this essay, see Zahi Zalloura, "The Ethics of Montaigne's Des Boyteux: The Case of Martin Guerre," *Yearbook of Comparative and general Literature* 51 (2003–4), 69–84.

16. John O'Brien, "Suspended Sentences," in *Le Visage Changeant de Montaigne / The Changing Face of Montaigne,* ed. Keith Cameron and Laura Willett (Paris: Champion, 2003), 92.

CHAPTER 3. MONTAIGNE'S FRATERNITY

1. Etienne de La Boétie, *Discours de la Servitude Volontaire,* ed. Simone Goyard-Fabre (Paris: Flammarion, 1983) [English: *On Voluntary Servitude,* trans. David Lewis Schaefer, in *Freedom Over Servitude,* ed. D. L. Schaefer (Westport, Conn.: Greenwood Press, 1998), 189–222. Henceforth all parenthetical text references will be to these editions.

2. Jacques Derrida, *Politics of Friendship,* trans.George Collins (New York : Verso, 1997) [French: *Politiques de l'amitié* (Paris: Galilée, 1994)].

3. On this point see Stephen Greenblatt, "Montaigne Witnesses the Death of His Friend Etienne de La Boétie," in *A New History of French Literature,* ed. Denis Hollier (Cambridge, Mass.: Harvard University Press, 1989), 224. Marc D. Schachter sees the relationship between Montaigne and La Boétie as based on "a kind of hybrid of love and friendship." "The Friendship Which Possesses the Soul: Montaigne Loves La Boétie," *Journal of Homosexuality* 3–4 (2001): 6. See also see Nancy Freilick, "Friendship, Transference, and Voluntary Servitude," in *The Changing Face of Montaigne,* ed. Keith Cameron and Laura Willet (Paris: Champion, 2003), 195–206.

4. Jean-Luc Nancy, *The Experience of Freedom* (Stanford: Stanford University Press, 1993), 123.

5. Trevor Hope, "Sexual Indifference and the Homosexual Male Imaginary" *Diacritics* 24 (1994): 170. On the homosocial in Montaigne, see Carla Freccero, "Psychoanalysis, Montaigne and the Melancholic Subject of Humanism," *Montaigne Studies* 9 (1997): 17–34.

6. Lawrence D. Kritzman, *The Rhetoric of Sexuality and the Literature of the French Renaissance* (Cambridge: Cambridge University Press, 1991), 66.

7. Montaigne, Michel de. "Extraict d'une lettre," in *Œuvres complètes, ed. Maurice Rat* (Paris: Bibliothèque de la Pléiade/Gallimard, 1962), 1247–60.

8. The source is the same as the one cited in the epigraph to this chapter.

9. Donald Frame, *Montaigne: A Biography* (New York: Harcourt, 1965), 79.

10. According to Jean-Michel Delacompté, "L'amitié, sanctuaire de *notre liberté volontaire,* c'est-à-dire qui ne dépend que de nous, par un refus, par un arrachement aux contraintes d'autrui qui nous environnent." *Et qu'un seul soit l'ami* (Paris: Gallimard, 1995), 181.

CHAPTER 4. MONTAIGNE ON HORSEBACK, OR THE SIMULATION OF DEATH

This essay was translated from the French by Malcolm Debevoise.

1. On the idea of balance, see Floyd F. Gray, *La Balance de Montaigne: Exagium, essai* (Paris: Nizet, 1982).

2. See Sigmund Freud, *Totem and Taboo: Some Points of Agreement between the Mental Lives of Savages and Neurotics,* trans. James Strachey (New York: Norton, 1962).

3. On the theme of falling, see the following: Georges Van Den Abbeele, *Travel as Metaphor: From Montaigne to Rousseau* (Minneapolis: University of Minnesota Press, 1992); Richard L. Regosin, *Montaigne's Unruly Brood: Textual Engendering and the Challenge to Paternal Authority* (Berkeley: University of California Press, 1996); Laurent Jenny, "Histoire d'une chute," in *L'Expérience de la chute: De Montaigne à Michaux* (Paris: Presses Universitaires de France, 1997), 30–37; and Michel Jeanneret, *Perpetuum mobile: Métamorphoses des corps et des œuvres, de Vinci à Montaigne* (Paris: Macula, 1997).

4. I have profited greatly from Derrida's theoretical analysis of death in his *Apories: mourir—s'attendre aux "limites de la vérité"* (Paris: Galilée, 1996), 25. With respect to "the *experience* of aporia," Derrida asks: "Que serait une telle *expérience*? Le mot signifie aussi passage, traversée, endurance, épreuve du franchissement, mais peut-être une traversée sans ligne et sans frontière indivisible (35) ("What is this *expérience*? The word also signifies passage, crossing, endurance, the ordeal of crossing over, but perhaps a crossing over without a line, without an indivisible boundary" [35]).

5. Tom Conley, *The Graphic Unconscious in Early Modern French Writing* (Cambridge: Cambridge University Press, 1992), 125.

6. Jenny asks: "Must it be admitted that the shock to the soul and the return to the world coincided in a single oxymoronic moment?" in "L'expérience de la chute," 35.

7. Marcel Tetel, *Présences italiennes dans les "Essais" de Montaigne* (Paris: Champion, 1992), 130.

CHAPTER 5. THE ANXIETY OF DEATH

1. See Jean-Paul Sermain, "*Insinuatio, circumstantia, visio et actio:* L'Itinéraire rhétorique du chapitre III, 4: 'De la Diversion,'" *Bulletin de la Société des Amis de Montaigne* 7 (1985): 127.

2. See my chapter "Montaigne's Family Romance," in *The Rhetoric of Sexuality and the Literature of the French Renaissance* (Cambridge: Cam-

bridge University Press, 1991), 73–92. See also my essay "Montaigne and Psychoanalysis," in *Approaches to Teaching Montaigne's "Essays,"* ed. Patrick Henry (New York: Modern Language Association of America, 1993), 110–16.

3. Montaigne made this addition to the 1588 edition of the *Essais* in the essay entitled "De la vanité" (III, 9). I am here using Frame's translation, p. 752, n. 14.

4. Richard Regosin, "Sources and Resources: The 'Pretexts' of Originality in Montaigne's *Essais,*" *Substance* 21 (1978): 114.

5. Randle Cotgrave defines the verb "ruser" as: "to beguile, to deceive, to shift, to use tricks, to deale cunningly, to proceed by sleights." *A Dictionarie of the French and English Tongues* (1611; reprint, Columbia: University of South Carolina Press, 1968).

6. Jacques Lacan, *Ecrits: A Selection* (New York: Norton, 1977), 166.

7. Sigmund Freud, *Beyond the Pleasure Principle* (New York: W.W. Norton, 1961), 147.

CHAPTER 6. EXCAVATING MONTAIGNE

1. See Lawrence D. Kritzman, "Montaigne's Family Romance," in *The Rhetoric of Sexuality and the Literature of the French Renaissance* (Cambridge: Cambridge University Press, 1991), 73–92.

2. See Marjorie Henry Ilsley, *A Daughter of the Renaissance: Marie le Jars de Gournay: Her Life and Her Works* (The Hague, Neth.: Mouton, 1963); see also Elayne Dezon-Jones, *Fragments d'un discours féminin* (Paris: Corti, 1988).

3. Richard Regosin, "Montaigne and His Readers," in *A New History of French Literature,* ed. Denis Hollier (Cambridge, Mass.: Harvard University Press, 1989), 248–53.

4. "Préface de Marie de Gournay à l'édition de 1595 des 'Essais,'" ed. François Rigolot, *Montaigne Studies 1* (1989): 53. Subsequent references to this edition are identified parenthetically in the text. I have also consulted the "Préface" of the 1595 L'Angelier edition housed at the Houghton Library, Harvard University.

5. Inscription in Montaigne's library. See "Chronologie de Montaigne," in Montaigne, *Œuvres complètes,* ed. Albert Thibaudet and Maurice Rat (Paris: Bibliothèque de la Pléiade, 1962), xvi–xvii.

6. According to Rigolot, "Elle [Marie de Gournay] se présente sans hésiter comme l'éditrice idéale des *Essais,* à la fois parce qu'elle a connu leur auteur personnellement et dans l'intimité (elle peut donc, en cas d'ambiguité, restituer les "intentions" de Montaigne dans leur pureté), parce qu'elle s'est

refusée à corriger le texte par respect pour la volonté de son 'Père' et en-
fin, tout simplement, parce que l'amour filial qui l'habite compensera toute
défaillance éventuelle de sa part ('mon affection suppléant à mon incapacité')" (11).

7. Adam Phillips, *On Flirtation* (Cambridge, Mass.: Harvard University
Press, 1994), 100.

8. According to Tilde A. Sankovitch, "It is *she* who conceives a desire for him—that is, for the Book he incarnates—and it is *she* who takes
possession of the *Essays* in an ecstasy, a trance, of pleasure." "Marie le
Jars de Gournay: The Self-portrait of an Androgynous Hero," in *French
Women Writers and the Book* (Syracuse, N.Y.: Syracuse University Press,
1988), 78.

9. On Marie de Gournay as a reader, see Cathleen Bauschatz, "Marie de
Gournay's 'Préface de 1595': A Critical Evaluation," *Bulletin de la Société
des Amis de Montaigne*, 7th ser., 3–4 (Jan.–June 1986): 73–82.

10. This phrase is borrowed from Julia Kristeva's *New Maladies of the
Soul* (New York: Columbia University Press, 1995).

11. Quoted in Dezon-Jones, *Fragments*, 193.

12. Donald Frame, *Montaigne: A Biography* (New York: Harcourt,
Brace and World, 1965), 276.

13. Sankovitch, "Marie le Jars de Gournay," discusses her own coming
of age in terms of a "mimicry of ritual initiation" (79).

14. Quoted in Alan Boase, *The Fortunes of Montaigne: A History of the
Essays in France, 1580–1669* (London: Methuen, 1935), 52.

15. Quoted in Richard Regosin, "Montaigne's Dutiful Daughter," in
*Montaigne's Unruly Brood: Textual Engenderings, Monstrous Progeny, and
the Challenge to Paternal Authority* (Berkeley: University of California Press,
1996), 78. Regosin states: "I would argue that Marie de Gournay is guilty of
having misspoken, and more seriously, that she is guilty of having spoken at
all" (52).

16. "Preface de Marie de Gournay," 27.

CHAPTER 7. THE SOCRATIC MAKEOVER

1. Among the more interesting analyses of the essay, see the following:
Terence Cave, *The Cornucopian Text: Problems of Writing in the French Renaissance* (Oxford: Clarendon Press, 1979), 302–12; Hope Glidden, "The
Face in the Text: Montaigne's Emblematic Self-portrait (Essais III:12)," *Renaissance Quarterly* 46, no. 1 (1993): 71–79; David Quint, *Montaigne and
the Quality of Mercy: Ethical and Political Themes in the Essays* (Princeton,
N.J.: Princeton University Press, 1998); Joshua Scodel, "The Affirmation

of Paradox: A Reading of Montaigne's 'De la Phisionomie' (III, 12)," *Yale French Studies* 64 (1983): 209–37; and Zahi Zalloua, *Montaigne and the Ethics of Skepticism* (Charlottesville, N.C.: Rockwood Press, 2005).

2. See the following treatises: Barthélemy Coclès, *Physiognomania* (1533); Michel Lescot, *Physionomie* (1540); and Jean d'Indagine, *Chiromance* (1549).

3. Raymond La Charité, "Montaigne's Silenic Text: 'De la phisionomie,' in *Le Parcours des Essais: Montaigne, 1588–1988*, ed. Marcel Tetel and G. Mallary Masters (Paris: Aux Amateurs de Livres, 1989), 66–67.

4. Quint, *Montaigne and the Quality of Mercy*, 133.

5. Adam Phillips, *On Flirtation* (Cambridge, Mass.: Harvard University Press, 1994), 12.

6. Slavoj Zizek, *Tarrying with the Negative: Kant, Hegel, and the Critique of Ideology* (Durham, N.C.: Duke University Press, 1993), 128.

7. On the role of Xenophon, see Floyd Gray, "Montaigne and the Memorabilia," *Studies in Philology* 58 (1961): 130–39.

8. According to Zalloua, "'De la phisionomie' at once tests and attests to the essayist's ethical relation to the other. In his writing of Socrates, Montaigne . . . resists this 'natural,' or rather naturalized, hermeneutic impulse . . . to encapsulate the meaning of his ideal other, to inscribe Socrates unproblematically in any preestablished and authorized lineages or discourses . . . to portray him as an unequivocal being" (*Montaigne and the Ethics of Skepticism,* 63).

9. See Tobin Siebers, *Morals and Stories* (New York: Columbia University Press, 1992), 63.

10. As Slavoj Zizek has concluded, "Every recognition of the subject in an image or signifying trait . . . already betrays its core; every jubilant 'that is me' already contains the seed of 'that's not me.'" *The Parallax View* (Cambridge: MIT Press, 2006), 244.

CHAPTER 8. ROMANCING THE STONE

1. Gérard Defaux, *Marot, Rabelais, Montaigne: L'Ecriture comme présence,* Geneva: Slatkine, 1987); Hugo Friedrich, *Montaigne,* trans. Robert Rovini (Paris: Gallimard, 1968). The same logocentric readings persist even today. For example, in his introduction Ulrich Langer has stated that "Montaigne himself is always present." *The Cambridge Companion to Montaigne,* ed. Ulrich Langer (Cambridge, Cambridge University Press, 2005), 2.

2. See Charles-Augustin Sainte-Beuve, *Port-Royal,* vol. 2 (Paris: Bibliothèque de la Pléiade, 1958); Albert Thibaudet, *Montaigne,* ed. Floyd Gray (Paris: Gallimard, 1963).

3. Richard L. Regosin, "The Text of Memory's Experience as Narration in Montaigne's Essays," in *The Dialectic of Discovery*, ed. John D. Lyons and Nancy L. Vickers (Lexington, Ky. and Indianapolis, Ind.: French Forum, 1984), 105.

4. Jacques Derrida, *Force de loi* (Paris: Galilée, 1994).

5. See Robert Cottrell, "Representation and the Desiring Subject in Montaigne's 'De l'experience,'" in *Le Parcours des Essais: Montaigne, 1588–1988,* ed. Marcel Tetel and G. Mallary Masters (Paris: Aux Amateur de Livres, 1989), 97–109.

6. Judith Butler, *Gender Trouble: Feminism and the Subversion of Identity* (New York: Routledge, 1990), 163 n. 43.

7. Lawrence Kritzman, "Montaigne et l'écriture excrementale," in *Destruction/Découverte: Le fonctionnement de la rhétorique dans les "Essais" de Montaigne* (Lexington, Ky.: French Forum, 1980), 147–49; see also Gisèle Mathieu-Castellani, *Montaigne: L'écriture de l'essai* (Paris: Presses Universitaires de France, 1988).

8. Antoine Compagnon, *Nous: Michel de Montaigne* (Paris: Seuil, 1980).

9. Sigmund Freud, *The Standard Edition of the Complete Works of Sigmund Freud* (London: Hogarth Press, 1955), 17:240.

10. See Jules Brody, "Les Oreilles de Montaigne," *Romanic Review* 74 (1983):121–35.

11. Plato, *Symposium*, trans. Alexander Nehamas and Paul Woodruff (Indianapolis, Ind.: Hackett, 1989).

12. Xenophon, *Conversations of Socrates*, trans. Hugh Tredennick and Robin Waterfield, ed. Robin Waterfield (New York: Penguin, 1990). See also *The Socratic Movement*, ed. Paul Vander-Waerdt (Ithaca, N.Y.: Cornell University Press, 1994).

13. Kaja Silverman, *World Spectators* (Stanford, Calif.: Stanford University Press, 2000), 9.

14. Petronius, *Satyricon* and the *Apocologyntosis*, trans. J. P. Sullivan (New York: Penguin, 2005).

15. Jean Laplanche and J. B. Pontalis, *The Language of Psycho-analysis,* trans. Donald Nicholson-Smith (New York: Norton, 1974), 313.

16. Floyd F. Gray, *Gender, Rhetoric and Print-Culture in French Renaissance Writing* (Cambridge: Cambridge University Press, 2000), 134–42.

17. Martial, *Epigrams,* ed. D. B. Shackelton Bailey (Cambridge, Mass.: Harvard University Press, 1993), 3.

18. Philippe Lacoue-Labarthe, *Poetry as Experience,* trans. Andrea Tarnowski (Stanford, Calif.: Stanford University Press, 1999), 67. According to Gisèle Mathieu-Castellani, "S'arrêter à ce qui n'est pas, mais *peut* être, feindre les choses, concevoir les formes de toutes choses qui se peuvent imaginer,

représenter les choses qui peuvent être vraisemblables, bâtir son ouvrage sur le possible . . . si telle est la definition de la poésie, elle n'est pas si éloignée de l'essai idéal, de l'essai tel qu'il se rêve." *Montaigne ou la verité du mensonge* (Geneva: Droz, 2000), 42.

19. Jacques Lacan, *The Seminars of Jacques Lacan—Book VII: The Ethics of Psychoanalysis, 1959–60,* trans. Dennis Porter (New York: Norton, 1992), 319.

WORKS CITED

PRIMARY SOURCES

Aristotle. "On the Soul." In *The Complete Works of Aristotle,* vol. 1, ed. Jonathan Barnes, 641–92. Bollingen Series, 71. Princeton, N.J.: Princeton University Press, 1984.

Bodin, Jean. *De la demonomanie des sourciers.* Paris: Jacques du Puys, 1580.

La Boétie, Etienne de. *Discours de la servitude volontaire.* Edition Simone Goyard-Fabre. Paris: Flammarion, 1983. English transl.: "On Voluntary Servitude." Trans. David Lewis Schaefer. In *Freedom Over Servitude,* ed. D. L. Schaefer, 189–222. Westport, Conn.: Greenwood Press, 1998.

Coclès, Barthélemy. *Physiognomania.* 1533.

Cotgrave, Randle. *A Dictionarie of the French and English Tongues.* 1611. Reprint, Columbia, S.C.: University of South Carolina Press, 1968.

Gournay, Marie le Jars de. "Préface de Marie de Gournay à l'édition de 1595 des 'Essais,'" ed. François Rigolot. *Montaigne Studies* 1 (1989): 7–60.

d'Indagine, Jean. *Chiromance.* 1549.

Lescot, Michel. *Physionomie.* 1540.

Martial. *Epigrams.* Ed. D. B. Shackelton Bailey. Cambridge, Mass.: Harvard University Press, 1993.

Montaigne, Michel de. "Chronologie de Montaigne." In Montaigne, Œuvres complètes, ed. Albert Thibaudet and Maurice Rat, xvi–xvii. Paris: Bibliothèque de la Pléiade/Gallimard, 1962.

———. Les Essais. Ed. Pierre Villey. Paris: Presses Universitaires de France, 1965. English transl.: The Complete Essays of Montaigne. Trans. Donald M. Frame. Stanford, Calif.: Stanford University Press, 1958.

———. "Extraict d'une lettre." In Montaigne, Œuvres complètes, ed. Albert Thibaudet and Maurice Rat, 1247–60. Paris: Bibliothèque de la Pléiade/Gallimard, 1962.

Ovid. Metamorphoses. Trans. A. D. Melville. Oxford: Oxford University Press, 1986.

Paré, Ambroise. Des Monstres, des prodiges, des voyages. Paris: Livre Club du Libraire, 1964. English transl.: On Monsters and Marvels. Trans. Janis L. Pallister. Chicago: University of Chicago Press, 1982.

———. "Des noueurs d'esguillette." In Des monstres et des prodiges, ed. Jean Céard. Geneva: Droz, 1971.

Petronius. "Satyricon" and the "Apocologyntosis". Trans. J. P. Sullivan. New York: Penguin, 2005.

Pico della Mirandola, Gianfrancesco. De Imaginatione. Venice, 1501; Strasbourg, 1507. French transl.: Traité de l'imagination. Trans. Antoine de Baif. Paris: Weschel, 1557.

Plato. Symposium. Trans. Alexander Nehamas and Paul Woodruff. Indianapolis, Ind.: Hackett, 1989.

Richeome, Louis. Trois discours pour la religion catholique, des miracles, des saincts & des images. Bordeaux: S. Millanges, 1597.

Seneca. Epistles. Trans. Richard M. Gunnere. 3 vols. Loeb Classical Library. Cambridge, Mass. Harvard University Press, 1996.

Sextus Empiricus. Outlines of Scepticism, 2nd ed. Ed. and Trans. Julia Annas and Jonathan Barnes. Cambridge: Cambridge University Press, 2000.

Xenophon. Conversations of Socrates. Trans. Hugh Tredennick and Robin Waterfield. New York: Penguin, 1990.

SECONDARY SOURCES

Bauschatz, Cathleen. "Marie de Gournay's 'Préface de 1595': A Critical Evaluation." Bulletin de la Société des Amis de Montaigne, 7th ser., 3–4 (Jan.–June 1986): 73–82.

Bloom, Harold, ed. "Introduction." In Michel Montaigne: Modern Critical Views. New York: Chelsea House, 1987.

Boase, Alan. The Fortunes of Montaigne: A History of the Essays in France, 1580–1669. London: Methuen, 1935.

Brody, Jules. "Les Oreilles de Montaigne." *Romanic Review* 74 (1983): 121–35.

Bundy, Murray Wright. *The Theory of the Imagination in Classical and Medieval Thought*. University of Illinois Studies in Language and Literature, 12. Urbana, Ill.: University of Illinois Press, 1927.

Butler, Judith. *Gender Trouble: Feminism and the Subversion of Identity*. New York: Routledge, 1990.

Calder, R.M. "Montaigne, 'Des Boyteux' and the Question of Causality." *Bibliothèque d'humanisme et Renaissance* 45 (1983): 445–60.

Cameron, Keith, and Laura Willett, eds. *Le Visage Changeant de Montaigne / The Changing Face of Montaigne*. Paris: Champion, 2003.

Cave, Terence. *The Cornucopian Text: Problems of Writing in the French Renaissance*. Oxford: Clarendon Press, 1979.

Céard, Jean. *La Nature et les prodiges*. Geneva: Droz, 1977.

Compagnon, Antoine. *Nous: Michel de Montaigne*. Paris: Seuil, 1980.

Conley, Tom. "An Allegory of Prudence." *Montaigne Studies* 4, nos. 1–2 (1992): 156–79.

———. *The Graphic Unconscious in Early Modern French Writing*. Cambridge: Cambridge University Press, 1992.

———. "Montaigne Moqueur: 'Virgile' and Its Geographies of Gender." In *High Anxiety: Masculinity in Crisis in Early Modern France*, ed. Kathleen P. Long, 93–106. Kirksville, Mo., Truman State University Press, 2001.

Cottrell, Robert D. "Representation and the Desiring Subject in Montaigne's 'De l'experience'." In *Le Parcours des "Essais": Montaigne, 1588–1988*, ed. Marcel Tetel et G. Mallary Masters, 97–110. Paris: Aux Amateur de Livres, 1989.

———. *Sexuality/Textuality: A Study of the Fabric of Montaigne's "Essais"*. Columbus: Ohio State University Press, 1981.

Davis, Natalie Zemon. *The Return of Martin Guerre*. Cambridge, Mass.: Harvard University Press, 1983.

Defaux, Gerard. *Marot, Rabelais, Montaigne: L'Ecriture comme présence*. Geneva: Slatkine, 1987.

Delacompté, Jean-Michel. *Et qu'un seul soit l'ami*. Paris: Gallimard, 1995.

Derrida, Jacques. *Apories: Mourir—s'attendre aux "limites de la vérité."* Paris: Galilée, 1996.

———. "Donner la mort." In *L'Ethique du don: Jacques Derrida et la pensée du don* [Colloque de Royaumont, Dec. 1990], ed. Jacques Derrida, Jean-Michel Rabaté, and Michael Wetzel, 11–108. Paris: Métailié-Transition, 1992.

———. *Force de loi*. Paris: Galilée, 1994.

———. *Mémoires—for Paul de Man*. Trans. Cecile Lindsay, Jonathan Culler, and Eduardo Cadava. New York: Columbia University Press, 1989.

———. *Politiques de l'amitié.* Paris: Galilée, 1994. English transl.: *Politics of Friendship.* Trans. George Collins. New York: Verso, 1997.

———. "Roland Barthes." In *The Work of Mourning,* ed. Pascale-Anne Brault and Michael Naas, 31–67. Chicago: University of Chicago Press, 2001.

Dezon-Jones, Elayne. *Fragments d'un discours féminin.* Paris: Corti, 1988.

Dubois, Claude-Gilbert. *L'Imaginaire de la Renaissance.* Paris: Presses Universitaires de France, 1985.

Entin-Bates, Lee R. "Montaigne's Remarks on Impotence." *Modern Language Notes* 91 (1976): 640–54.

Foucault, Michel. *Le Souci de soi.* Paris: Gallimard, 1984.

———. "Theatrum Philosophicum." *Critique* 282 (November 1970): 885–908.

Frame, Donald. *Montaigne: A Biography.* New York: Harcourt, 1965.

Freccero, Carla. "Psychoanalysis, Montaigne and the Melancholic Subject of Humanism." *Montaigne Studies* 9 (1997): 17–34.

Freilick, Nancy. "Friendship, Transference, and Voluntary Servitude." In *The Changing Face of Montaigne,* ed. Keith Cameron and Laura Willet, 195–206. Paris: Champion, 2003.

Freud, Sigmund. *Beyond the Pleasure Principle.* New York: Norton, 1961.

———. *The Standard Edition of the Complete Works of Sigmund Freud.* London: Hogarth Press, 1955.

———. *Totem and Taboo: Some Points of Agreement Between the Mental Lives of Savages and Neurotics.* Trans. James Strachey. New York: Norton, 1962.

Friedrich, Hugo. *Montaigne.* Trans. Robert Rovini. Paris: Gallimard, 1968.

Garavini, Fausta. "La Présence des 'monstres' dans l'élaboration des *Essais*: A propos de I, iii,'Nos affections s'emportent au-delà de nous.'" In *Le Parcours des "Essais": Montaigne, 1588–1988.* ed. Marcel Tetel and G. Mallary Masters, 33–46. Paris: Aux Amateurs de Livres, 1989.

Gasché, Rudolphe. "Theatrum Theoreticum." In *The Honor of Thinking,* 188–208. Stanford, Calif.: Stanford University Press, 2007.

Gelin, Henri. "Les Noueries d'aiguillette en Poitou," *Revue des Etudes Rabelaisiennes* 8 (1910): 122–33.

Glidden, Hope. "The Face in the Text: Montaigne's Emblematic Self-portrait (*Essais* III:12)." *Renaissance Quarterly* 46, no. 1 (1993): 71–97.

Gray, Floyd F. *La Balance de Montaigne: Exagium, essai.* Paris: Nizet, 1982.

———. *Gender, Rhetoric and Print-Culture in French Renaissance Writing.* Cambridge: Cambridge University Press, 2000.

———. "Montaigne and the Memorabilia." Studies in Philology 58 (1961): 130–39.

Greenblatt, Stephen. "Anti-Dictator: Montaigne Witnesses the Death of His Friend Etienne de La Boétie." In *A New History of French Literature,* ed. Denis Hollier, 223–28. Cambridge, Mass.: Harvard University Press, 1989.

———. "Limping Examples: Exemplarity, the New Historicism, and Psychoanalysis." In *Creative Imitation: New Essays on Renaissance Literature in Honor of Thomas M. Greene.* Vol. 95, ed. David Quint et al., 281–95. Binghamton, N.Y.: Medieval and Renaissance Texts and Studies, 1992.

Hartle, Ann. *Michel de Montaigne: Accidental Philosopher.* Cambridge: Cambridge University Press, 2003.

Hope, Trevor. "Sexual Indifference and the Homosexual Male Imaginary." *Diacritics* 24 #2–3 (1994): 169–83.

Huet, Marie-Hélène. *Monstrous Imagination.* Cambridge, Mass.: Harvard University Press, 1993.

Huguet, Edmond. *Dictionnaire de la langue française du seizième siècle.* 7 vols. Paris: Librairie Arienne Edouard Champion, 1925–67.

Ibrahim, Annie, ed.. *Qu'est-ce qu'un monstre?* Paris: Presses Universitaires de France, 2005.

Ilsley, Marjorie Henry. *A Daughter of the Renaissance: Marie le Jars de Gournay: Her Life and Her Works.* The Hague: Mouton, 1963.

Jeanneret, Michel. "Débordements rabelaisiens," *Nouvelle Revue de Psychanalyse* 43 (1991): 105–23.

———. *Perpetuum Mobile: Métamorphoses des corps et des œuvres, de Vinci à Montaigne.* Paris: Macula, 1997. English transl.: *Perpetuel Motion: Transformative Shapes in the Renaissance from da Vinci to Montaigne.* Trans. Nina Pollen. Baltimore, Md.: Johns Hopkins University Press, 2001.

Jenny, Laurent. "Histoire d'une chute." In *L'Expérience de la chute: De Montaigne à Michaux,* 30–37. Paris: Presses Universitaires de France, 1997.

Kristeva, Julia. *New Maladies of the Soul.* New York: Columbia University Press, 1995.

Kritzman, Lawrence D. *Destruction/découverte: Le Fonctionnement de la rhétorique dans les "Essais" de Montaigne.* Lexington, Ky.: French Forum, 1980.

———. "Montaigne and Psychoanalysis." In *Approaches to Teaching Montaigne's "Essays",* ed. Patrick Henry, 110–16. New York: Modern Languages Association of America, 1993.

———. "Montaigne et l'écriture excrementale." In *Destruction/Découverte: Le Fonctionnement de la rhétorique dans les "Essais" de Montaigne,* 147–49. Lexington, Ky.: French Forum, 1980.

————. "Montaigne's Family Romance." In *The Rhetoric of Sexuality and the Literature of the French Renaissance*, 73–92. Cambridge: Cambridge University Press, 1991.

————. "Pedagogical Graffiti and the Rhetoric of Conceit." In The Rhetoric of Sexuality and the Literature of the French Renaissance, 57–72. Cambridge: Cambridge University Press, 1991.

Lacan, Jacques. *Ecrits: A Selection*. Trans. Alan Sheridan. New York: Norton, 1977.

————. *The Seminars of Jacques Lacan. Book VII: The Ethics of Psychoanalysis, 1959–60*. Trans. Dennis Porter. New York: Norton, 1992.

————. "The Signification of the Phallus." In *Ecrits: A Selection*, trans. Alan Sheridan, 281–91. New York: Norton, 1977.

La Charité, Raymond. "Montaigne's Silenic Text: 'De la phisionomie." In *Le Parcours des "Essais": Montaigne, 1588–1988*, ed. Marcel Tetel and G. Mallary Masters, 59–69. Paris: Aux Amateurs de Livres, 1989.

Lacoue-Labarthe, Philippe. *Poetry as Experience*. Trans. Andrea Tarnowski. Stanford, Calif.: Stanford University Press, 1999.

Langer, Ulrich. Introduction to *The Cambridge Companion to Montaigne*. Ed. Ulrich Langer, 1–8. Cambridge: Cambridge University Press, 2005.

Laplanche, Jean, and J. B. Pontalis. *The Language of Psycho-analysis*. Trans. Donald Nicholson-Smith. New York: Norton, 1974.

Laqueur, Thomas. *Making Sex: Body and Gender from the Greeks to Freud*. Cambridge, Mass.: Harvard Uuniversity Press, 1990.

Lyons, John D. *Before Imagination*. Stanford, Calif.: Stanford University Press, 2005.

————. "Ethics, Imagination, and Surprise." *Montaigne Studies* 14 (2002): 95–204.

————. *Exemplum: The Rhetoric of Example in Early Modern France and Italy*. Princeton, N.J.: Princeton University Press, 1989.

Mathieu-Castellani, Gisèle. "L'Essai, corps monstrueux." In *Montaigne: L'Ecriture de l'essai*, 221–40. Paris: Presses Universitaires de France, 1988.

————. *Montaigne ou la verité du mensonge*. Geneva: Droz, 2000.

McKinley, Mary B. *Words in a Corner: Studies in Montaigne's Latin Quotations*. French Forum Monographs, 26. Lexington, Ky.: French Forum, 1981.

Meijer, Marianne S. "Guesswork or Facts: The Connection between Montaigne's Last Three Chapters (III:11, 12 and 13)." *Yale French Studies* 64 (1983): 167–79.

Nancy, Jean-Luc. *L'Expérience de la liberté*. Paris: Galilée, 1980.

Norton, Glyn P. *Montaigne and the Introspective Mind*. The Hague: Mouton, 1975.

O'Brien, John. "Reasoning with the Senses: The Humanist Imagination." *South Central Review,* 10, no. 2 (1993): 3–20.

———. "Seeing the Dead: The Gaze as Commemoration," *Montaigne Studies* 4, nos. 1–2 (Sept. 1992): 97–110.

———. "Suspended Sentences." In *Le Visage Changeant de Montaigne / The Changing Face of Montaigne,* ed. Keith Cameron and Laura Willett, 195–206. Paris: Champion, 2003.

Park, Katharine, and Lorraine J. Daston. "Unnatural Conceptions: The Study of Monsters in Sixteenth- and Seventeenth-Century France and England." *Past and Present* 92 (1981): 20–54.

Phillips, Adam. *On Flirtation.* Cambridge, Mass.: Harvard University Press, 1994.

Polachek, Dora E. "Montaigne and the Imagination: The Dynamics of Power and Control." In *Le Parcours des "Essais": Montaigne, 1588–1988,* ed. Marcel Tetel and G. Mallary Masters, 135–45. Paris: Aux Amaterus de Livres, 1989.

Quint, David. *Montaigne and the Quality of Mercy: Ethical and Political Themes in the "Essays".* Princeton, N.J.: Princeton University Press, 1998.

Reeser, Todd W. *Moderating Masculinity in Early Modern Culture.* North Carolina Studies in Romance Languages, 283. Chapel Hill: University of North Carolina Press, 2006.

Regosin, Richard L. "Montaigne and His Readers." In *A New History of French Literature,* ed. Denis Hollier, 248–53. Cambridge, Mass.: Harvard University Press, 1989.

———. "Montaigne's Dutiful Daughter." In *Montaigne's Unruly Brood: Textual Engendering and the Challenge to Paternal Authority,* 48–79 Berkeley: University of California Press, 1996.

———. "Montaigne's Monstrous Confession." *Montaigne Studies* 1 (1989): 73–87.

———. *Montaigne's Unruly Brood: Textual Engendering and the Challenge to Paternal Authority.* Berkeley: University of California Press, 1996.

———. "Sources and Resources: The "Pretexts" of Originality in Montaigne's *Essais.*" *Substance* 21 (1978): 103–15.

———. "The Text of Memory's Experience as Narration in Montaigne's Essays." In *The Dialectic of Discovery,* ed. John D. Lyons and Nancy L. Vickers, 145–58. Lexington, Ky.: French Forum, 1984.

Rigolot, François. *Les Métamorphoses de Montaigne.* Paris: Presses Universitaires de France, 1988.

Sainte-Beuve, Charles-Augustin. *Port-Royal.* Vol. 2. Paris: Bibliothèque de la Pléiade, 1958.

Sankovitch, Tilde A. "Marie le Jars de Gournay: The Self-Portrait of an Androgynous Hero." In *French Women Writers and the Book,* 73–99. Syracuse, N.Y.: Syracuse University Press, 1988.

Sayce, Richard A. *The Essays of Montaigne: A Critical Exploration.* Evanston, Ill.: Northwestern University Press, 1972.

Schacter, Marc D. "The Friendship Which Possesses the Soul: Montaigne Loves La Boétie." *Journal of Homosexuality* 41, 3–4 (2001): 5–22.

Schofield, Malcolm. "Aristotle on the Imagination." In *Essays on Aristotle's 'De Anima,'* ed. Martha C. Nussbaum and Amélie Oksenberg Rorty, 249–79, Oxford: Oxford University Press, 1992.

Scodel, Joshua. "The Affirmation of Paradox: A Reading of Montaigne's 'De la Phisionomie' (III, 12)." *Yale French Studies* 64 (1983): 209–37.

Sermain, Jean-Paul. "*Insinuatio, circumstantia, visio et actio:* L'Itinéraire rhétorique du chapitre III, 4: 'De la diversion'." *Bulletin de la Société des Amis de Montaigne* 7 (1985): 123–40.

Siebers, Tobin. *Morals and Stories.* New York: Columbia University Press, 1992.

Silverman, Kaja. *World Spectators.* Stanford, Calif.: Stanford University Press, 2000.

Starobinski, Jean. "Imagination." In *Actes de l'association de littérature comparée,* ed. François Jost, 952–63. The Hague: Mouton, 1966.

———. *Montaigne en mouvement.* Paris: Gallimard, 1982.

Telle, Emile V. "Montaigne et le procès Martin Guerre." *Bibliothèque d'humanisme et Renaissance* 37 (1975): 387–419.

Tetel, Marcel. *Présences italiennes dans les "Essais" de Montaigne.* Paris: Champion, 1992.

Thibaudet, Albert. *Montaigne.* Ed. Floyd Gray. Paris: Gallimard, 1963.

Van Den Abbeele, Georges. *Travel as Metaphor: From Montaigne to Rousseau.* Minneapolis: University of Minnesota Press, 1992.

Vander-Waerdt, Paul. ed. *The Socratic Movement.* Ithaca, N.Y.: Cornell University Press, 1994.

Zalloua, Zahi. *Montaigne and the Ethics of Skepticism.* Charlottesville, N.C.: Rockwood Press, 2005.

Zizek, Slavoj. *The Parallax View.* Cambridge: MIT Press, 2006.

———. *Tarrying with the Negative: Kant, Hegel, and the Critique of Ideology.* Durham, N.C.: Duke University Press, 1993.

INDEX

Aesop, 166
affect: cognition and, 39, 80, 89, 96, 117, 121, 129; displacement of, 98, 107–8, 113–14, 117
Alcibiades, 139, 182–83
alienation, 57, 114–15
allegory, 15, 42, 92, 99, 108, 150
alterity: experience and, 58, 88; friendship and, 79–81; of kidney stone, 170; in Martin Guerre, 64, 68; masks and, 44–45, 110, 126; miracles and, 48–50; openness to, 22, 36–37, 57, 79, 155, 161–62, 182–83; self-identity and, 6–7, 10, 80, 98, 156, 162; sexuality and, 65–69, 185–88; singularity and, 74, 192; through imagination, 2, 5–6, 190; universal diversity and, 162, 165–66; valences of future and, 7, 17, 166; writerly act and, 13, 16, 32, 92, 156. *See also* difference; otherness

androcentric tradition, 41–42, 44, 48, 83
anxiety, 12, 39, 43, 104–21, 130
"The Anxiety of Death: Narrative and Subjectivity in 'De la diversion{sqtœ," 24, 104–20
Apollo, 163, 186, 189
Apologie (Montaigne), 8, 18
Apology (Plato), 149
aporia: Being and, 2–3, 138; of cognitive engendering, 156–57; of death, 87–88, 94–95, 99–103; of experience, 151, 201n4; of law, 166; of self-portraiture, 7, 17; of time, 5–6, 19
Apories (Derrida), 201n4
Areopagites, 65
Ariosto, 14
Aristophanes, 187
Aristotle: on friendship, 74, 80, 86; human nature and, 76, 139; imagination and, 9, 13, 16,

nation and, 9–10, 36–37, 177;
as innate, 76–78; logic and, 13,
52–54; miracles and, 51–61
record, 49–50, 104
Reeser, Todd, 67
reflexivity, 9, 29, 31, 92–94, 173
register, 16, 48–49, 155
Regosin, Richard, 8, 57, 116,
122, 157; on de Gournay, 122,
203n13; on Montaigne's monster, 196n4, 198n2
religion, 75, 81, 84, 100, 145
Renaissance texts, 36, 58, 198n4
repetition, 106, 109, 111, 119–20
"Representing the Monster," 51–69
repression, 19, 108, 114, 118–20,
173
Republic (Plato), 183–84, 189–90
resurrection, 94–95, 98, 103
rhetoric: detours and, 108, 111,
119; female voice and, 126–33;
language and, 54–55, 89, 95–
98, 140, 163; as performance,
106–7, 175, 177, 189; pros-
theses of, 24, 74, 86, 103, 129;
ruse of, 109, 118–20, 202n5; of
self-portraiture, 2–3, 22, 102–3,
105, 148, 152–53
Richeome, Louis, 57
Rigolot, François, 202n6
"Romancing the Stone," 25, 154–92

Sainte-Beuve, Charles-Augustine,
154
Sankovitch, Tilde A., 203nn8,13
Satires (Juvenal), 107
Satyricon (Petronius), 185–89
Sayce, Richard, 59
scientific knowledge, 57, 157,
168–71, 192, 198n8
seeing. *See* visualization
self-examination: mastery and,
11–13, 31, 98, 111, 113–14;

self-knowledge and, 1–2, 8, 23,
155–56, 168–71, 182, 184; self-
reflexivity and, 21, 25, 29, 31,
154; writerly space of, 12–13,
17, 82, 89–96, 100. *See also*
psychoanalysis
self-portraiture: alterity and, 7, 156;
death and, 98, 100–103, 105,
121; monstrousness and, 16, 30,
32–34, 49–50, 62; Montaigne
and, 2–3, 19–20, 22, 25, 144–
53; narrative performance of,
5–6, 10, 177. *See also* identity
self-reflection. *See* self-examination
Seminar (Lacan), 191
Seneca, 10, 67, 190. *See also* classical thought; philosophy; Stoics
sensations: biology and, 15, 169,
172, 184–85; cognition and, 9,
96, 100, 155, 161, 189–90
servitude, 73–86
sexuality: celibacy and, 180–81;
character of Quartillia and,
185–89; erotic pleasure and, 14,
38, 66, 69, 177–78; female desire
and, 31–32, 42–43, 45, 65–69,
126–33, 185–89; homosexuality and, 83, 129, 187–89; in
"Martin Guerre," 63–69; monster theory and, 23–24, 29–69,
196n10; oedipal drama of, 130,
171–72; as work of art, 196n7.
See also desire; gender
Shakespeare, William, 87
Siebers, Tobin, 152
signification: meaning and, 8, 20, 35,
52–53, 57, 113–16, 157; as phallic, 56, 173, 185–87, 197n13;
through rhetoric, 112–13
Silverman, Kaja, 183
simulation: of authentic self, 47,
114, 140–41, 146, 175; of death,
24, 87–103, 173; of dialogic

DATE DUE